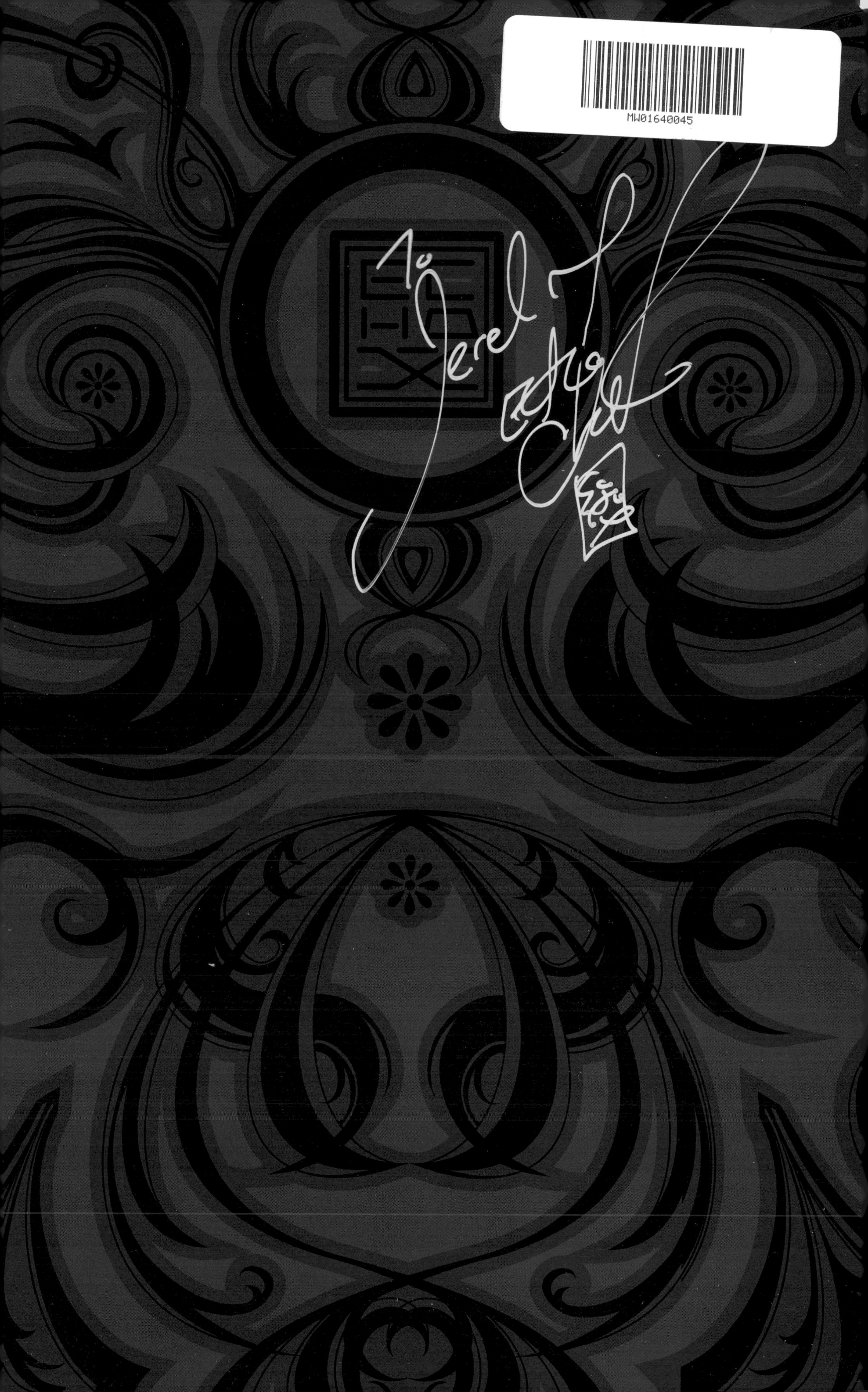
MW01640045

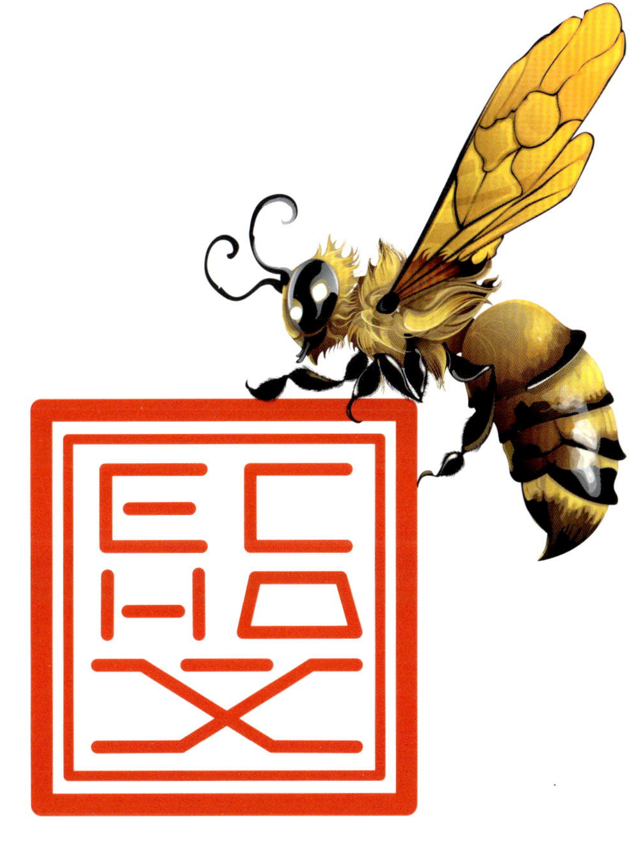

echo nouveau

the art and life of a working girl: 1995-2010

all art and text by
echo chernik

designed and edited by
lazarus chernik

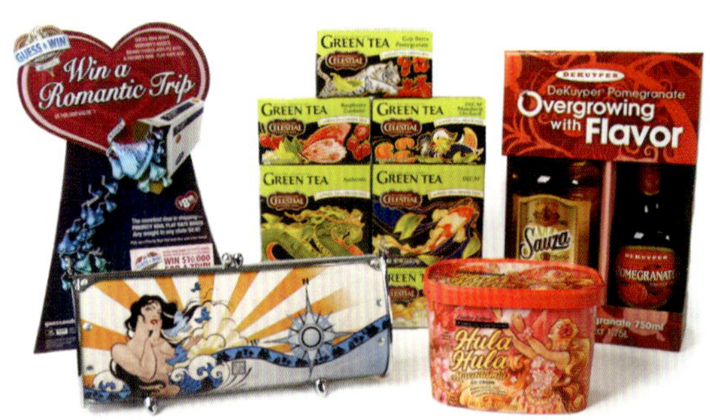

Echo Nouveau
The Art and Life of a Working Girl: 1995-2010
The Collected Commercial Art of Echo Chernik

Cover Art: "Oh Pour L'Amour Du Chocolat" and "Freyja" by Echo Chernik

To Runa and Katheryn Chernik, my best creations yet.
To Holly and Robert McKinney who always supported my creative path.
To Glenn Chernik, who always believed in us, no matter what the obstacle.
And to the memory of Barbara Chernik.

Credits

All Art & Illustration by the Studio of Echo Chernik - consisting of the artist, the creative efforts of Lazarus Chernik, several beautiful models and the occasionally creative studio cat.

Photography: Echo Chernik, Lazarus Chernik. Portrait on page 98 by Ricardo Sevilla
Content: Echo Chernik and Lazarus Chernik
Editing: Echo Chernik, Lazarus Chernik and Holly McKinney
Design & Layout: Lazarus Chernik
Website: http://www.echo-x.com/echonouveau

Printed in Colombia

ISBN 978-0-615-45951-6

Aries
Taurus
Gemini
Cancer
Leo
Libra
Virgo
Scorpio
Sagittarius
Capricorn
Aquarius
Pisces

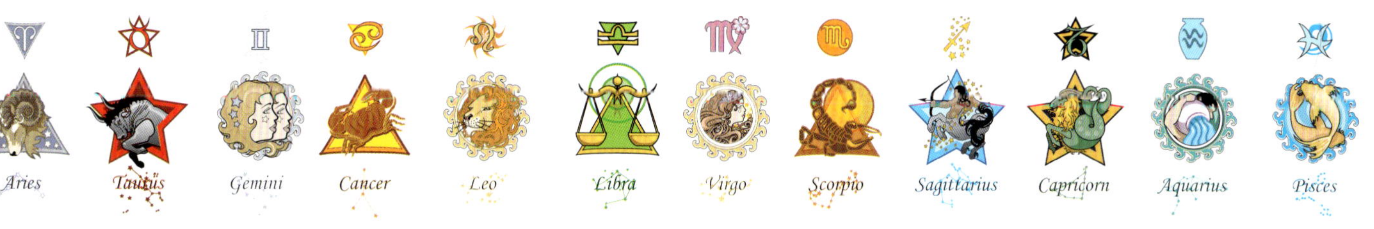

CONTENTS

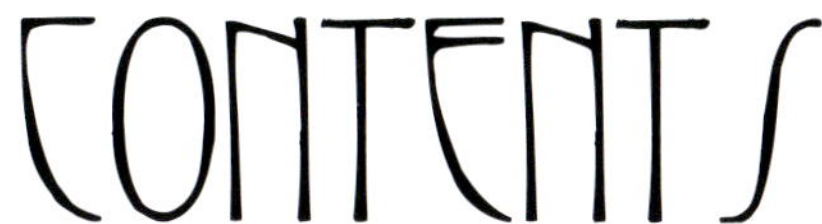

What is an Illustrator

and how often do you have to feed it?

What exactly does an Advertising Illustrator do? I get that question a lot. This book is more than a compilation of the past fifteen years of my career as an illustrator; but a discussion of the age old question "How do you become a booked solid, in-demand illustrator doing what you love, and what is it like?" This book is not only for my fans, but for those of you who wish to pursue a career in art. It is also for those parents currently sporting the same wide eyed "This is out of my comfort-zone, but my child is talented and I want to be supportive" stare that my own once donned.

Illustration falls under the umbrella of Commercial Art and is the creation of art with the intent to visually convey a story or idea. Commercial artists also include a wide variety of professions including illustrators, graphic designers, web designers, animators, typographers, art directors, creative directors and many others. They can be on staff or work freelance. Illustrators require superior drawing skills, a marketable style and most importantly, the ability to communicate. There is a wide range of illustration specialities, including Advertising, Medical, Technical, Book Cover, Editorial, Comic Book, Cartoon and hundreds more. Illustrators are not fine artists who execute other people's visions, but visual communicators who contribute to the mainstream market. An illustrator must possess not only exceptional, versatile talent and artistic ability, but also the desire and skill to communicate an idea or story visually through design. You must be a team player, willing to collaborate with others and adhere to input to create the best art for the particular job.

To be a successful Illustrator, you must be strong enough to accept critique, to sometimes defend your creative choices on the design, and to know when to set your ego aside in order to get the job done. You must enjoy each new project as a challenge - some will have exciting opportunities to explore one's creative freedom, others can be almost tedious in nature. Each project is a collaborative effort, working with creative directors, art directors, commercial artists and often the clients themselves. It's a field wrought with exciting artistic challenges, late nights, hard work, and incredible rewards.

As an illustrator's body of work develops, it will push them into their niche and define their career. If an illustrator has a quick-and-loose style that lends them to be hired frequently by magazines then they may be considered an Editorial Illustrator. The majority of my career has been with Poster and Advertising work. However, I also have a wide range of work in the publishing, packaging, and editorial sectors. Although I specialize in the highly decorative style that is Art Nouveau, not all of the pieces in this book are in that style. I always illustrate in the style that is best for each project. Some pieces require a more realistic approach, others need simpler line work. The ability to consider and illustrate in the style that suits the end result, and the ability to always put the success of the project first, is what keeps you busy as an illustrator. Every piece in this book was commissioned for a client, published or presented, and span the first fifteen years of my career.

If you choose to be freelance, you will learn something early on: "When it rains, it pours." You will have no work, and lose sleep in a panic. Then suddenly, when you're just about to sell the studio cat for spare parts, you will have more work than you could possibly handle and no time to shop for that new car you can suddenly purchase outright. If you prefer to know where your paycheck is coming from each week, then this is not the career for you. If you are driven by the thrill of anticipation of what juicy creative project is just an email notification away.... read on.

The path of the Freelance Illustrator does not come with an instruction manual or any sort of safety net. It is a path defined by the love of creativity, and is navigated purely by will, hard-work, and luck. As a Commercial Arts instructor for several years, I defined what have been the most important elements to my success as an Illustrator. I have compiled years of wisdom and experiences in this book, with the hopes that my learned sage advice will help those starting down this path. And for the rest of you - enjoy the art!

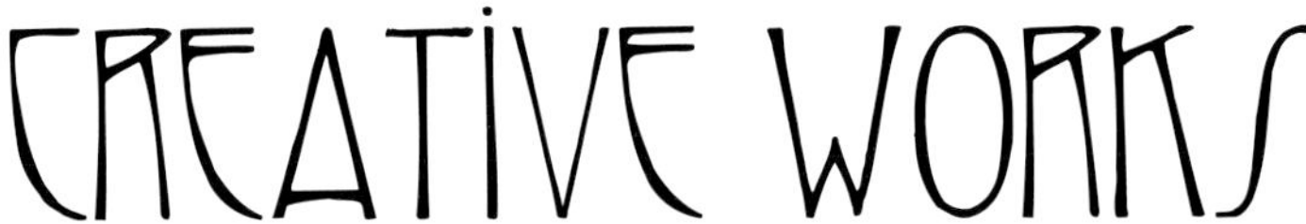

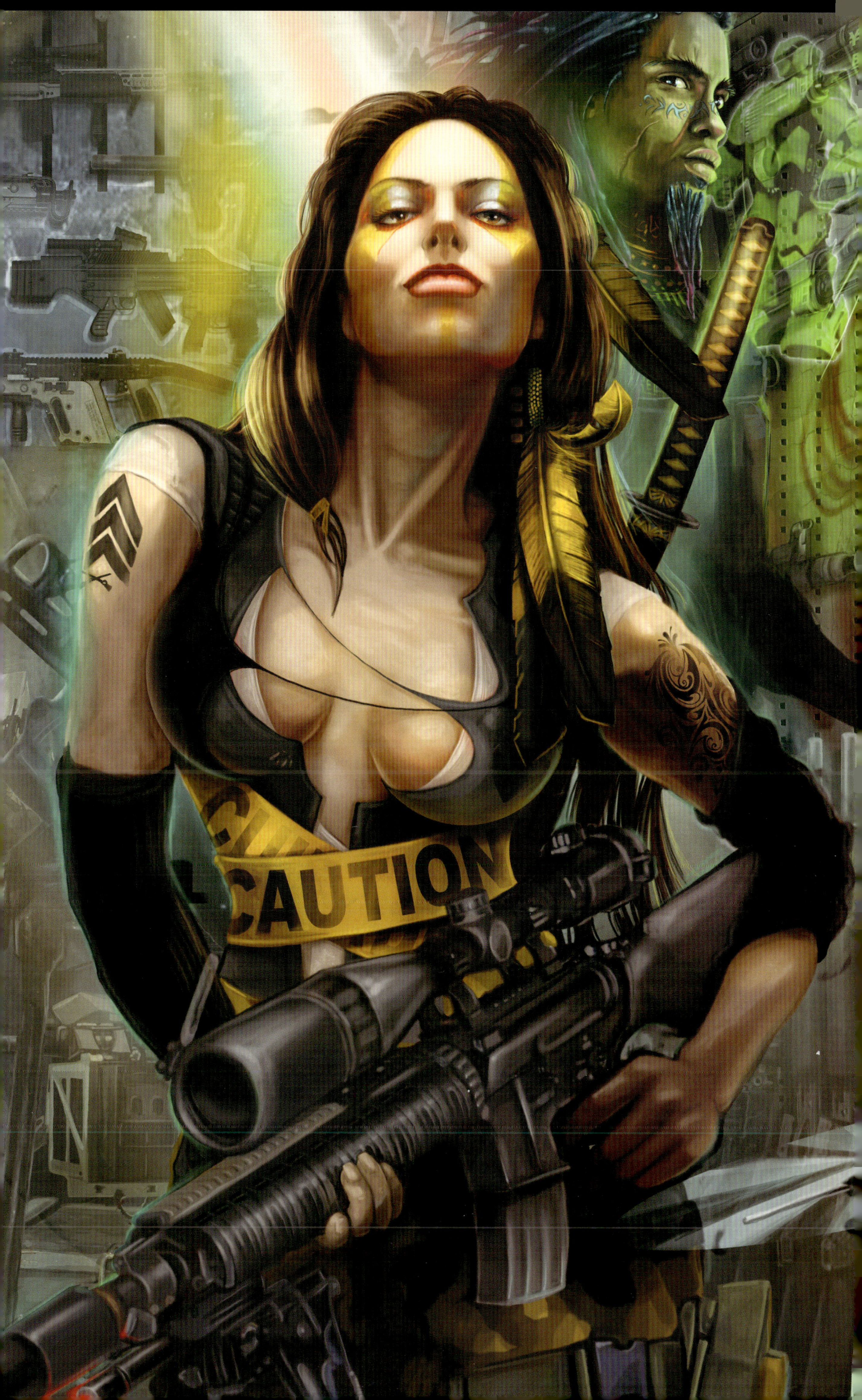
CAUTION

Portfolio

The face that you show the world

Your portfolio is your identity. It is what speaks to art buyers around the world. It is an ever changing and developing creature, requiring constant maintenance and attention. It should consist of only your strongest pieces, and over time, these will change. The early pieces will start to fall away as it evolves into a more mature, professional embodiment of all that is you. It is important to keep it shiny, orderly, trimmed, and out in public. Published pieces are preferable, but everyone needs to start somewhere. To become published, you need to develop a body of work to market yourself with and create a look to your work that will make you stand out.

Developing a "style" is much more intimidating sounding than it really is. Young artists often become too concerned with trying to develop a 'look', when all you really need to do is follow your heart and do what you love. Billions of decisions are made in the creation of a single piece of art. You subconsciously fill your work with thousands of small decisions that are inherently you. You are influenced by artists that you like, the subject matter you enjoy, and by the very world around you. The manner that you filter this influence, combined with your own decision-making process creates art that is unique. *This* is your style. A good way to see "you" in your work is to lay all of your pieces out on a wall, sit back and stare at them. You will see similarities that you have subconsciously chosen to involve in your work - and this is your 'look'.

You should also be concerned with the subject matter of your portfolio. Good advice that I received many years ago was to only show pieces that you would like to do again. If you promote yourself with a clown in one of your illustrations, then be prepared to be hired to draw clowns. Decide what sort of work you would *like* to illustrate. Do you enjoy drawing lanky women in fashionable clothing? Then you may want to tailor your work towards fashion illustration. Prefer detail-oriented photorealism? Maybe medical or scientific illustration is a good direction. Inspired to reproduce life with exotic results? Editorial illustration might be for you. Fantasy? Games and publishing is your best bet. Create a collection targeted towards the work that you want, and encompasses subject matter that you really enjoy. Do not try to force yourself into a "style" that you do not enjoy. When you love what you do, the passion that you put into your pieces is apparent to all.

Promote yourself constantly. Create a web site to showcase your portfolio and make it as professional looking as possible. If you cannot market yourself, no one will believe that you can contribute successfully to their marketing effort. Start with an easy to remember domain name. Make sure the pieces are your strongest and they are easy to navigate. Resist the urge to put everything you have ever done on the site. Keep it professional - omit personal information, amateur design elements, and desperate wording such as "please hire me". There are several portfolio portals to choose if you cannot make your own. Professional portal sites such as creativeshake.com, theispot.com and altpick.com attract quality clients, and are worth the investment, and most offer a free section to start you out. Discussion board art sites (e.g., deviantart.com) are often seen as "hobbyist sites", but I find them to be useful free promotion, and there are art directors who frequent the sites for fun. There are companies (e.g., the Black Book, Workbook, and the Directory of Illustration) that offer packaged marketing campaigns. For one price, they offer printed pages in annual portfolio directories as well as corresponding web pages and direct-mail campaigns. You can do your own mailings and emailings from address lists from Adbase.com. Utilize social media applications but keep it business-oriented. Facebook (et. al.) is invaluable for keeping agents, clients, fans, and followers of your work up to date on your portfolio and your client's successes. There is nothing wrong with being friendly - but I suggest maintaining a private page for personal opinions. Advertising is expensive, but it is important to stay in people's minds. I have had clients who tell me that they saw me on a site four or five years ago, and have been waiting for the right project to come along. So, even if you do not feel you are getting results, you may not see them immediately. Keep promoting yourself, and ask your client where they found you? This will help you target your marketing efforts, and invest your advertising budget wisely.

People ask me about artist representatives. Some agencies will only shop for artists through a rep because reps are careful to only represent proven professionals. Your representative handles your promotions, mailings, presentations, negotiations, billings, and can act as a mediator if communication breaks down. In return, they receive a percentage of each fee. When approached by a rep, you must feel comfortable working with them and they must bring you enough work to make it worth while. I recommend working together for a trial period, and building your advertising together over time, to make sure that you like the way that they run your business. It can be a very strong relationship if built properly, and you should always feel in control of your decisions.

The Business

Equally as important as talent

Your number one goal as a professional artist is to make a living. Illustrators get paid when the project is completed correctly and on time. To be successful, any freelance illustrator has to learn the ins and outs of business. Time management skills, budgeting, self-promotion and negotiations are important skills. It is imperative that you develop good working habits and a dedicated studio space. Not everyone is equipped with the self control and discipline required to avoid afternoon soap operas and the lure of the afternoon nap, so you might need to rent a separate studio.

They can't hire you if they can't find you. Self promotion is key to becoming a successful illustrator. You must constantly and aggressively market your portfolio. When an advertising agency has a concept for a project, they then have to find an illustrator to match the style that they are envisioning. So, they start thumbing through illustration directories, visit artist representative websites, search the Internet, and pull out the old sample cards that they've received.

Hopefully, your artistic vision will capture someone's attention and become a sought after 'look'. Sometimes art buyers* could love your work and even hang it on their wall, but they have no idea how they can fit it in their project. This is where marketability comes in. How can what you do be used in modern publishing? Trends change. It could be that what you love to do may not be catching on yet, and you might need to alter your style slightly to make it more palatable. It took me years of working in an art nouveau influenced style to finally see it reflected in the mainstream, but I have many marketable styles in my repertoire for a wide range of projects. I have had clients and art directors follow my work silently for years then call and apologize that it took so long to find a way to use me. So be patient and confident, and consistent with your marketing efforts.

Always remember you are a professional businessperson. All of the talent in the world does not matter if you do not make your deadlines and are not skilled in basic corporate etiquette. You may be sitting there painting in your favorite boxer shorts and tank, but you are a professional consultant that is expected to act like one. Make your deadlines, do not be late for meetings, and be considerate of your client's business. Get EVERYTHING in writing, send follow-up letters reiterating phone discussions and get them to reply in agreement. These simple tricks will make you stand out as a professional, increase your value, and improve your marketability.

Successful artists find a way to always stay in the field no matter what. Be versatile. If you cannot get work as an illustrator, become a graphic designer. Work at a sign shop or run copies at the local office supply store if you can't find anything else. While you are there, learn as much as you can about the technology, the printing process, spot colors, varnishes, laminates, binding - everything. Learn about typography, color separation, and web page design. Even veteran illustrators will need to accept a typography job or a 'not their-style' job now and again to supplement during lean times. It is good to have a full arsenal at your fingertips, and it is the ability to be versatile that will keep you busy when it is slow. The wider your base of understanding of what happens to your artwork once you submit it, the more you can anticipate the art directors needs, and this will set you apart from the rest.

I recommend that everyone own *The Graphic Artist's Guild's Guide to Pricing and Ethical Guidelines* (found at all major booksellers - or free with a GAG membership (gag.org)). It is an invaluable resource which will explain important concepts such as contracts, copyrights, licensing, rush fees, kill fees and bidding on jobs, and provides sample contract and bid forms for your use. It contains contract samples, and rates for current jobs, divided by industry. You may find that a Graphic Artist's Guild membership is right for you. The GAG is a great resource to start when researching business hurdles specific to the self-employed such as taxes (hire an accountant!), health insurance, creation of a fictitious name, and licensing for in-home businesses.

It takes about ten years to become established as a working illustrator. I was told that early on, and sure enough, at ten years and three months I realized I was booked for several months out, and working steady. The key to becoming a successful freelance illustrator is versatility, mixed in with a smidgen of talent, a whole lot of drive, and the occasional caffeine drip.

For more information on the business of art visit www.echo-x.com/echonouveau

** Although anyone can hire an illustrator, an Art Buyer is a titled position in larger advertising agencies. This person's job is to scout and hire talent for a pitch on a new project. Because the agency will bill the client for the talent, they may work with you through the bid process. If the project is won, will pass you on to the creative team that you will be working with.*

The Professional Creative Process

Beyond Working in Your Pajamas

I receive so many questions about how I work. How do you find clients? Do you show them sketches? How do you land the job? How do you make art? The general advertising illustration job goes something like this (give or take):

The advertising agency has a concept for an illustration. Sometimes they contact me requesting samples to present to their client in conjunction with their concepts (this is called a pitch). Other times, they contact me after a direction has been chosen, and they are ready to proceed with executing their vision. I then receive the creative brief. Sometimes it is a tight PDF file consisting of graphs, charts, notes, color swatches, logos, and reference, and other times it's a conference chat on the phone about the direction of the art. Sometimes the deadlines are manageable, more often they are yesterday. Sometimes I receive tight art direction with the concept clearly defined, other times, I am asked to pitch my own ideas. Depending on the urgency of the job and tightness of the specs, I may submit thumbnails to solidify direction and details. From there, I submit two or three directions in the form of pencil sketches, often accompanied with artist notes. Once the client approves the direction, a color rough may or may not be presented. Sometimes the ad agency will hire me to bring artwork to near finish purely to pitch to a client, and it may never see the light of day beyond the conference room. Once the rough is approved, I move to a finish. Throughout the process, I keep the art director in the loop by emailing or posting in-progress shots of the artwork, so that we can work together to stay on track. Occasionally I am responsible for creation of corresponding elements that need to be provided so that the illustration can be used in multiple dimensions and formats. It is always good to find out in advance if the art will be used in multiple dimensions. It is much easier to design the art if you can anticipate both usage in a vertical and horizontal format (see Arlo Guthrie p. 22).

All illustrators have a different method of working. Since I do so much advertising work (with the quick turnaround of changes that accompany this field), I have become primarily digital over the years. I am a traditionally trained oil painter and have worked in most media including photography, sculpture and print-making. I do my drawings by hand on vellum as I prefer the tactile nature of graphite. I scan my finished drawing into my computer and bring it into Adobe Photoshop. From there, I begin painting the figure. About halfway through, I bring it into Adobe Illustrator, and complete most of the vector work. Then it is a dance back and forth between the programs until it's finished. I also will occasionally create textures by hand or bring in real-world elements and scan them in to be integrated. Some of my pieces are completely Photoshop painting, others are exclusively vector. With some of my fine art pieces, I have recently taken to working in a more mixed-media manner, including acrylics or oils into my finished canvases.

It is important as a commercial illustrator to understand what is going on throughout the entire process and behind the scenes. Often the art director will report to a committee. In that case, you may need to tailor your presentation to give the committee certain control over parts of the artwork, to keep them away from the parts that you prefer not to change. This type of client management comes with experience, and the art directors usually appreciate it. They also appreciate when an illustrator foresees future potential uses for the artwork, and prepares it in a manner that they can easily manipulate. A lot of times, I will create leagues of extra bleed just in case, or finish off a truncated element (such as a bird), so that when the client decides that they want to pull that element out and use it on the side of the package, it is ready to go. They love when things are that easy. I always ask upfront what other formats the art may go into. I find out if they are printing with any required spot colors and get those color codes (e.g, Pantone 186c). Knowing where your art is going and how it may be used and then using the correct process for the success of the project separates the pro from the novice. Make your art director look good and they'll call you back for their next project.

If I have not said it before... make your deadlines. If you feel that you are going to miss your deadline (your ear was ripped off by vultures, and it is really making it difficult to concentrate) - communicate that immediately. Usually the client has a little wiggle room in their deadline. Tell them that they can have it by Tuesday, but you can make it perfect on Wednesday? If possible, they will usually try to carve out more time for quality. Learn to recognize when you will not be able to satisfy a deadline before accepting a job. As painful as it is, it's better to turn a job away than miss the deadline, or turn in sub par work.

Negotiations

Artists Love Getting Paid to Do What They Love

It is very hard for fledgling illustrators to know how much to charge for their work. Generally, you should figure out your 'base rate' and make adjustments for each project as it is negotiated. Once you have your base rate, you can apply pricing modifiers to it.

To calculate your 'base rate,' you need to determine what your living and studio expenses are. Your business has it's own expenses such as studio rental, advertising, and materials. Don't forget to calculate in any license fees, insurance, and taxes. Calculating what you need each month will help you decide the minimum that you must charge to stay afloat, and weed out the jobs that you simply cannot afford to take. Remember that you are not spending all of your time illustrating. A lot of time is spent on billing, advertising and self promotion. So, take this into account when determining your base rate. You must also learn to estimate how long a project will take you. Use these factors to determine the very minimum that you must bill, and then apply pricing multipliers.

Pricing multipliers vary and while calculated separately, are applied cumulatively. The first multipliers determine the base cost and include the variety of use (flyers only? featured branding campaign element?) and range and timeline of distribution (local for one use? nationwide for unlimited use?). Subsequent multipliers include copyright status (artist keeps rights? licensing? full buyout? work for hire?), rush fees and kill fees (usually 33%-50%). For example, an illustration of a character might have a base rate of $1,000 to produce, but a national client will generate more revenue from it so has a 250% multiplier (now $2,500). Because it's a national campaign it will be used more and more people will see it so another 200% (now $5,000). They needed it yesterday and you have to push projects aside to do it; that's 150% for the trouble to rush it (now $7,500). Full copyright buyout is a given so another 200% ($15,000). You want to earn more work from them in the future, so knock off 20% as a 'First-Time Discount' (now $12,000) and you trust them, so require only 33% up-front to serve as a kill fee ($4,000). The best way to fit into a budget is to adjust the timeline; one year renewable will satisfy most clients. These percentages are not fixed - just a guideline and require massaging per project. See the Graphic Artists Guild *Guide for Pricing and Ethical Guidelines* for more on this. Be flexible and you can generally negotiate an agreement that you are all pleased with.

What is their Budget? They usually have an idea of where they want to be, before they contact you. Sometimes the client will tell you what they are willing to pay (and it's always negotiable). Agencies are easiest to talk to, because they're billing it out to their client - so they often have a feeling what their client is expecting to pay for art. Other times they may ask you to bid on the job. In case of the latter, you write a letter with a synopsis of the job, terms of usage, licensing and what you would like to be paid for it. This can be extremely daunting if you are new, or if you really want the job. Never give an 'estimate' without knowing enough about a project. The best thing to do is try to get a range from the agency or client by asking, "Do you have a range that you'd like to be in for this project?" Sometimes you can get an idea of where your bid should land. Funny story - twice in my career of bidding on jobs, I was contacted by the ad agency and told that everything on the bid looked great, and if I could just double my numbers for them, they would send it over for client approval. It goes to show you that budgets vary. One persons "huge budget" is another's pocket change. Remember, just because you didn't win the bid, didn't mean your numbers were off. Quite often, clients simply move in another direction.

A contract is a detailed agreement that defines when you are getting paid and how the client gets to use the work that you created. Larger agencies that you trust will often file a purchase order for the job; this functions as a contract. For smaller clients, always get everything in writing. Make sure that you negotiate a partial upfront payment and a kill fee (a payment even if the job gets cancelled). Be careful signing a contract with "Work for Hire" written anywhere in it without understanding the full intent of the phrase. That text may override other clauses of the contract in favor of the client, and is only appropriate in very few cases. There are some clients that want artists to work "on spec". That means they want the art done to their specifications first before deciding if they want to pay for it - and they might not.

There are no set rules to this game. Be flexible with your rates but protect yourself. If a client refuses to put something in writing, you are probably better off without the job. If you are satisfied that what you are getting paid is what your time is worth, then you are good to go. In order to survive as a working illustrator, you must have the mad negotiating skills to navigate that road.

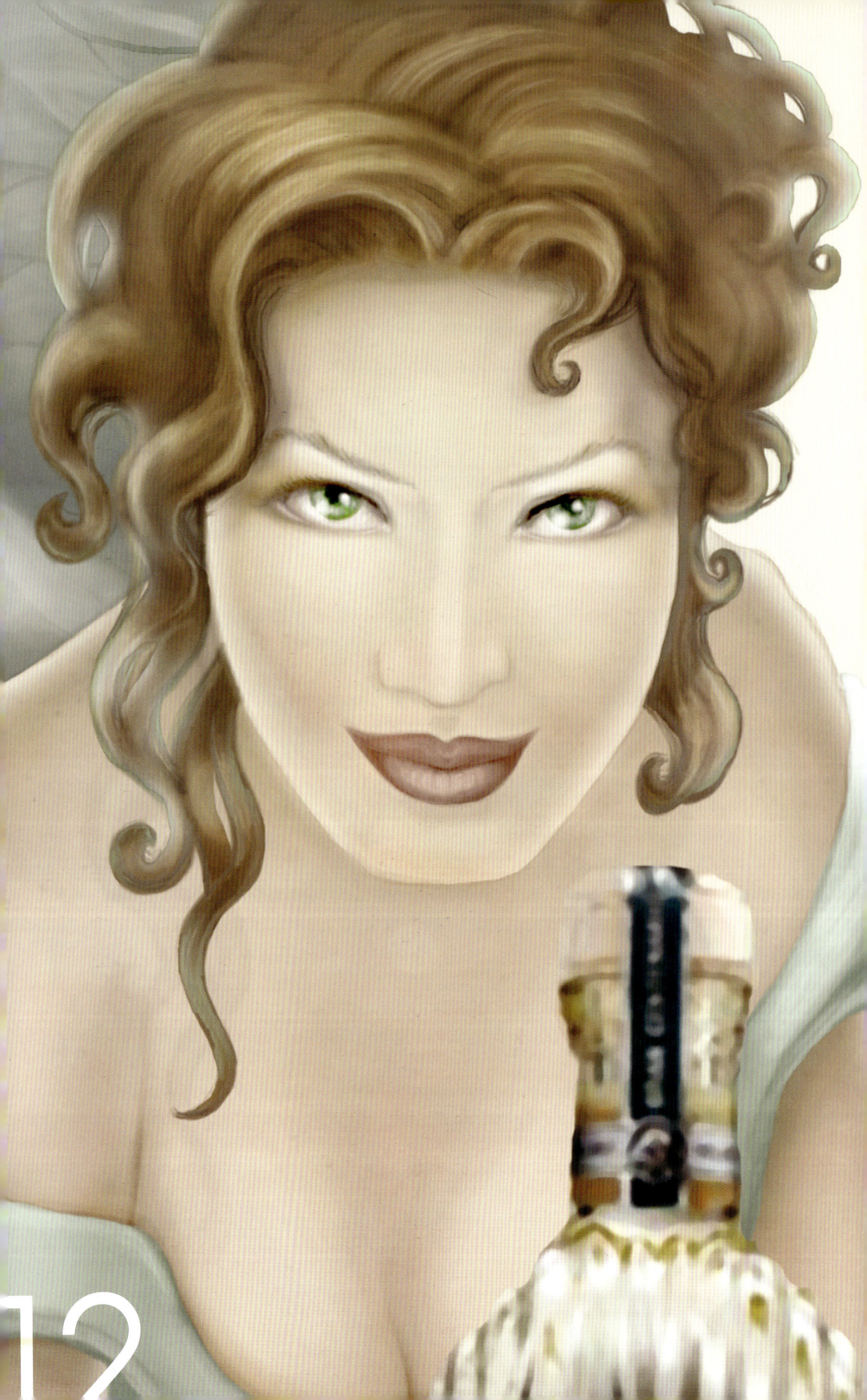

Advertising Campaigns

I find advertising illustration incredibly exciting. You never know what will come your way. Advertisements come in a variety of shapes and sizes, but they share one thing in common. Their number one (numero uno) important job is to sell a product or service, remain memorable to a consumer, and produce a profit.

Lazarus and I have both worked in advertising agencies, and it is a demanding business with long hours preparing for the all important Client Pitch. Agencies need to satisfy existing clients, and are also invited to pitch ideas for jobs that they have not won yet. Therefore, they will often compile in-house campaigns and concepts with the attempts to woo the client with their services. These illustration jobs are more likely to be juicy and fun, but less likely to actually make it onto the shelves. And some clients (Celestial Seasonings, for instance) have an internal art department.

The agency usually has a pretty defined idea of what they are looking for in terms of art by the time that they approach you - though there is often flexibility on the final design and execution. Sometimes they hire you for your style, other times they will give you an idea of the style they want you to execute. This sort of style flexibility is not for everyone.

Campaigns often require artwork that will have several uses. It may be featured in a magazine ad, but also on the website. I was recently asked to bid on a job which included magazine ads as well as corresponding billboards and flyers.

I love the diversity of each project. There are few words more exciting to me than, "Okay, our client is so-and-so, and this is what we're thinking....."

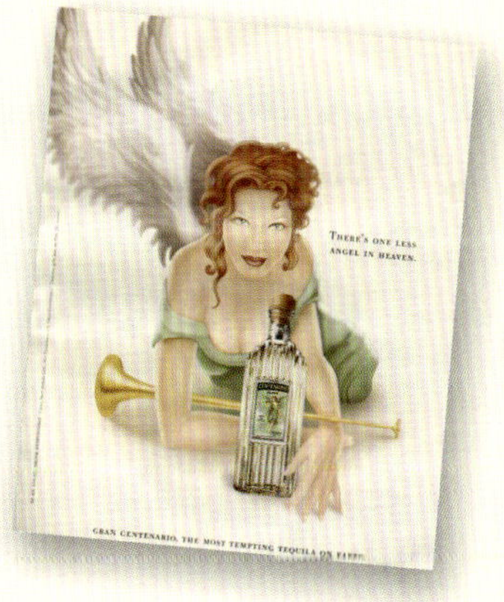

Heaven's Been Missing an Angel
Client: José Cuervo
Agency: Arnell Group
Year: 2004
Models: Echo Chernik

This is one of two illustrations commissioned through Arnell Group for José Cuervo. The concept was as follows: Their Gran Centenario brand of high end tequilas has traditionally been represented by the angel on the label. I was hired to create a "very, very soft" illustration of an angel that looked as if she had fallen from the sky. An angel event was held in LA to celebrate the campaign.

Model: I posed for the shot myself and Lazarus shot the reference. We did not have a bottle of GC or a vuvuzela lying around, so we used a shinai and a bottle of mead.

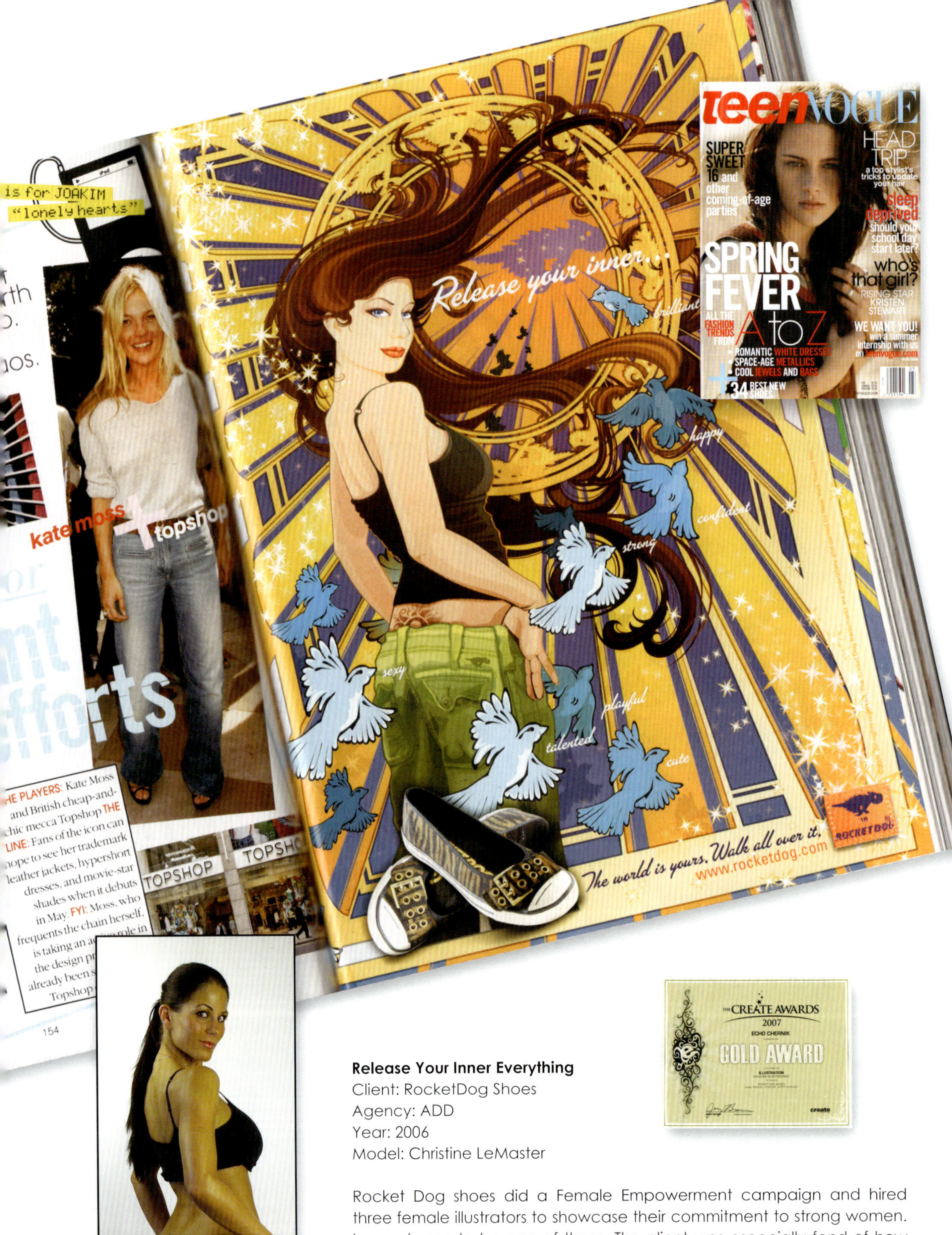

Release Your Inner Everything
Client: RocketDog Shoes
Agency: ADD
Year: 2006
Model: Christine LeMaster

Rocket Dog shoes did a Female Empowerment campaign and hired three female illustrators to showcase their commitment to strong women. I was chosen to be one of them. The client was especially fond of how I integrated their logo into the background. They loved it so much, that they changed the art direction of the other two illustrators to do the same. This is also one of the rare instances in which I did not deviate from the reference too much. Christine brought her own costuming - and that matched the perfect target audience for the ad. The art buyer for this job specifically hunted for artists through free fan art sites such as renderosity and deviantart - which goes to show, it pays to showcase your work in as many places as possible. You never know where someone will find you.

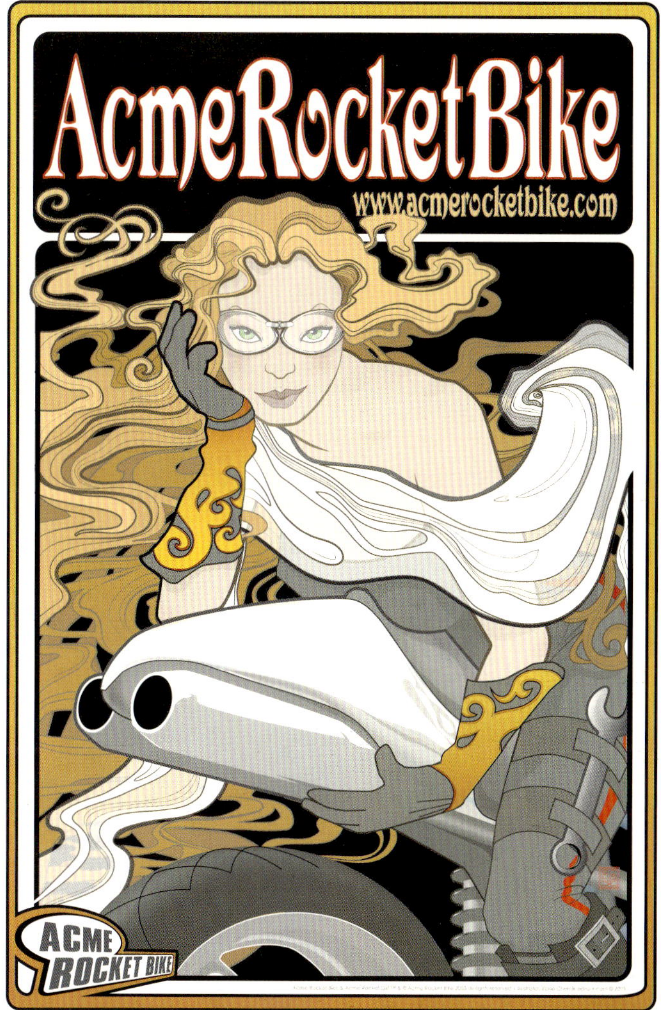

ACME was an amazing client that became a friend. Robert Steffano is a custom motorcycle builder in Northern California with numerous accolades and magazine features to his credit. His motorcycles are custom, and one of a kind. These posters were featured in several European magazines, including Italy's Desmo.

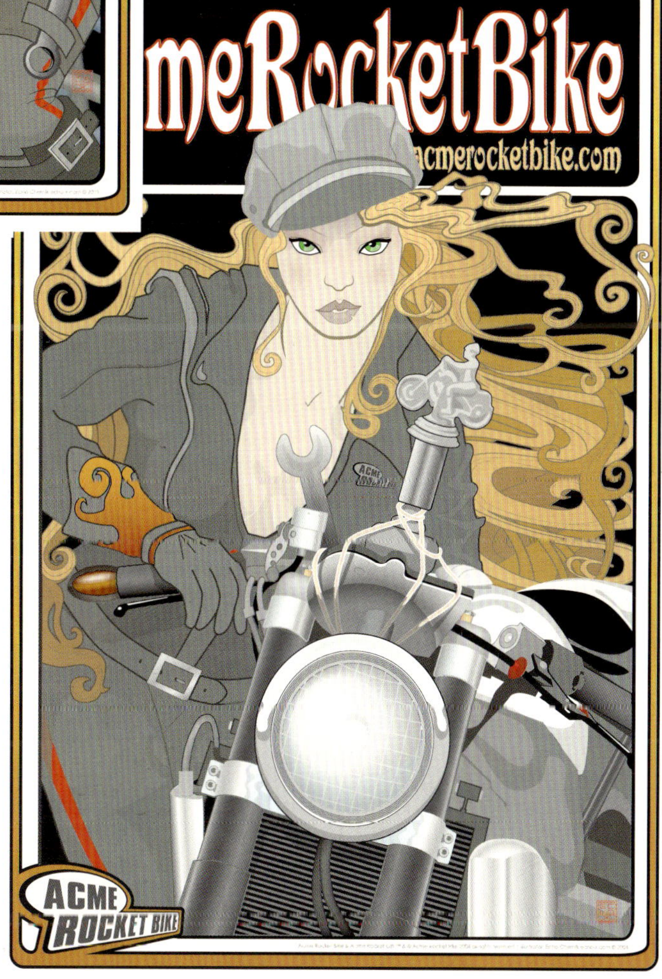

The first poster (ABOVE) features a modified Yamaha R1 in an update of Alphonse Mucha's classic retail poster "Cycles Perfecta" circa 1897. The second (RIGHT) uses Robert's custom Ducati Monster in a recreation of the poster for The Wild One starring Marlon Brando in 1953. Robert printed and framed a single large one of a kind poster for each of these bikes and gave them away to the purchaser. He was so pleased with the results that even he started referring to his strategy as "Buy a $60,000 poster and get a free motorcycle."

ACME Rocket Girl 1 & 2
Client: ACME Rocket Bike
Agency: Internal
Year: 2004
Model: Echo Chernik

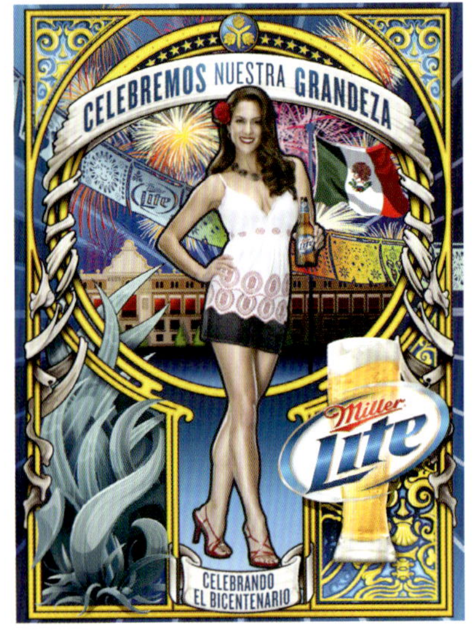

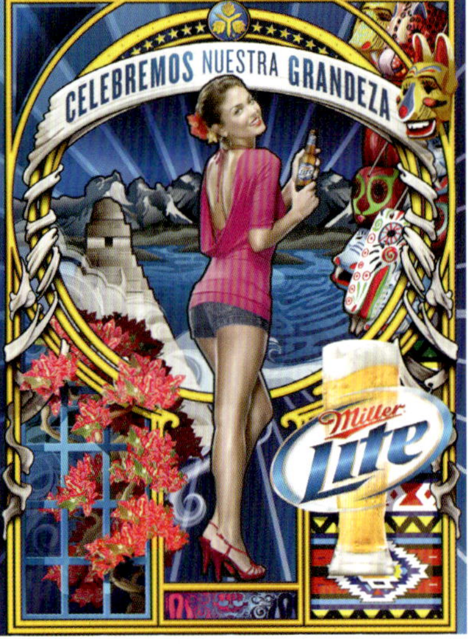

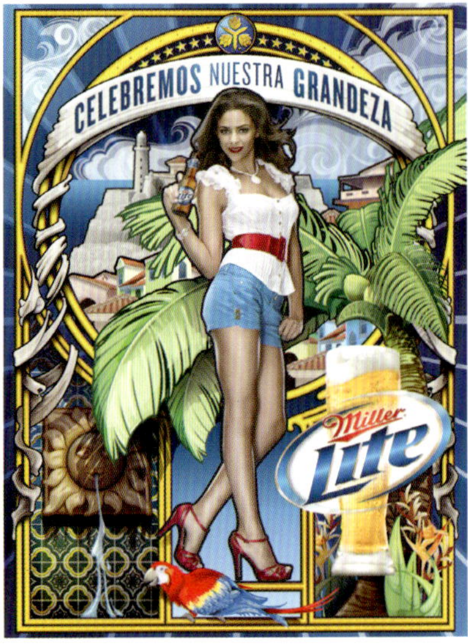

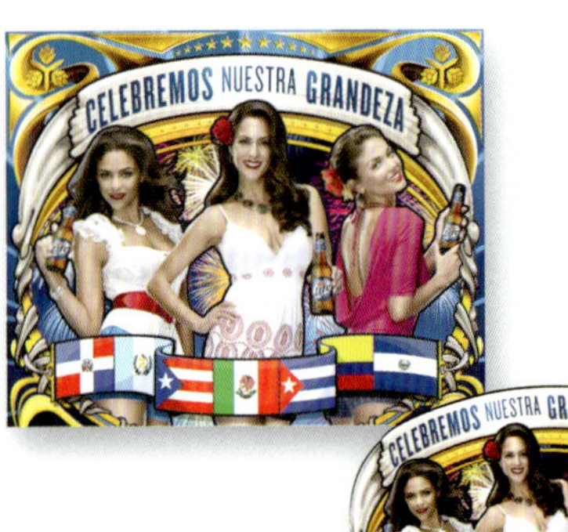

Hispanic Heritage Month
Client: Miller-Coors
Agency: Market Vision
Year: 2010
Models: Photos Provided

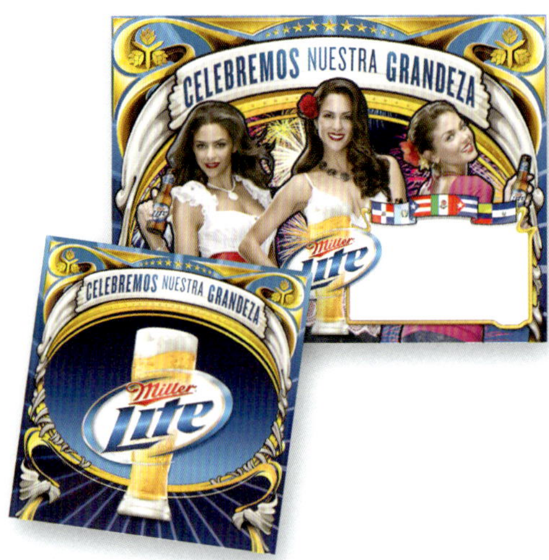

These illustrations for Miller are a celebration of Hispanic Heritage Month. When working with mainstream brands, you are often supplied with materials to drop into the posters (such as the Miller pilsner glass) and given art direction to conform to their brand theme. Clients will often supply pre-determined fonts to use, and Pantone color swatches as a set palette to work within. The concept for this piece was to utilize the photos taken for the previous years campaign and re-work them in a fresh new poster style. I also created a variety of coordinating pennants, hangtags, table tents, violators and cooler door pop-ups. Many of the elements were created in a manner that they could be pulled out and used as elements in other pieces.

The Step into Character campaign was a local New Orleans based promotion, and one of the first brand name clients that I had the pleasure of working with. My studio was on the east coast of Florida at the time I was working on this piece, and all through it I was watching hurricane Katrina speed through the Gulf of Mexico on it's eventual crash course with New Orleans. It is a surreal memory.

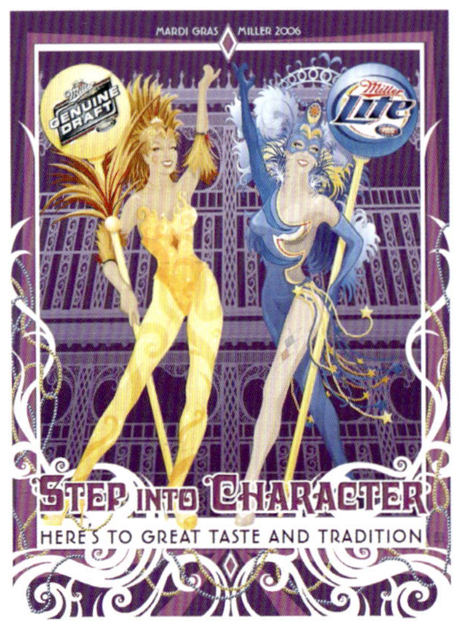

Step Into Character
Client: Miller-Coors
Agency: Upshot Media
Year: 2006

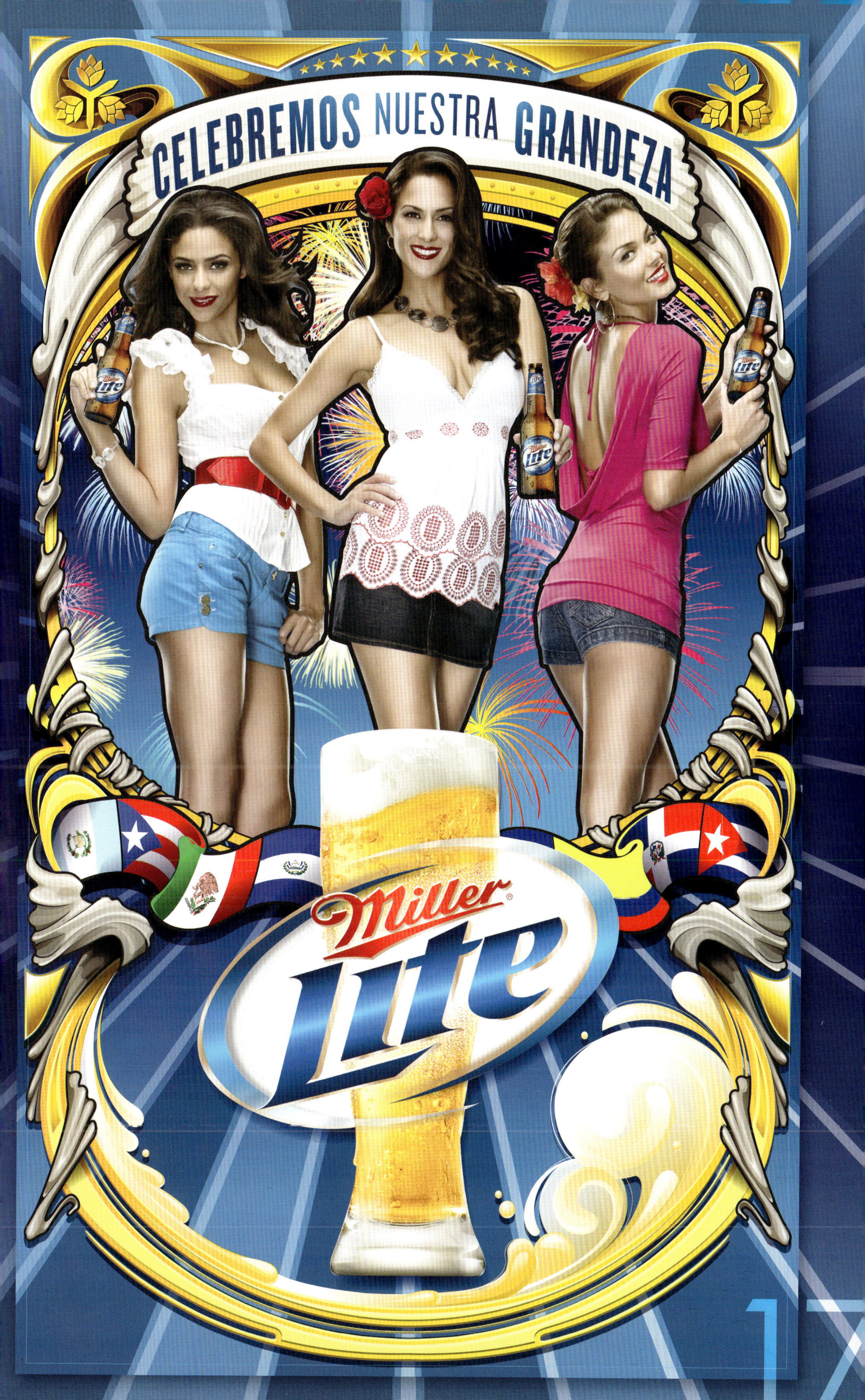
CELEBREMOS NUESTRA GRANDEZA
Miller
Lite

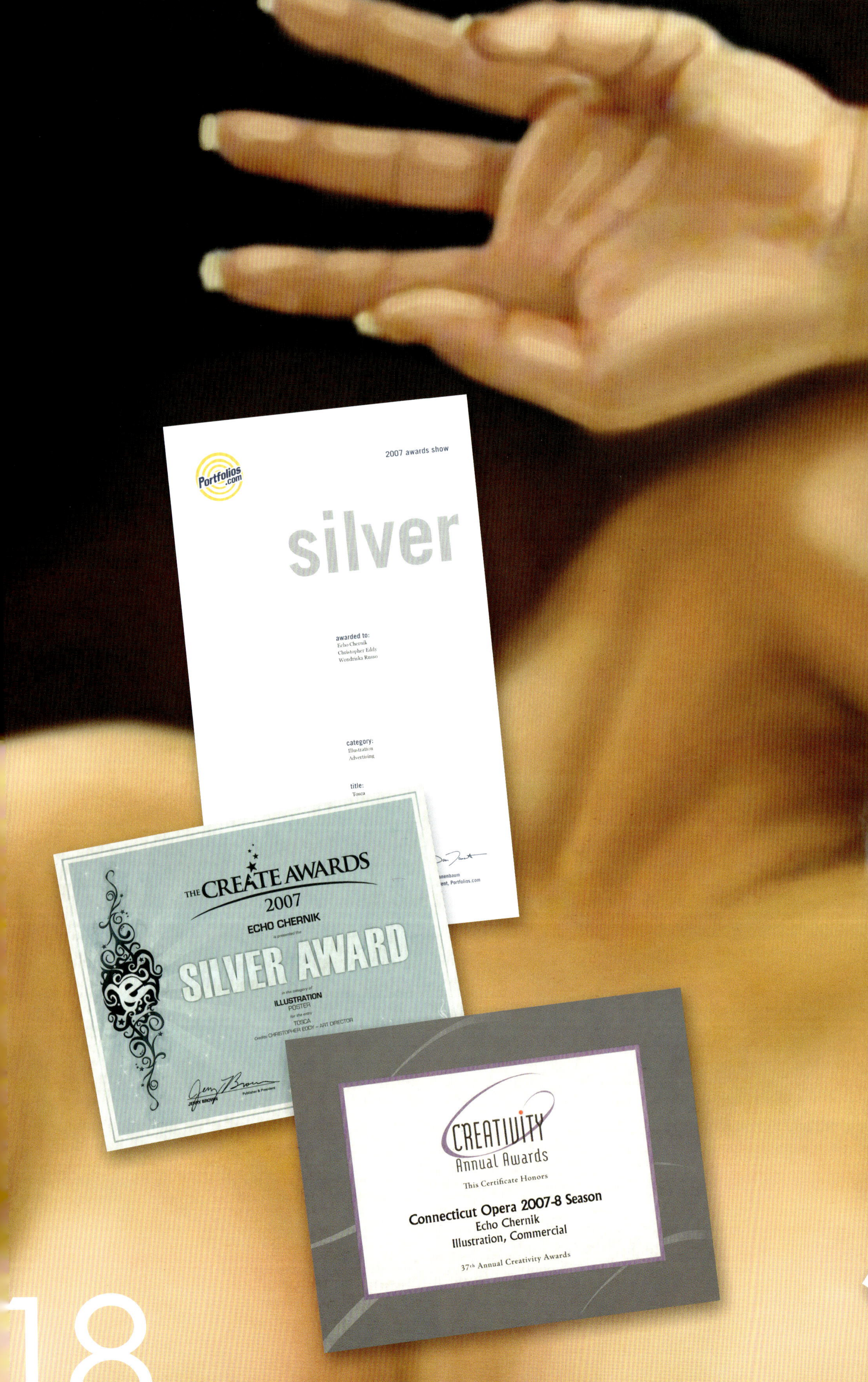
Portfolios .com
2007 awards show
silver
awarded to:
Echo Chernik
Christopher Eddy
Wondriska Russo
category:
Illustration
Advertising
title:
Tosca
THE CREATE AWARDS
2007
ECHO CHERNIK
SILVER AWARD
ILLUSTRATION
POSTER
TOSCA
Credits: CHRISTOPHER EDDY – ART DIRECTOR
CREATIVITY
Annual Awards
This Certificate Honors
Connecticut Opera 2007-8 Season
Echo Chernik
Illustration, Commercial
37th Annual Creativity Awards

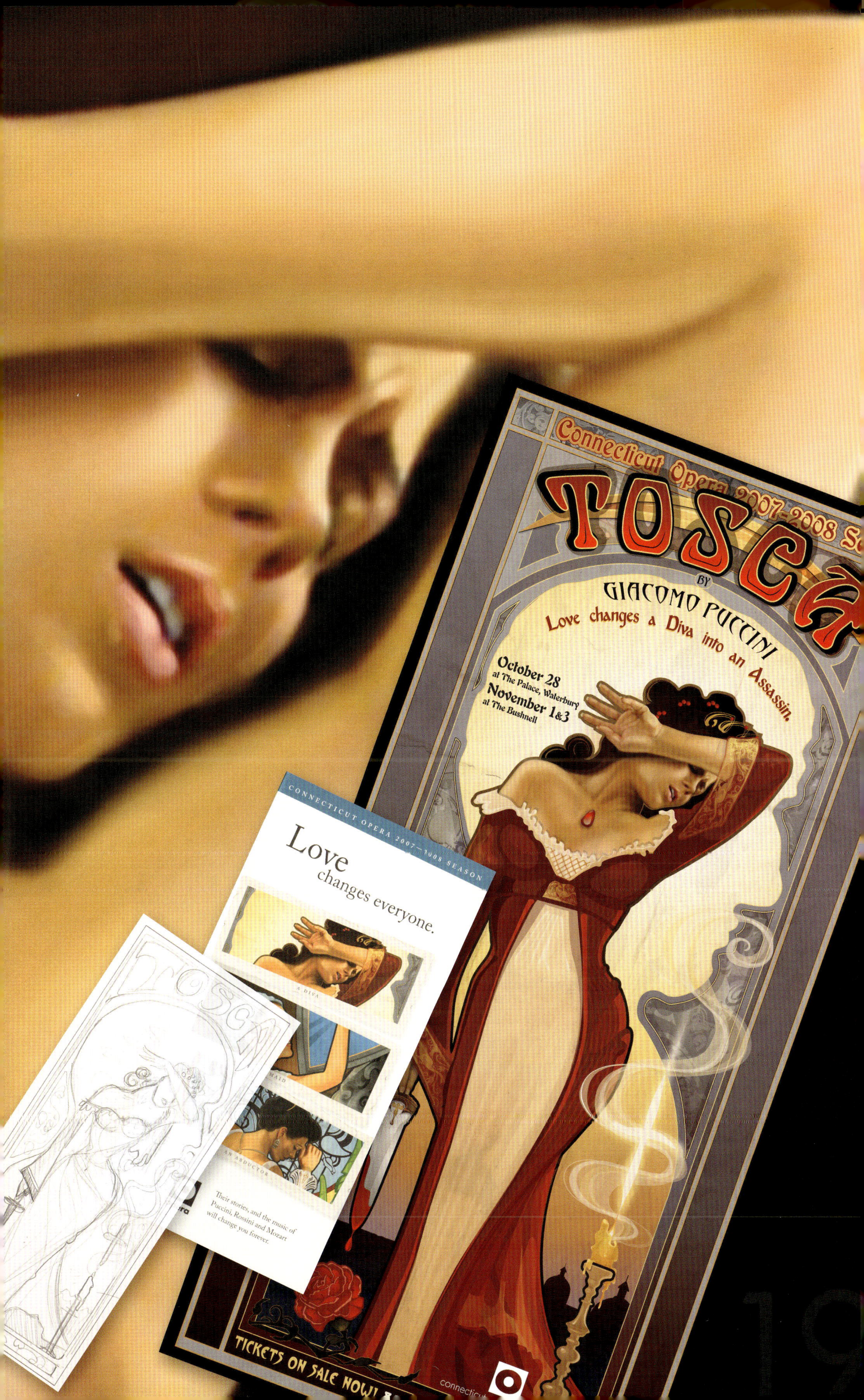
Connecticut Opera 2007-2008 Se
TOSCA
BY
GIACOMO PUCCINI
Love changes a Diva into an Assassin.
October 28
at The Palace, Waterbury
November 1&3
at The Bushnell
TICKETS ON SALE NOW!
CONNECTICUT OPERA 2007—2008 SEASON
Love
changes everyone.
A DIVA
Their stories, and the music of Puccini, Rossini and Mozart will change you forever.
TOSCA

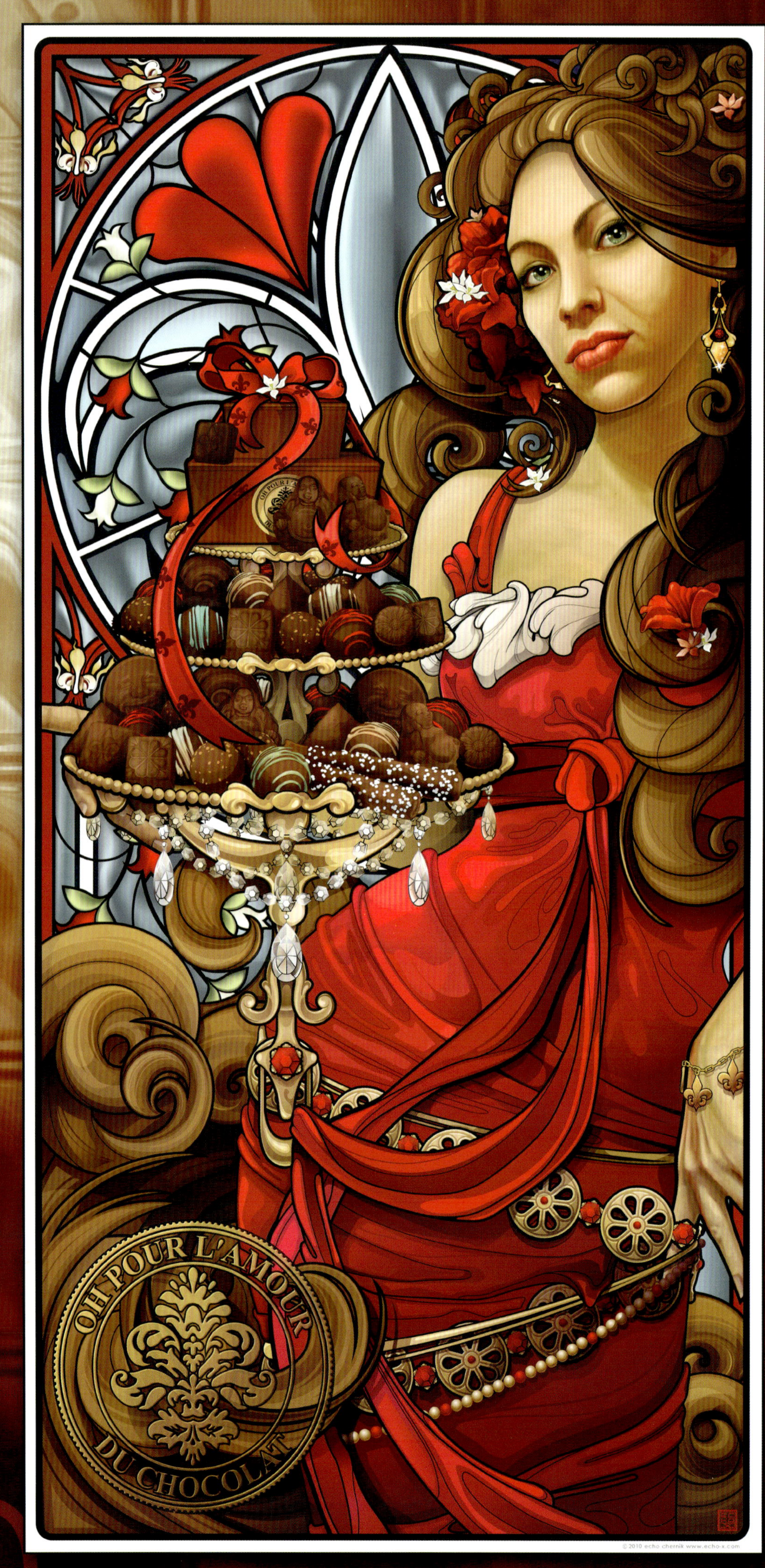
OH POUR L'AMOUR
DU CHOCOLAT

Posters

Art Nouveau style poster art invokes in us a sense of nostalgia for images and emotions of our childhood. Artists of the early twentieth century and before lacked photography and computers and to mass-produce advertisements in the manner of today. The public was communicated to with artworks, hand lettering, lithography, even wood block printing. One still enjoys the feeling of vintage advertisements by Alphonse Mucha, Steinlen, Toulouse-Lautrec, Erté, Anichini, to name some of my favorites. If you've never had the joy of seeing an exhibit, make sure to discover more about war propaganda posters, and the exquisite design of early Russian and Japanese woodblock posters at museums and the National Archives.

Designing posters requires one to capture and hold the eye of the viewer. They must be visually pleasing, and require a repeat visit, their goal generally being to sell you an item or event. They must communicate clearly their intent, and stay with you long after you've gone away. A poster artist must also be a skilled typographer. I was fortunate to be trained in typography in the days before computer lettering, and learned to appreciate the form, beauty and structure of type - elements that must be understood before one can manipulate and bend them to their will. An advertising illustrator must also know how to understand their target demographic, determine who their are selling to, and think like more than just a painter. In this case, I found my years of schooling at Pratt invaluable to my evolution in advertising.

My work is influenced not only by Art Nouveau, but also the symbolism of the Neoclassicists, decorative elements of Fileteado, the beauty of the Romantics, the delicate images of Japanese woodblocks and even the drama of futuristic Cyberpunk-style paintings. I embed a great deal of symbolism in each of my pieces. Whenever possible, I bring an edgy modern feel to the vintage style.

FACING
Oh For the Love of Chocolate
Client: Oh Pour l'Amour Du Chocolat
Agency: Internal
Year: 2010
Model: Tara Cadmus

RIGHT
Vanishing of the Bees
Client: Dogwoof Pictures
Agency: Internal
Year: 2009

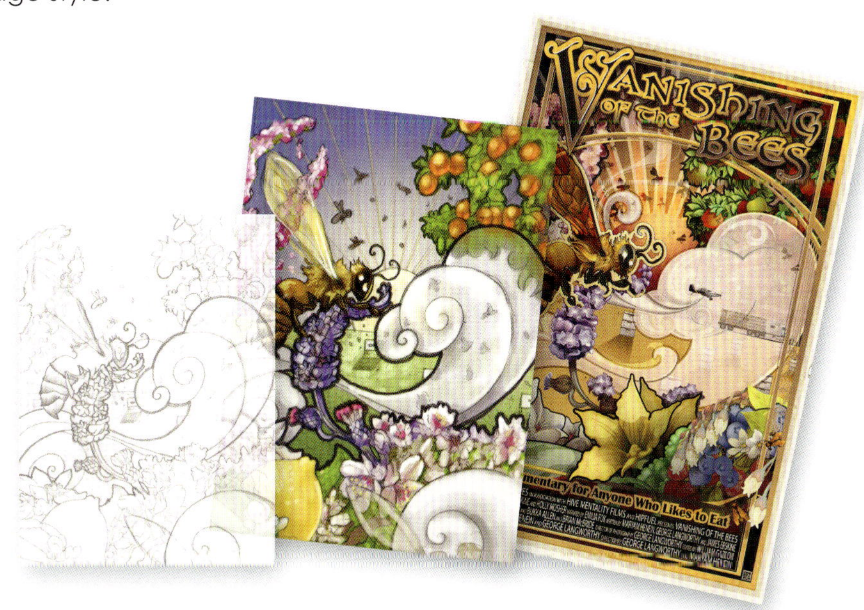

A project can change dramatically over the course of revisions.

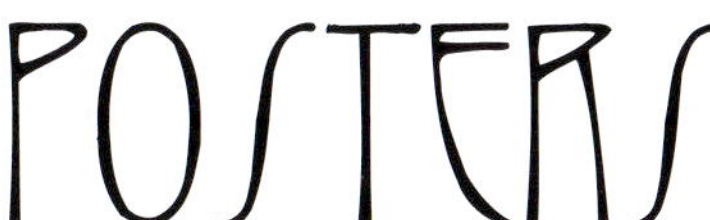

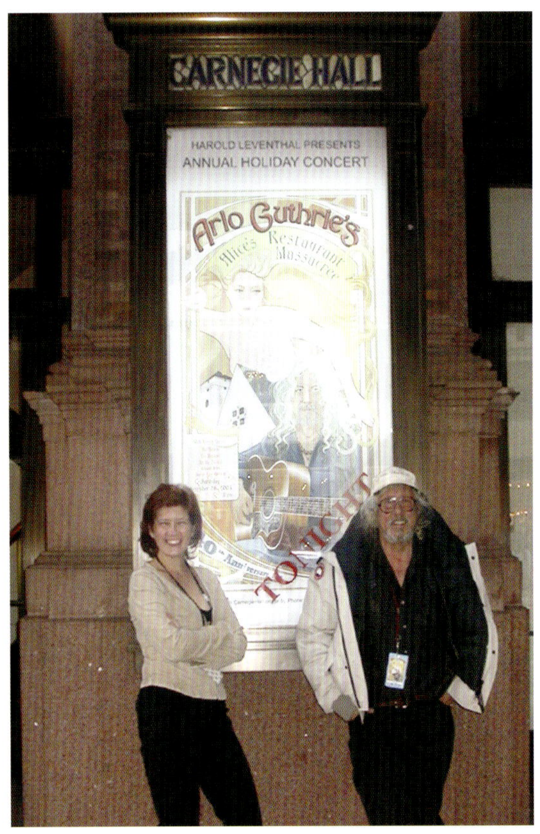

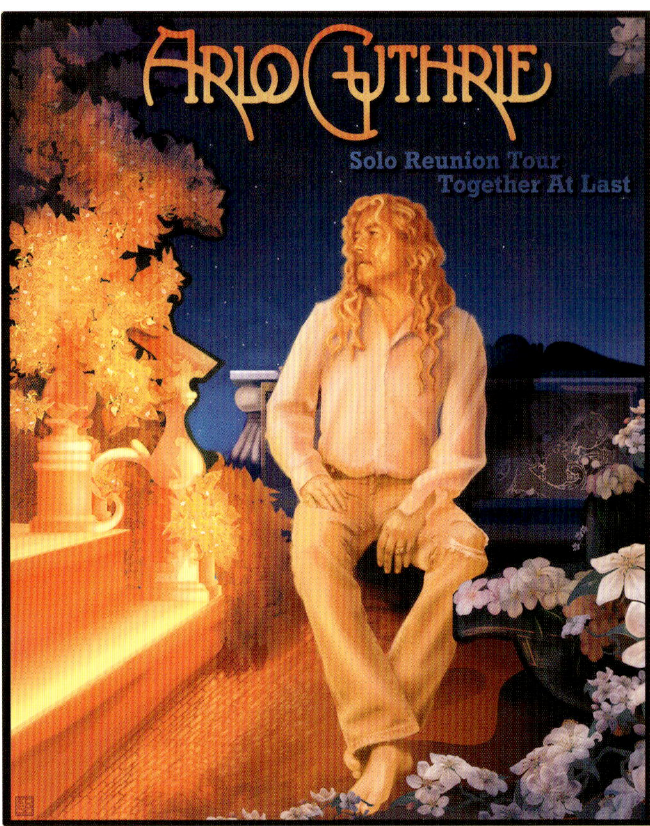

Clockwise: **40th Anniversary of Alice's Restaurant, Solo Reunion Tour, Lost World Tour, Journey On**
Client: Rising Son Records
Year: 2006-2010
Models: Arlo Guthrie, Meghan Perkins, Yaya Han, Josie Lee, Radhe and Jennifer

I was contacted back in 2006 to create the poster for the 40th anniversary of Alice's Restaurant. Since I grew up listening to the Guthries' music, it was pretty exciting. It is a lot of fun to collaborate with Arlo on various projects, as he is exceptionally creative. We've created four posters together, a CD cover and a maple syrup label. The Alice's Restaurant poster was designed in both 18x24, and as a tall vertical format to conform to the Carnegie Hall poster box display dimensions (see above). Both posters were designed simultaneously.

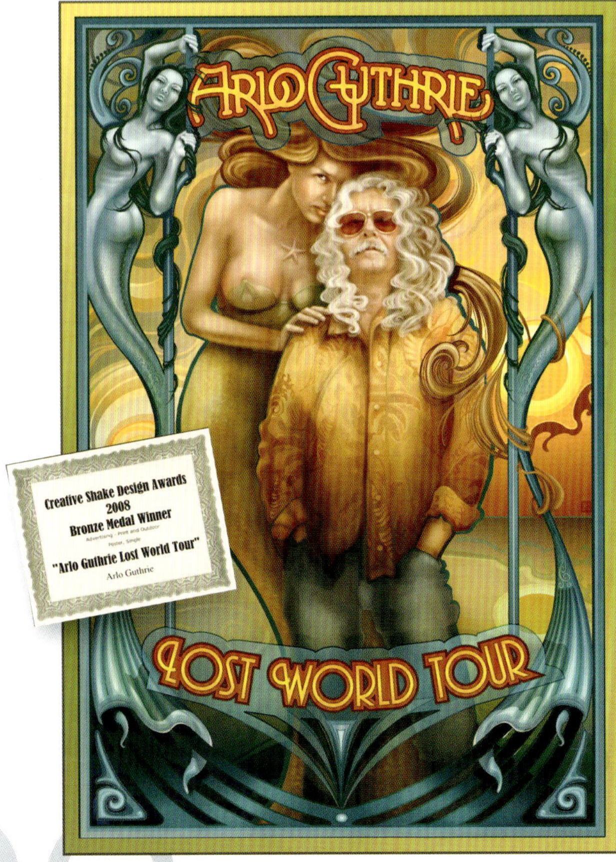

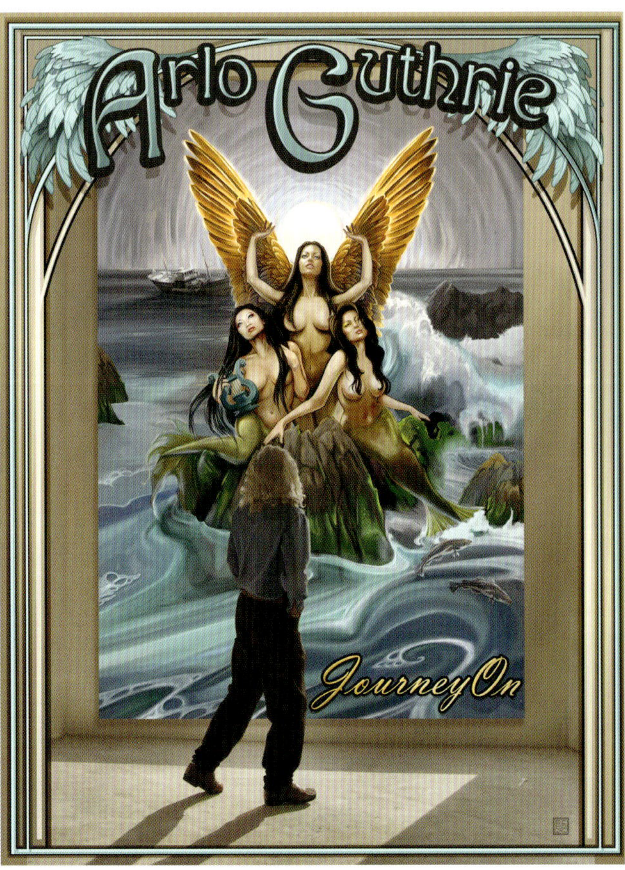

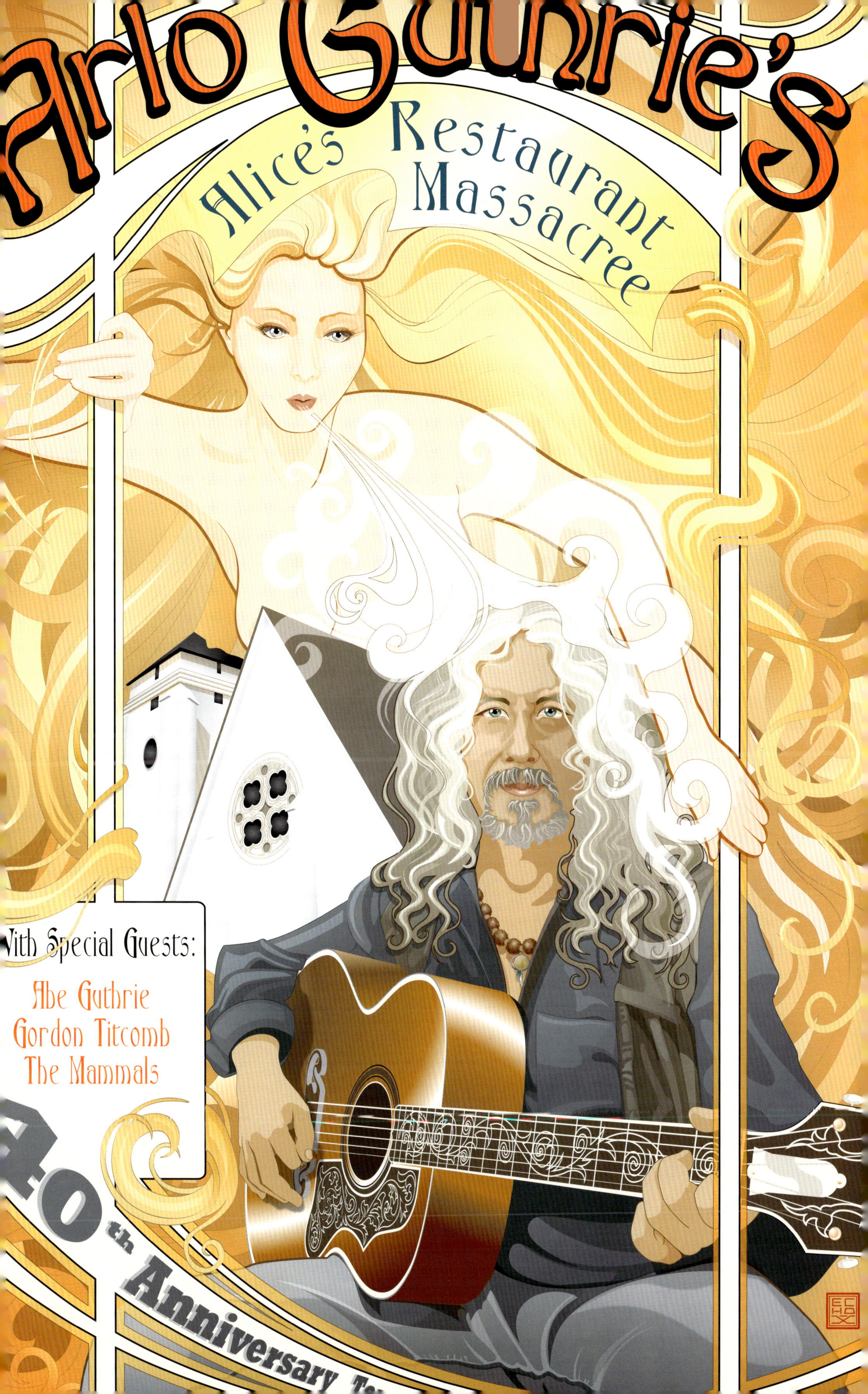

Arlo Guthrie's
Alice's Restaurant Massacree
Special Guests:
Abe Guthrie
Gordon Titcomb
The Mammals
40th Anniversary

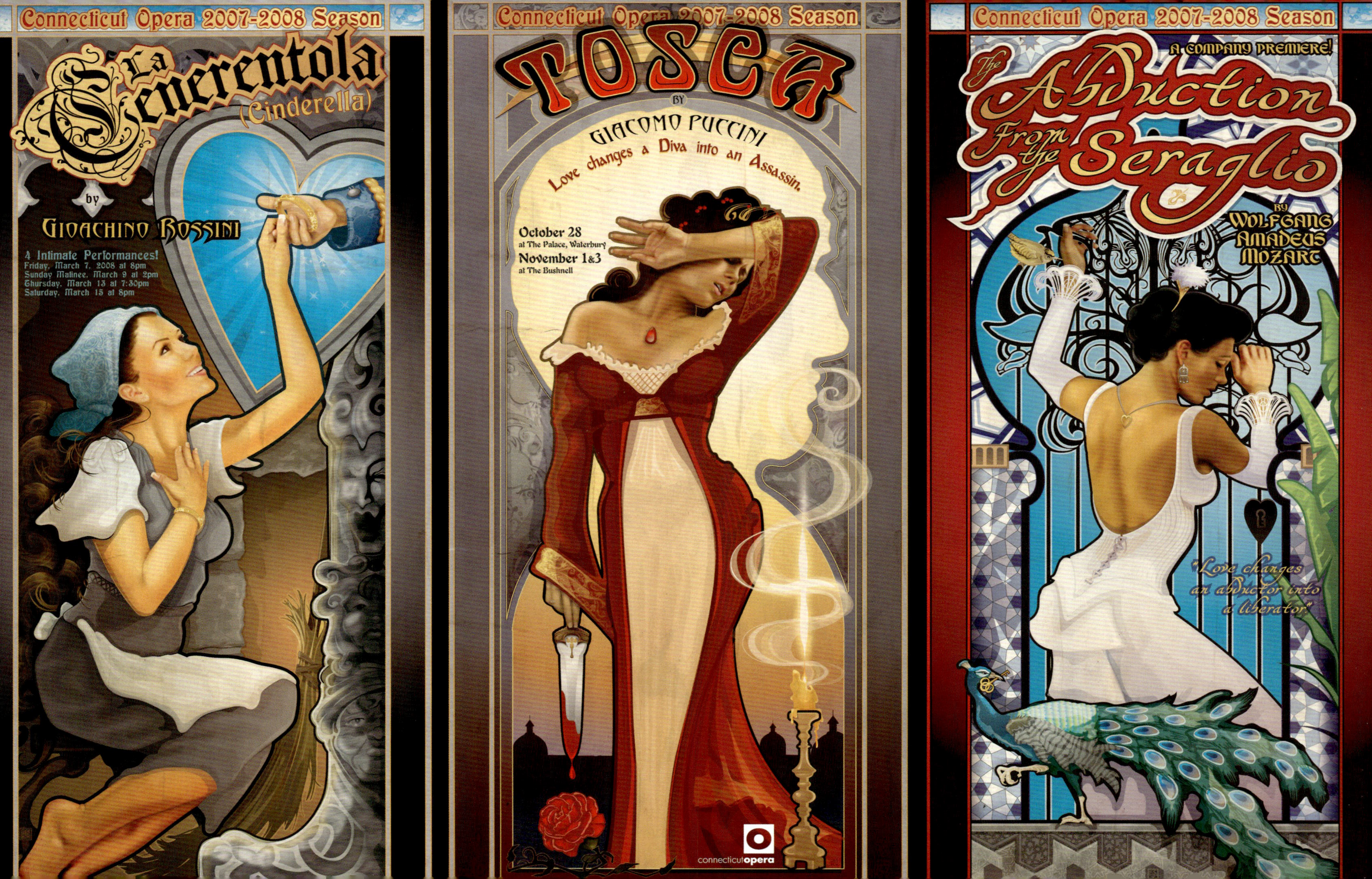
Connecticut Opera 2007-2008 Season
La Cenerentola
(Cinderella)
by
Gioachino Rossini
4 Intimate Performances!
Friday, March 7, 2008 at 8pm
Sunday Matinee, March 9 at 2pm
Thursday, March 13 at 7:30pm
Saturday, March 15 at 8pm
Connecticut Opera 2007-2008 Season
TOSCA
by
Giacomo Puccini
Love changes a Diva into an Assassin.
October 28
at The Palace, Waterbury
November 1&3
at The Bushnell
connecticutopera
Connecticut Opera 2007-2008 Season
A Company Premiere!
The Abduction From the Seraglio
by
Wolfgang Amadeus Mozart
"Love changes an abductor into a liberator"

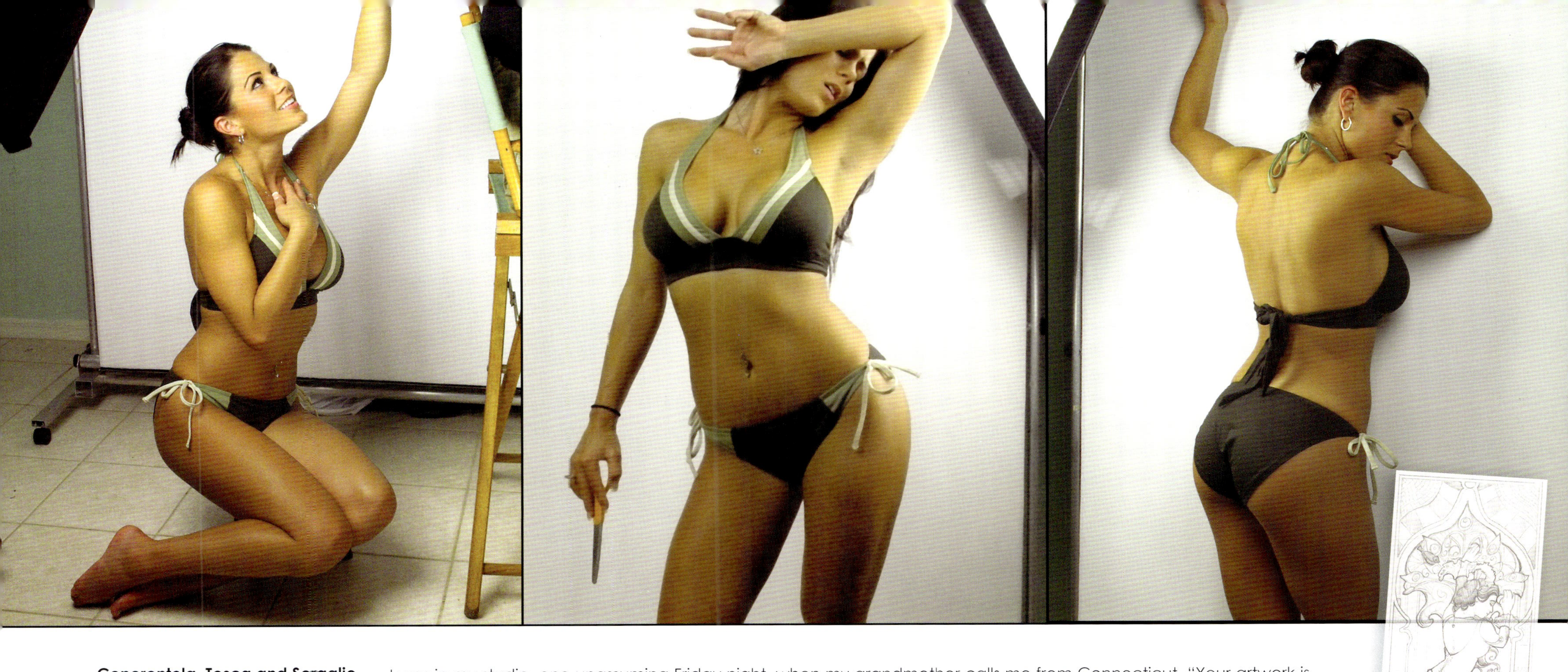

Cenerentola, Tosca and Seraglio
Client: Connecticut Opera
Agency: Wondriska Russo
Year: 2007-2008
Model: Christine LeMaster

I was in my studio, one unassuming Friday night, when my grandmother calls me from Connecticut. "Your artwork is on TV!", she tells me, a bit confused, I did what any recipient of an enigmatic phone call would do and Googled it. Apparently, the Connecticut Opera had run up a few hundred of the Tosca posters, and within a week, most had been stolen. The local news had done a segment on the poster thefts. This led to my local news doing similar; as well as half a dozen newspaper articles. You can find these on my website.

A fan of the Neoclassic style (Jacques-Louis David; "Oath of the Horatii", "Death of Socrates") and the high amount of symbolism it carries with it, I like to build symbolism into my pieces whenever possible. For instance, if you are familiar with Tosca, you will notice the shrouded Mario, the silhouette of Scarpia encompassing Tosca, the crucifix that she places over his heart, and the lies (as smoke) that seep from his lips.... You will notice symbolism in most of my works. When possible, I like my all details to have meaning versus being extraneous. Every detail should be a choice, there on purpose, and for a visual reason.

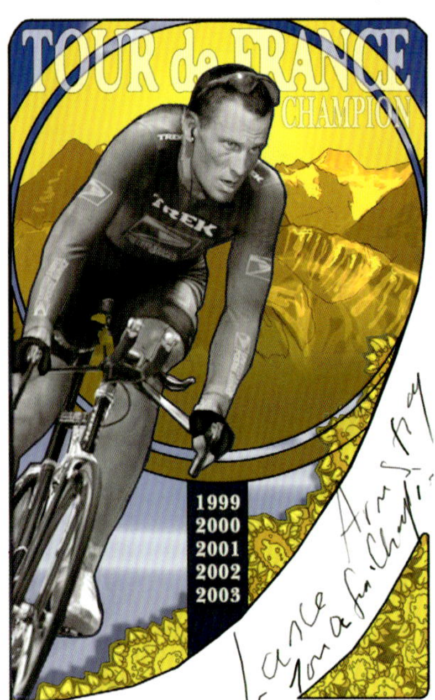

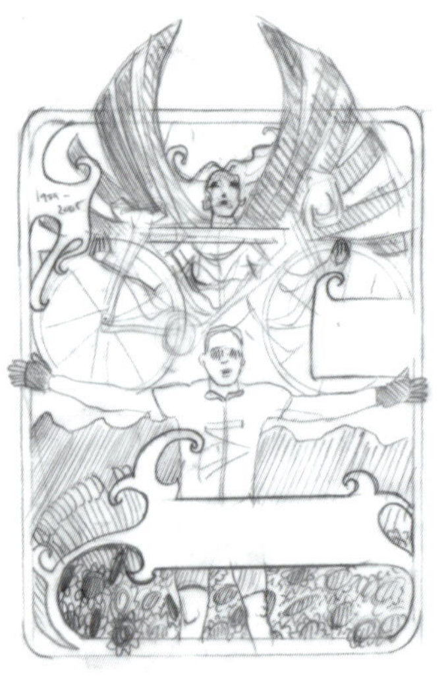

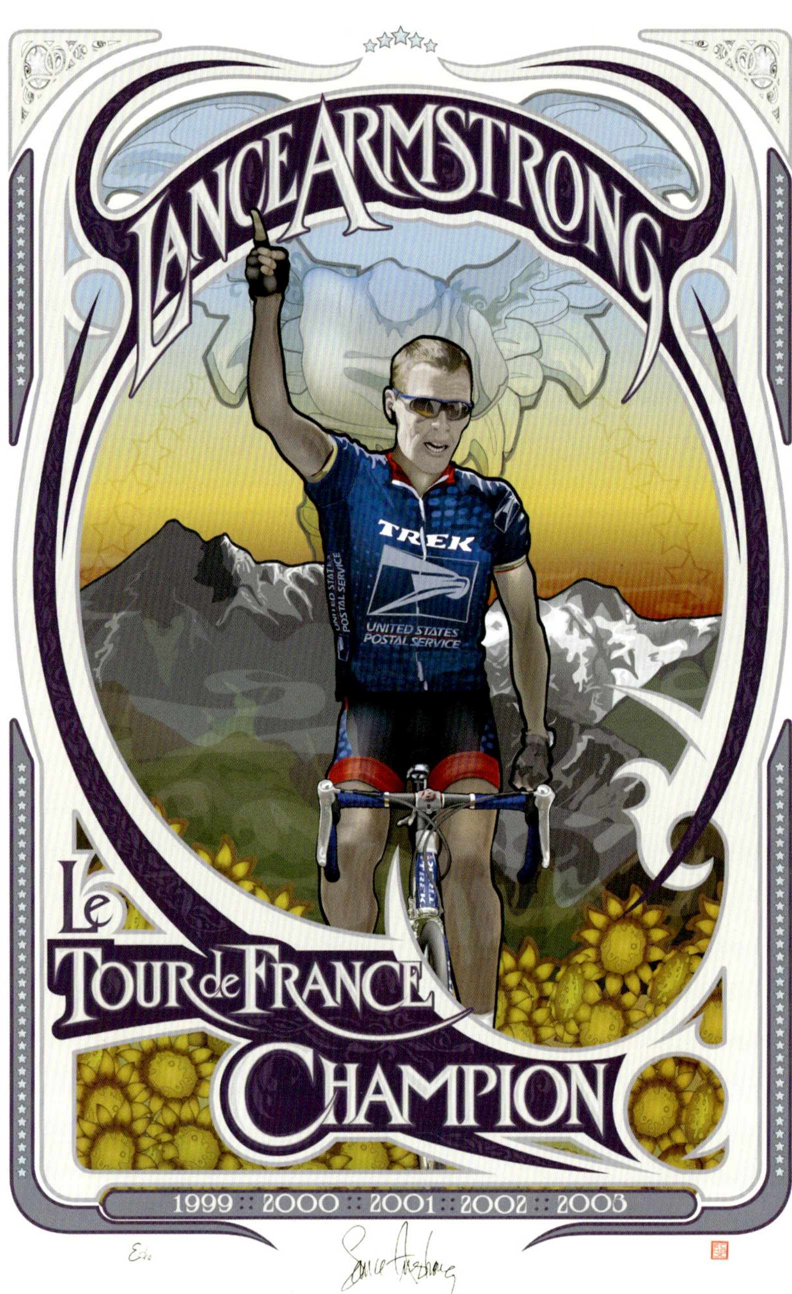

Le Tour de France Champion 5 Years Running
Client: Trek Bicycles
Agency: Internal
Year: 2003
Model: Lance Armstrong

Trek was the first pure advertising poster that I was commissioned for, after years of publishing and rpg illustration. The poster was commemorating Lance Armstrong's fourth (or fifth) consecutive Le Tour de France win. Two versions of the poster were commissioned, in case he lost the race. I prepared six or seven concepts, several based around the personification of Nike - Winged Victory. Ultimately the client chose to use this very particular photo reference of Lance; and my concept work was scrapped. The typography was later added by an internal designer. Ultimately the client loved the poster.

You learn early on as a commercial illustrator, that on some projects your vision does not match the clients. My philosophy is to push to create the best art possible, but if the client has something in mind that they are envisioning - as long as the end product pleases them, that's what the job is all about. Move on to the next project knowing that you did your best.

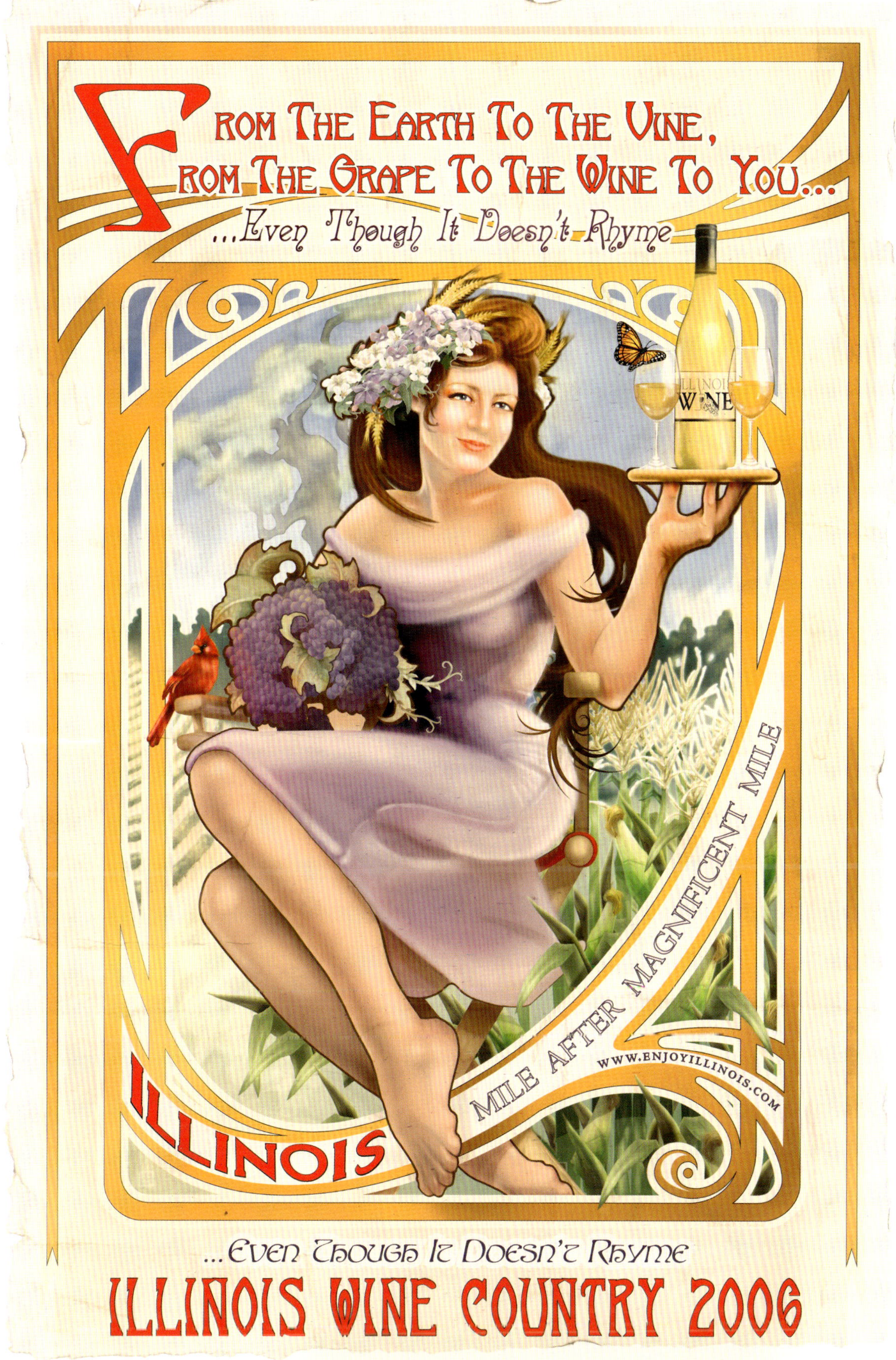

Illinois Wine Poster
Client: Illinois Dept. of Commerce
Agency: JWT
Year: 2006
Model: Echo Chernik

This poster was an advertisement for the State of Illinois tourism, and was hung in bus stations around Chicago. The original concept was for it to look like a Mucha illustration. Apparently, I captured Mucha's style so well that it made their lawyers nervous, and I was requested to submit this much softer version of poster. It is part of an ongoing campaign.

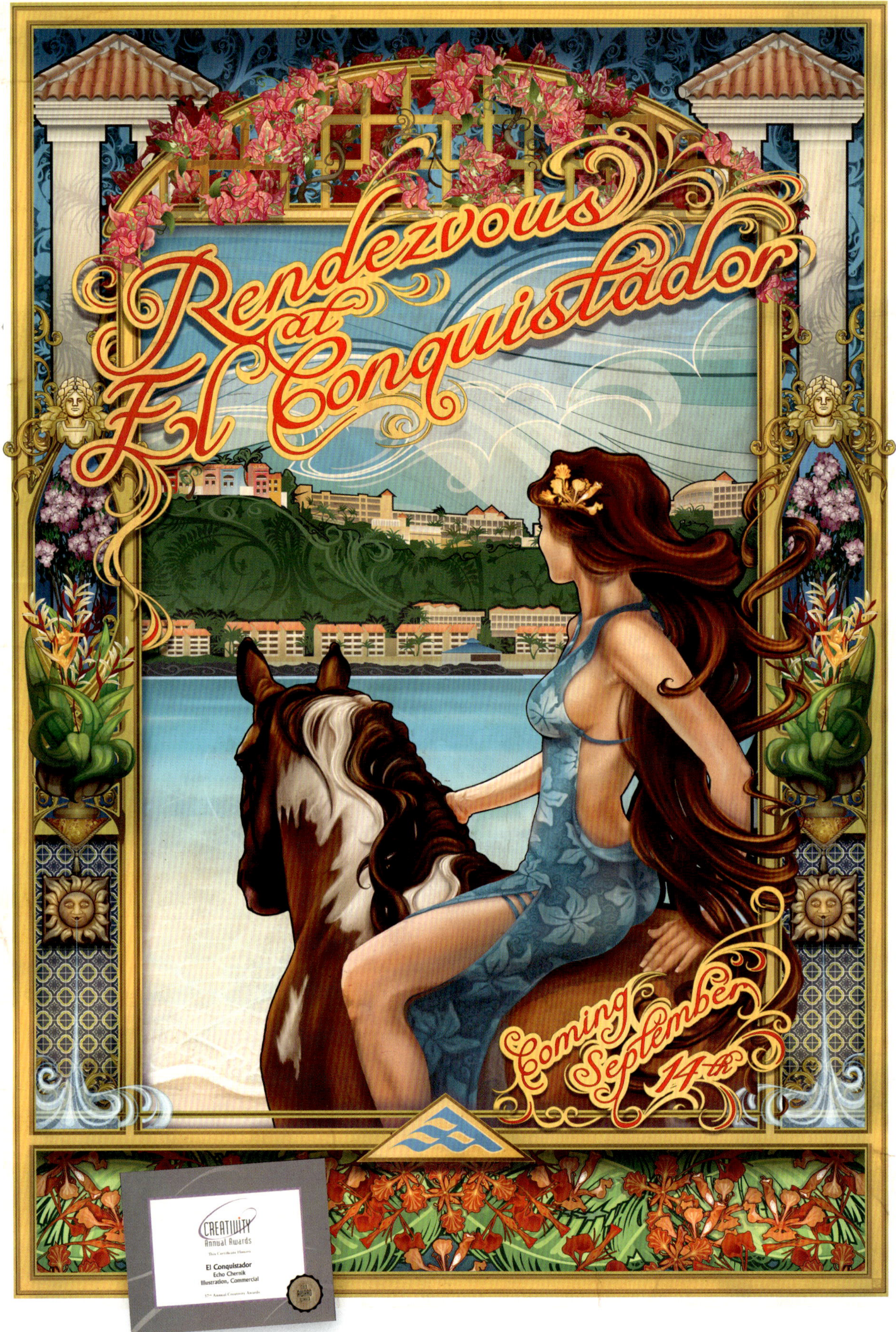

Rendezvous
Client: El Conquistador Resort
Agency: Zimmerman
Year: 2008
Model: Country Lane
Rep: Mendola Artists

This very large movie poster was promoting a short documentary on the El Conquistador resort in Puerto Rico celebrating the relaunch of their corporate center. I spent three days at the resort, photographing architectural elements, and concepting with the director. All of the elements in this poster are located at the resort, and I stayed at the blue villa on the cliff while visiting. It was one of my most enjoyable posters to create! There are several smaller spot illustrations and vertical banners that accompany it.

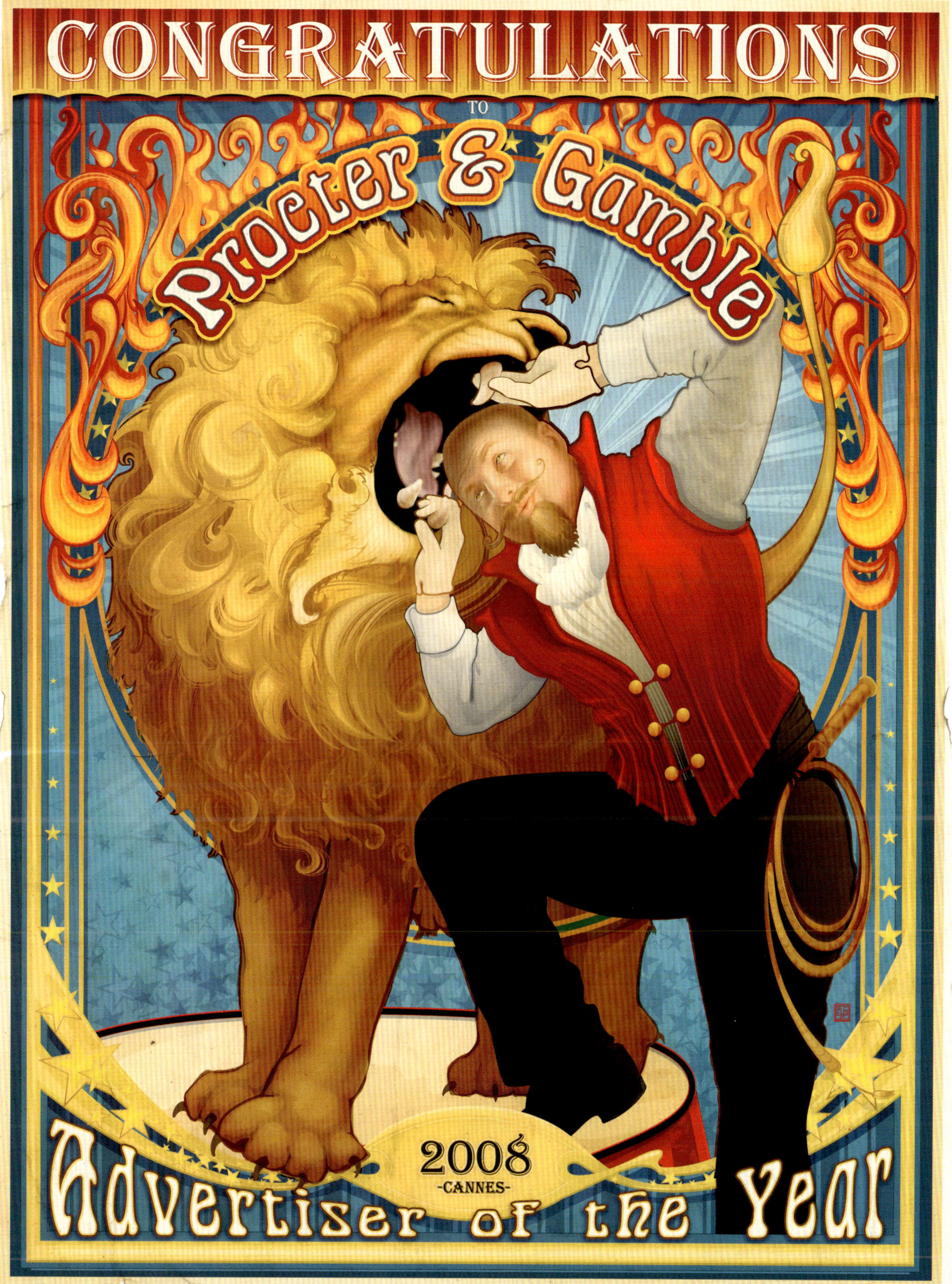

Cannes Lions' Reward
Client: Proctor & Gamble
Agency: Leo Burnett
Year: 2008
Model: Lazarus Chernik

Lazarus shows up at the studio after a business trip, to be greeted by me at the door, holding a vest and a whip. "Put this on, and meet me in the studio." You get used to such things at my studio. This was a rush job for Leo Burnett, to be presented to Proctor & Gamble as a congratulatory gift for winning at Cannes. They were a dream to work with! After it was done I received a letter from the chief creative director who was apparently blown away by it. I had two and a half days to complete the project.

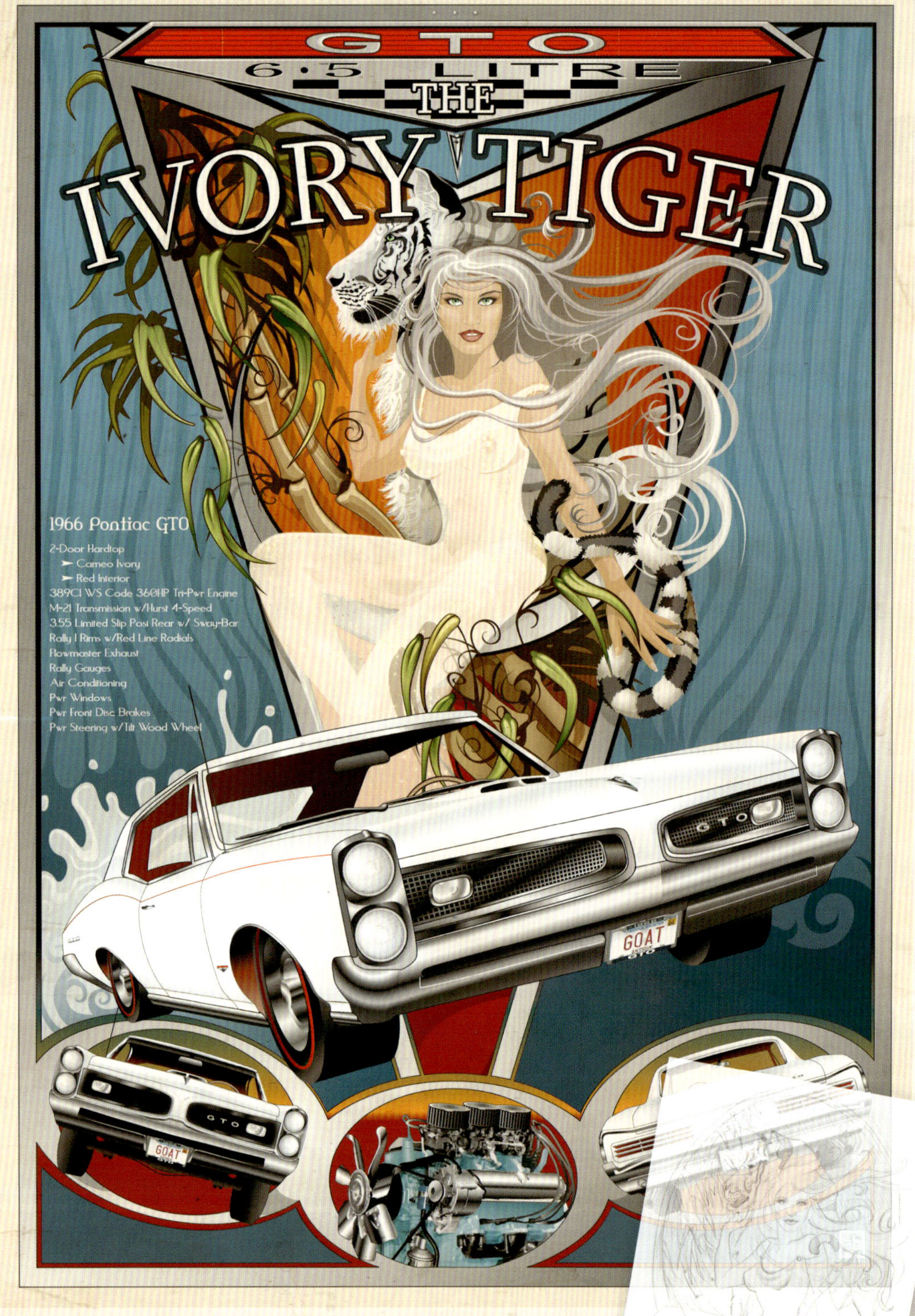

Ivory Tiger
Client: Rich Leone
Year: 2006
Model: Echo Chernik

This piece required Lazarus and I to work together from the beginning and is our most comprehensive collaboration to date. The client showcased his mint condition Pontiac GTO at shows across the country and wanted a poster to advertise with and sell. The client sent us photos of his Ivory Tiger and we both set to work. I created the figure, tiger and the organic elements while Laz produced the cars, engine, logo and all the geometric elements.

I use high-quality tracing vellum for all of my drawings. It allows me to draw, reposition and trace the same element over and over again until I arrive at a final design I'm happy with.

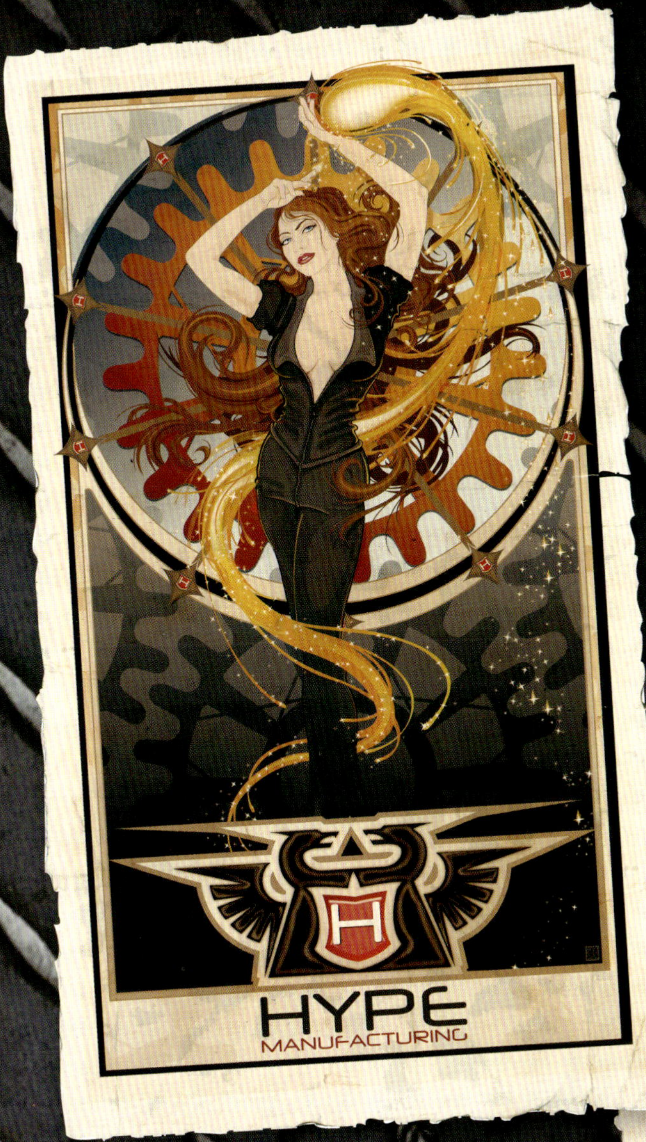

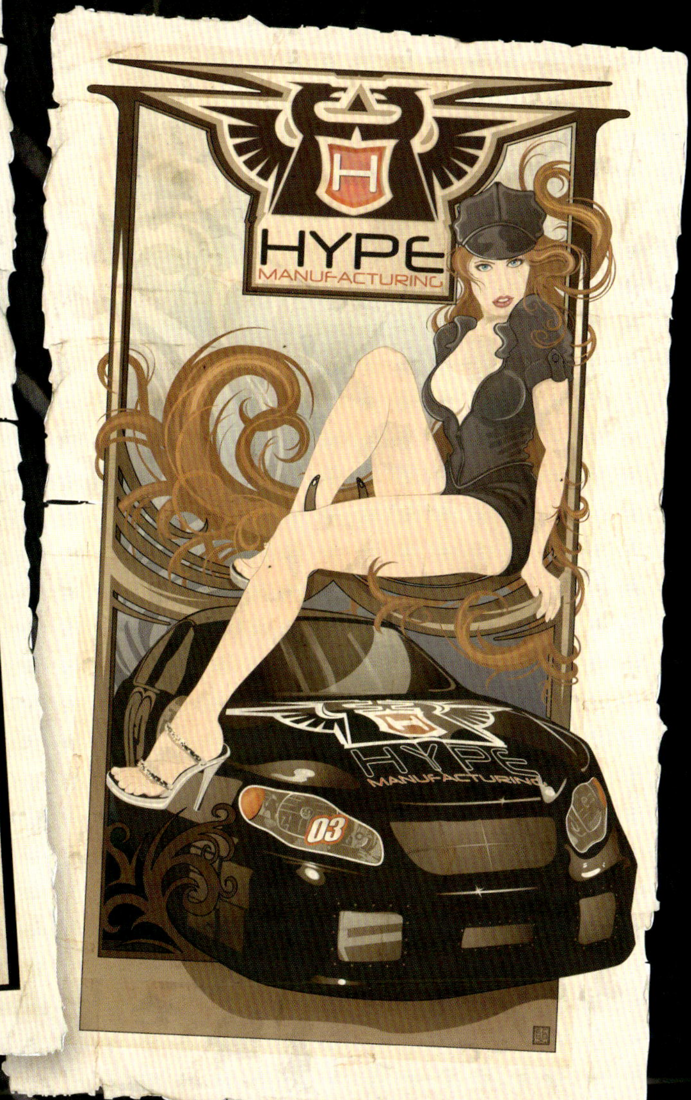

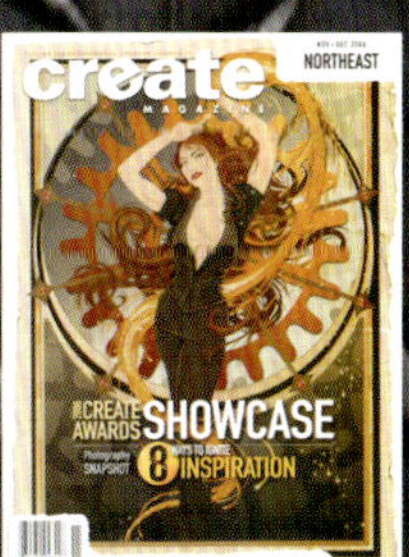

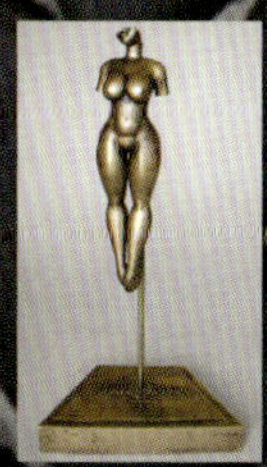
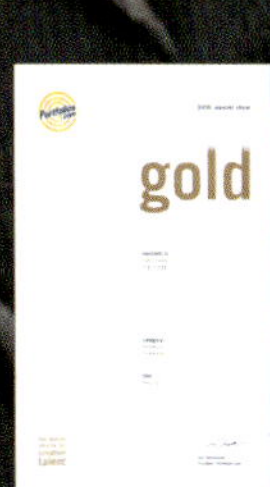

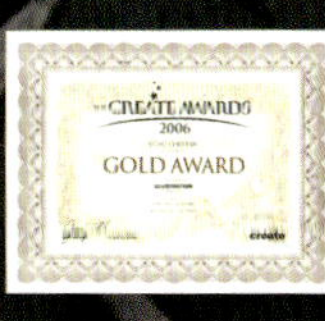

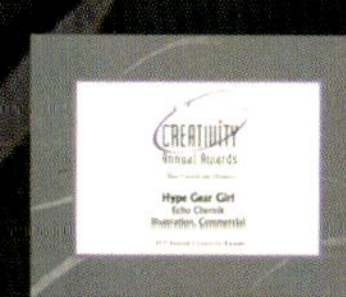
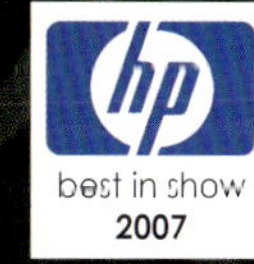

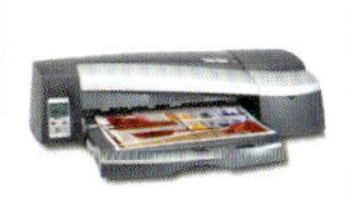

Hype Girl 1 (Spark Girl) and Hype Girl 2 (Speed Girl)
Client: Hype Manufacturing
Year: 2006
Model: Meghan Perkins

These sister illustrations were created for Hype Manufacturing, who manufactures racing car parts, to promote their car in Nascar. The posters won half a dozen Gold and Silver awards, and Spark Girl was featured on the cover of Create Magazine in the fall of 2006. There is nothing like promotion that can really catapult your career forward. It took me nearly three years to catch up with the seemingly endless barrage of work that resulted from that one magazine cover. I have been interviewed and featured in half a dozen magazines since then, but that one cover filled my dance card for the next few years.

It's beneficial for illustrators to enter their works into selective competitions. There are quite a few out there, but the right ones can give you exposure that is worth the entry fee many times over. I have been included in several issues of Spectrum Fantastic Art and I still receive leads from when my work was in Spectrum 14 many years ago.

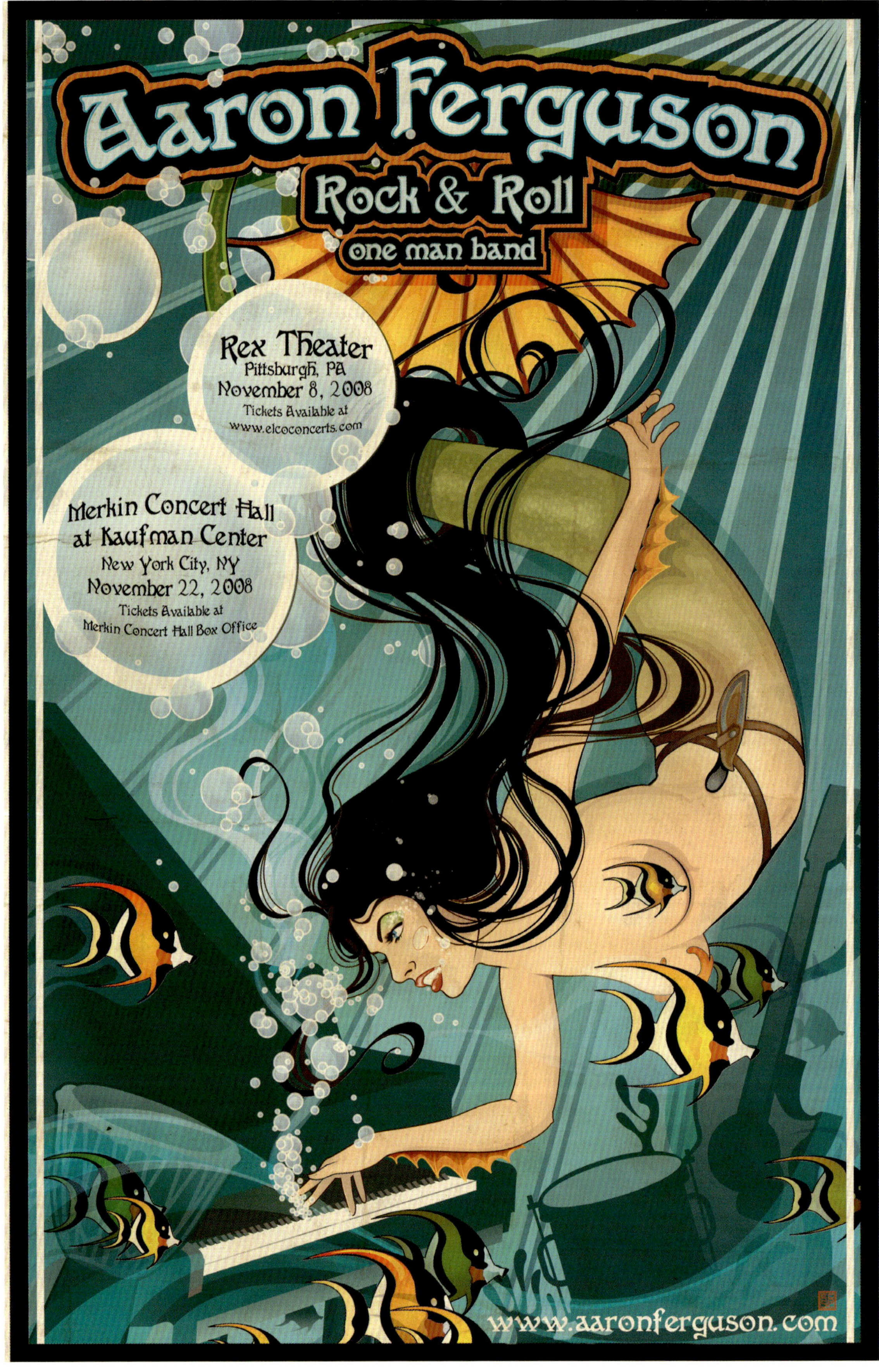

Rock & Roll Mermaid
Client: Aaron Ferguson
Agency: Internal
Year: 2008
Model: Meghan Perkins

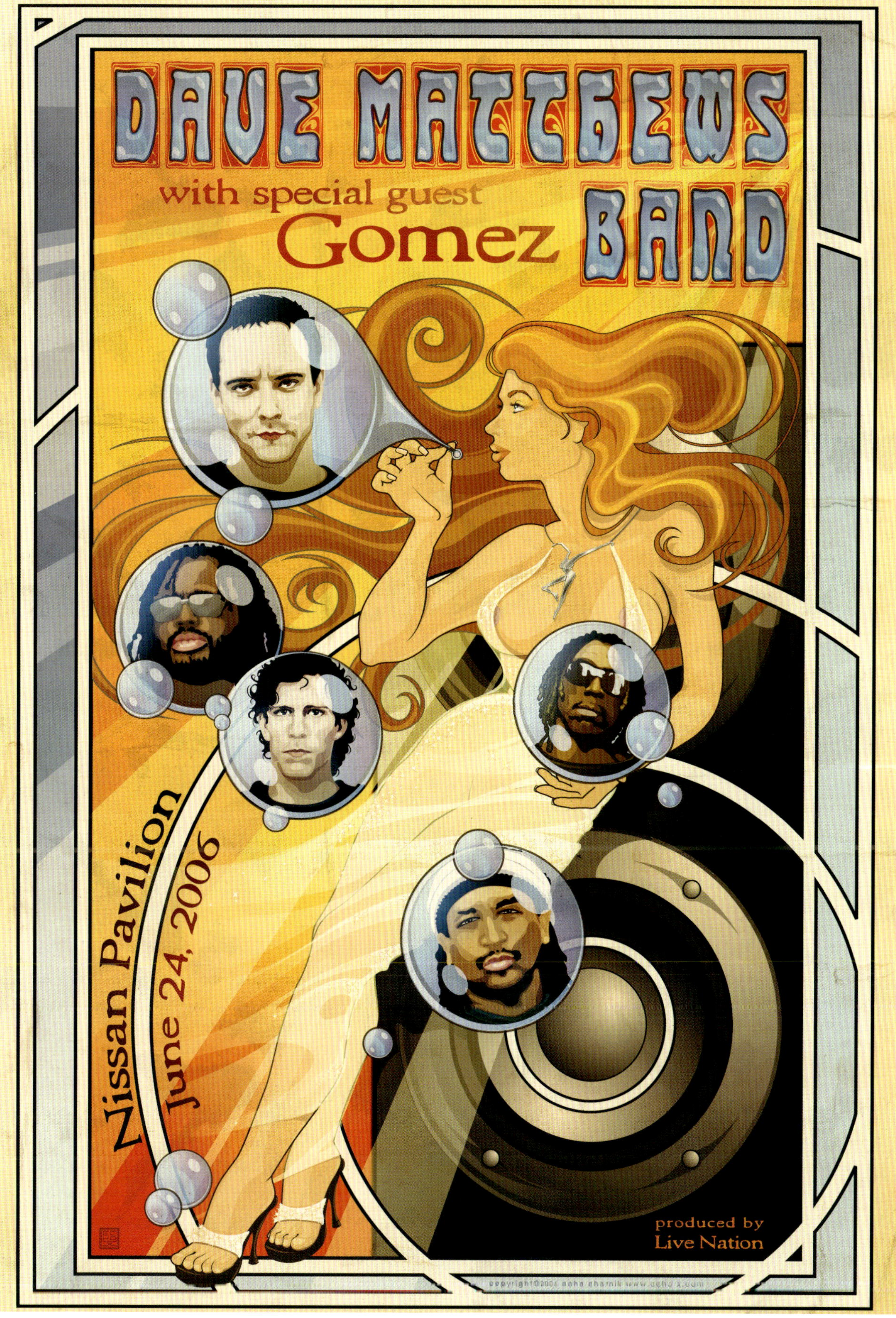

Bubble Girl
Client: Dave Matthews Band
Agency: LiveNation
Year: 2006
Model: Meghan Perkins

This poster was presented to a very small selection of people involved with the Dave Matthews Band, including the band itself. I had a very short deadline and a limited budget for the poster, but thought that it would be fun to tackle. It was a special edition run of only twenty-five.

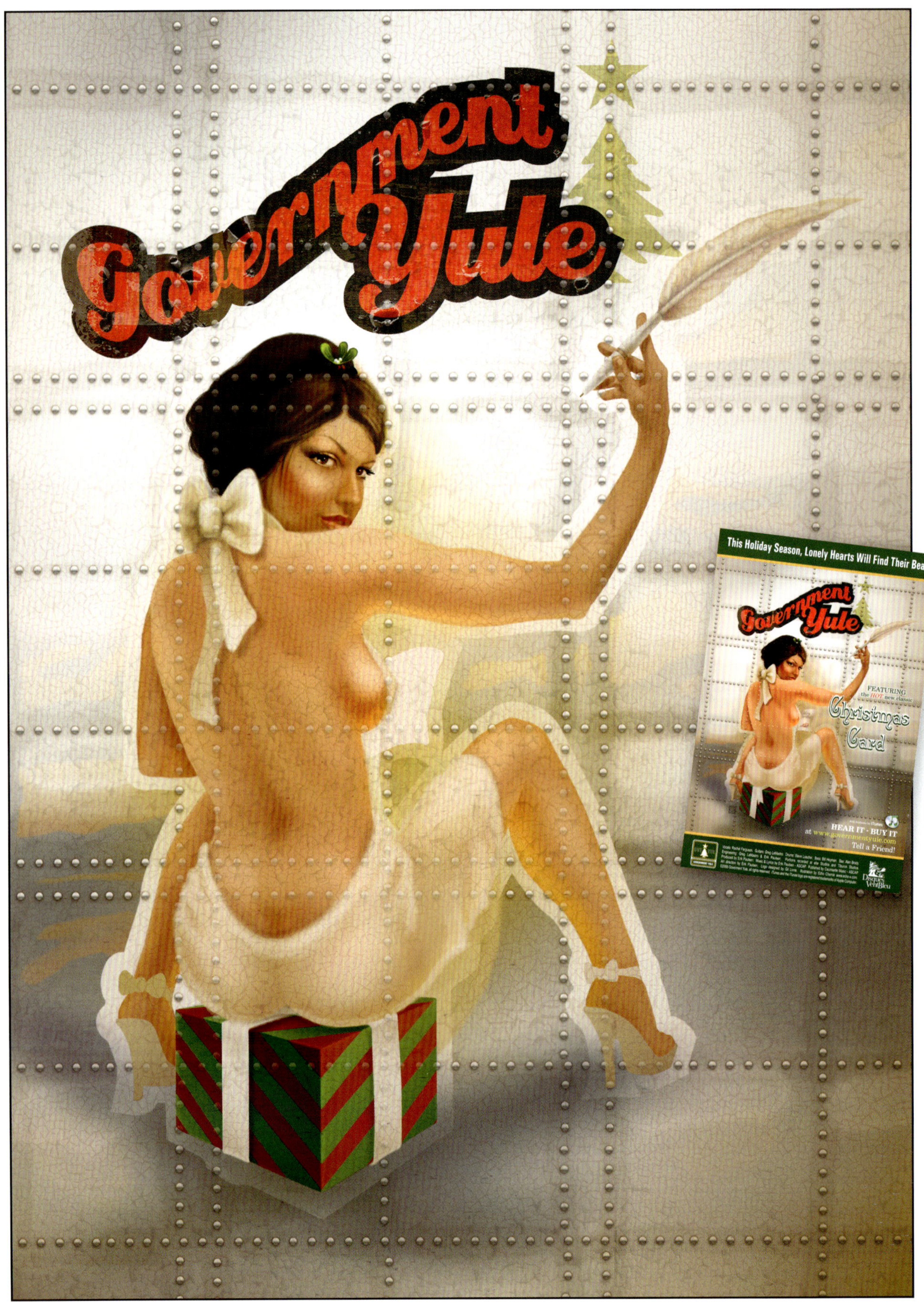

Bomber Girl
Client: Government Yule
Year: 2006
Model: Meghan Perkins

This piece was for the release of a private label holiday song. The concept was a sexy pin-up sweetheart writing to her military significant other in the style of pin-up girl bomber nose art.

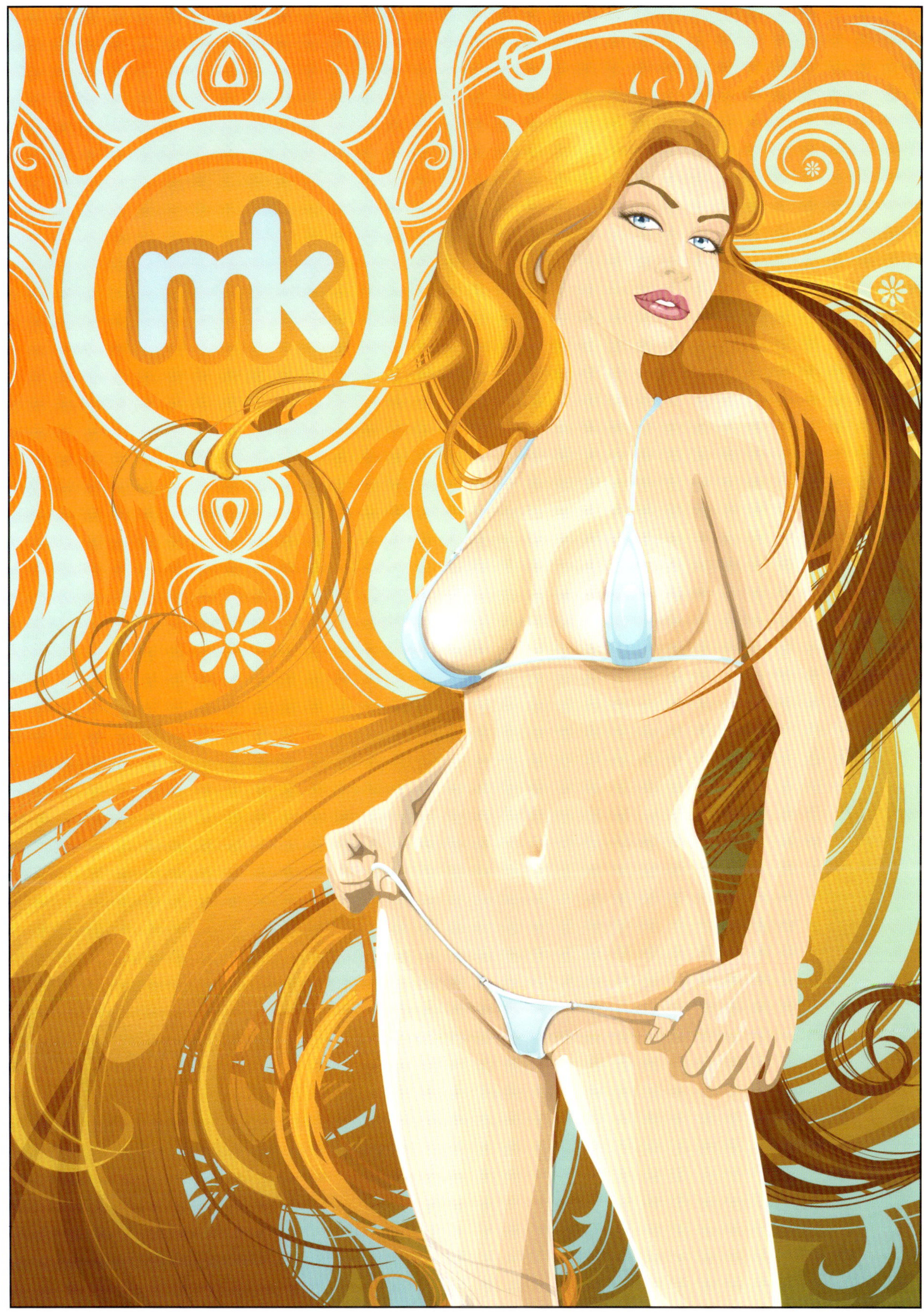

Microkitten Microkinis
Client: Microkitten Microkini
Year: 2009
Models: Christine LeMaster, Meghan Perkins

The client supplied the props for this piece. In other words, I received a very small sandwich bag with half a dozen miniscule thongs and bikini tops. The good news is, I got to keep the very, very small samples. The art direction emphasized that I make the bikini super-duper small. But in fact, when I sent the final piece to him, he insisted that I make it larger (apparently I had made it **too** small!).

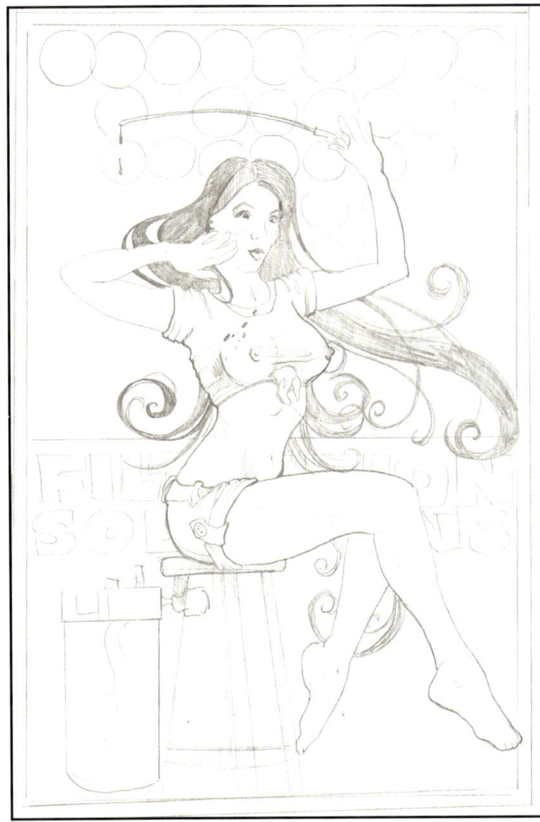

Alternate sketch a la Elvgren. We all agreed it was too "Oopsie - I'm a girl" and I wanted it to be more "So, I'm a sexy Mechanic - you got a problem with that?"

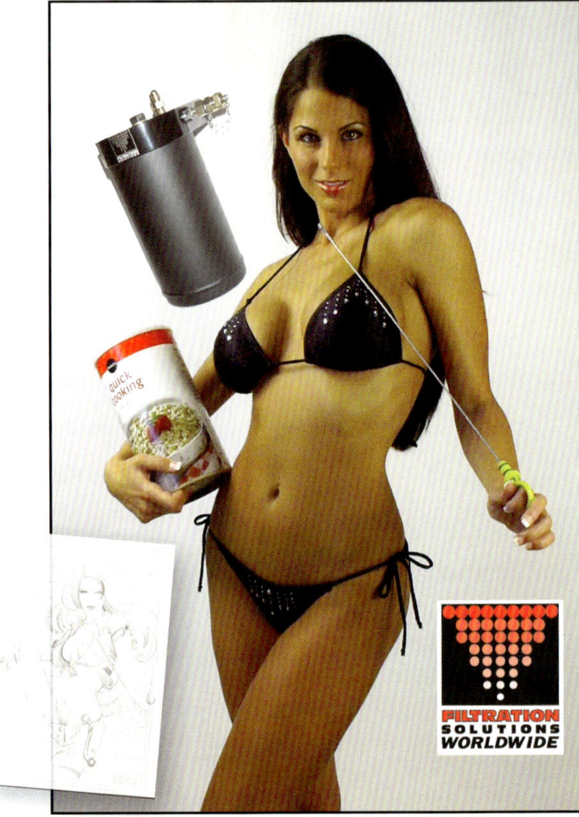

Christine LeMaster posing with a dipstick and a filter substitute. An actual filter hovers in the PSD file for reference. The logo placed for position only.

Soot Sucks!
Client: Filtration Solutions
Agency: Fasone & Partners, Inc.
Year: 2007
Model: Christine LeMaster

The 'Soot Sucks!' concept was simple - create a poster as a give-away to truck stops and commercial mechanics for the trucking industry. The poster hung in mechanic workshops around the country, nestled side by side with the usual pin-ups and centerfolds - but she HAD to stand out. I presented two concepts - an Elvgren inspired pin-up (as requested) and an alternative (the chosen direction). She isn't vapid or vacuous - she's a mechanic who's in on the joke, a capable, strong woman - as most of my women portray. The client hemmed and hawed about whether or not she should be sporting a nipple bump. That is, until the agency pointed out the phallus shaped dipstick dripping clear oil. Then the nipple bump was approved.

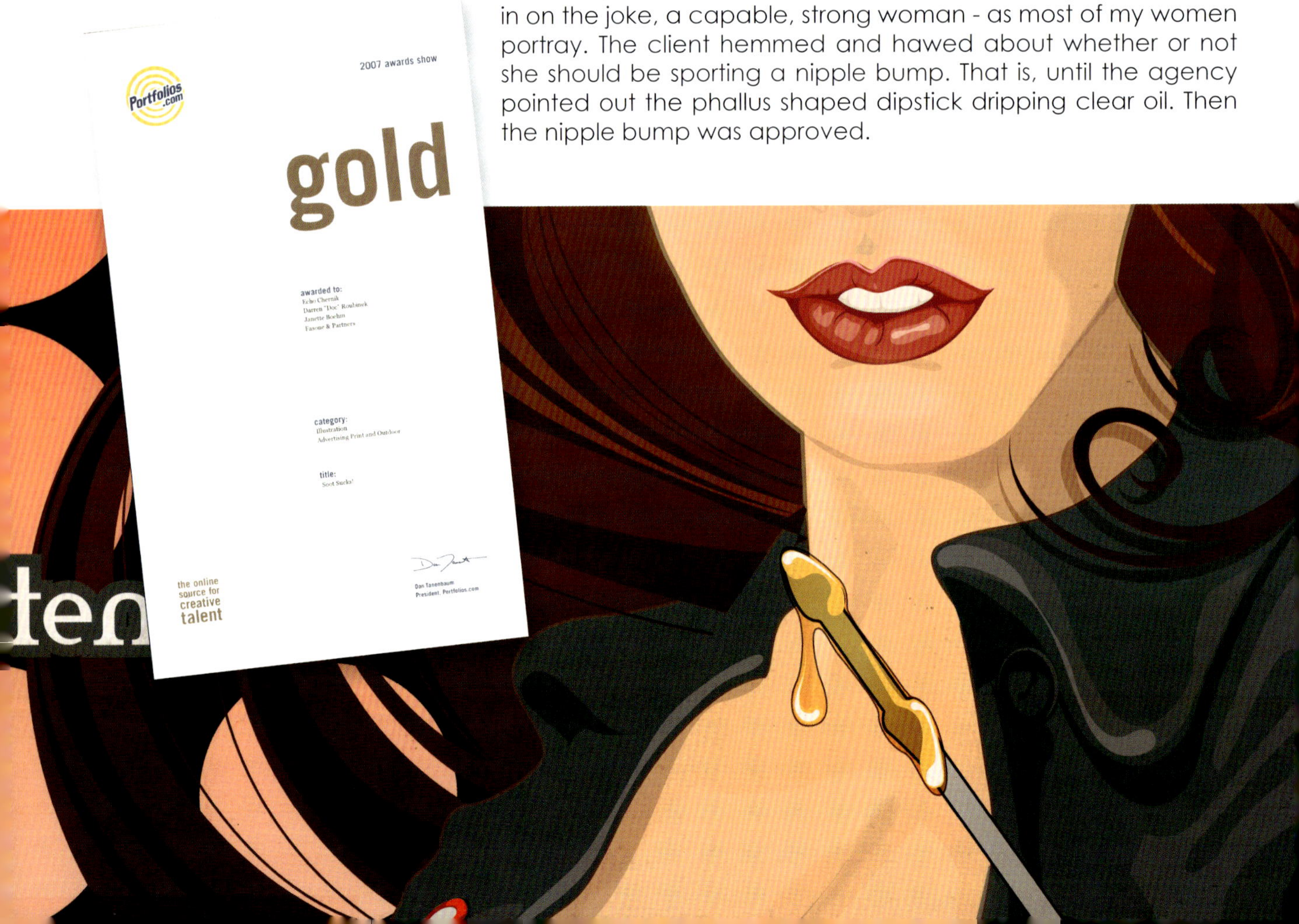

Portfolios.com

2007 awards show

gold

awarded to:
Echo Chernik
Darren "Doc" Roubinek
Janette Boehm
Fasone & Partners

category:
Illustration
Advertising Print and Outdoor

title:
Soot Sucks!

the online source for creative talent

Dan Tanenbaum
President, Portfolios.com

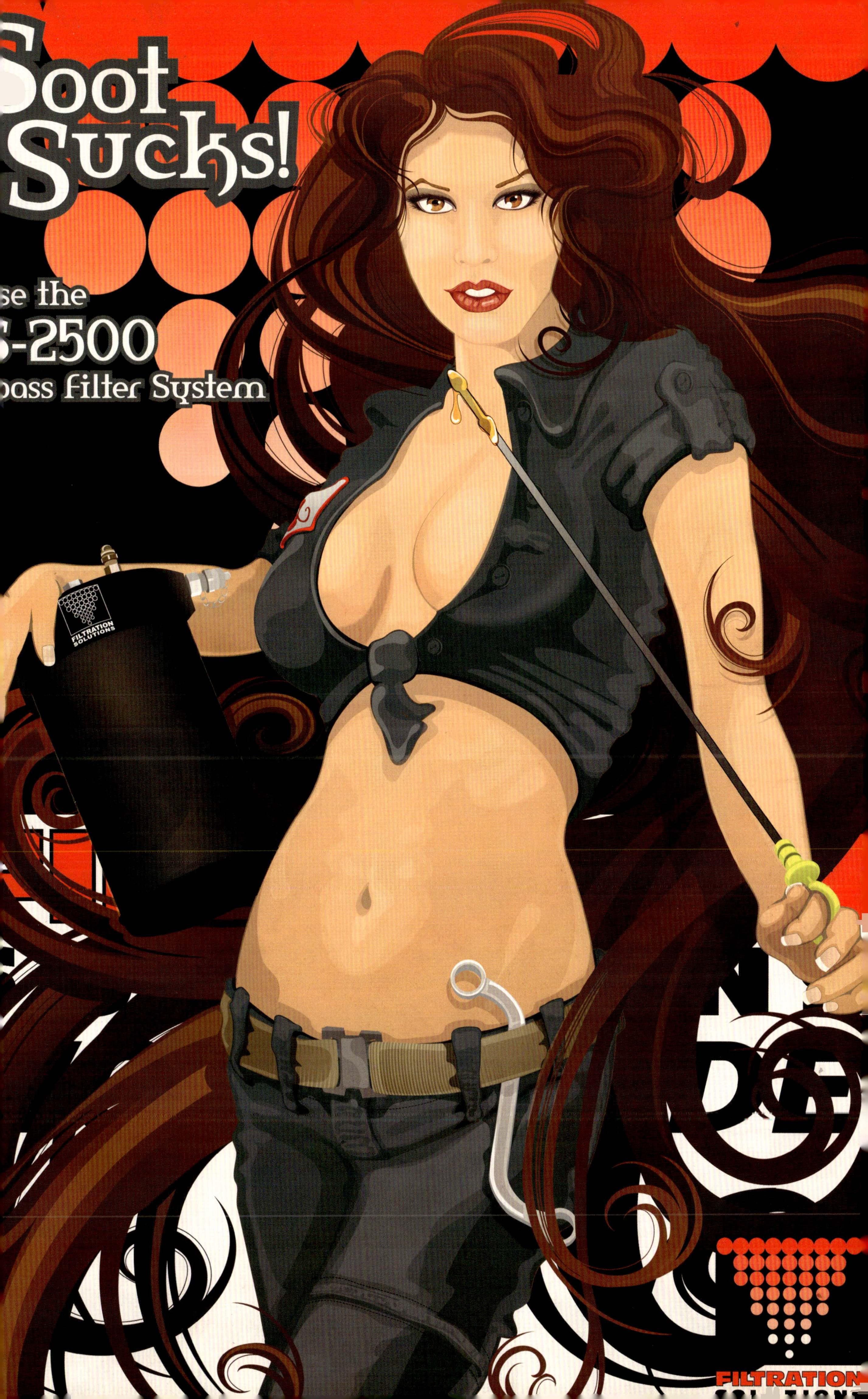

Soot Sucks!
se the
-2500
pass Filter System
FILTRATION SOLUTIONS
FILTRATION

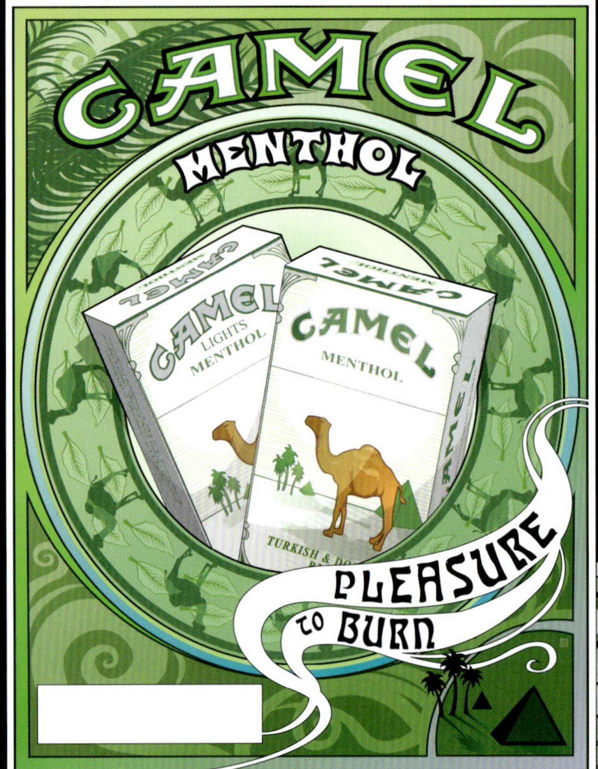

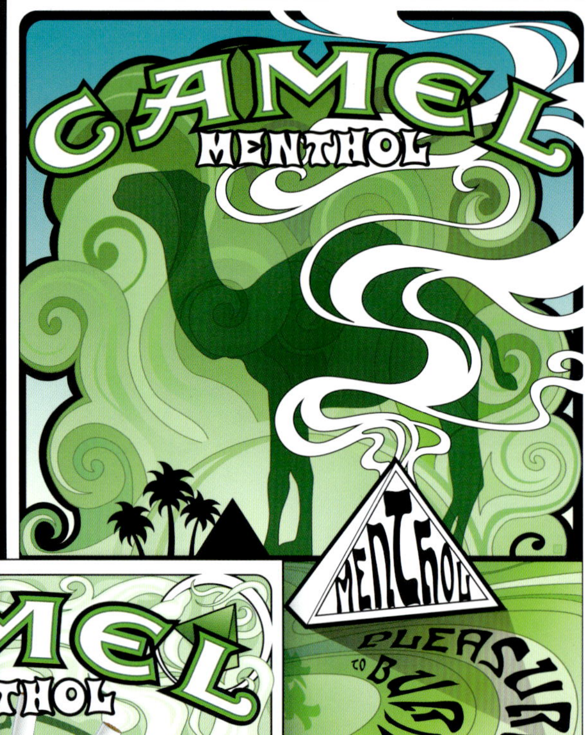

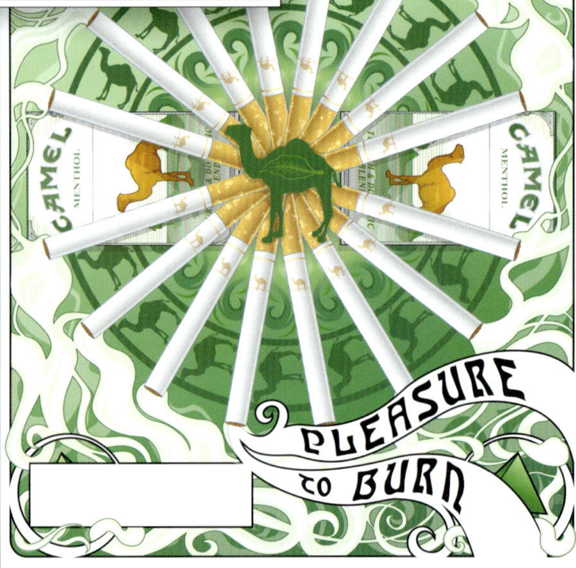

Camel Menthol
Client: Camel
Agency: Agent16
Year: 2003

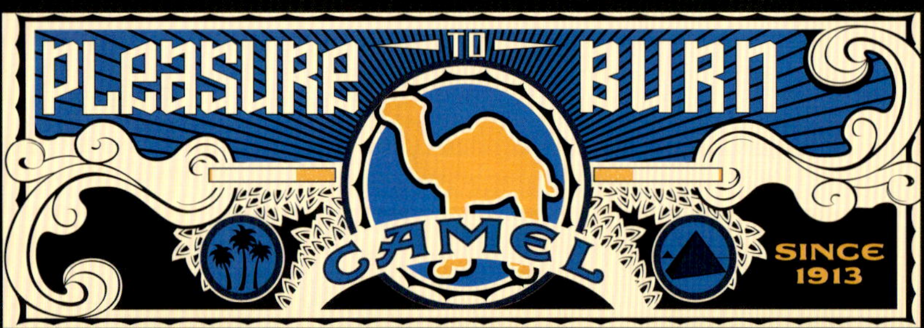

The above Menthol magazine advertisements for Camel cigarettes were part of a full out agency pitch. The agency hired twenty illustrators to complete finished illustrations, and the client was given its pick on what to use now and what to save for later use. I was supplied with color codes, mechanicals (a page layout with set dimensions and space for the surgeon generals warning) and told to have fun.

Funny insert. I am not a smoker, and for some of the reference shots for the rest of the campaign, I had to be schooled by a smoker on the right way to hold a cigarette using a pen.

Pleasure to Burn
Client: Camel
Agency: Agent16
Year: 2003
Model: Echo Chernik

In this case, I needed a Harley Davidson, and didn't have one handy. So, we asked the local retail store if we could borrow one of their bikes and they were very accommodating. I was mostly looking for hand placement for this shot, and re-shot the face in the studio. Interesting fact, I was five months pregnant when we shot this reference (hello baby!).

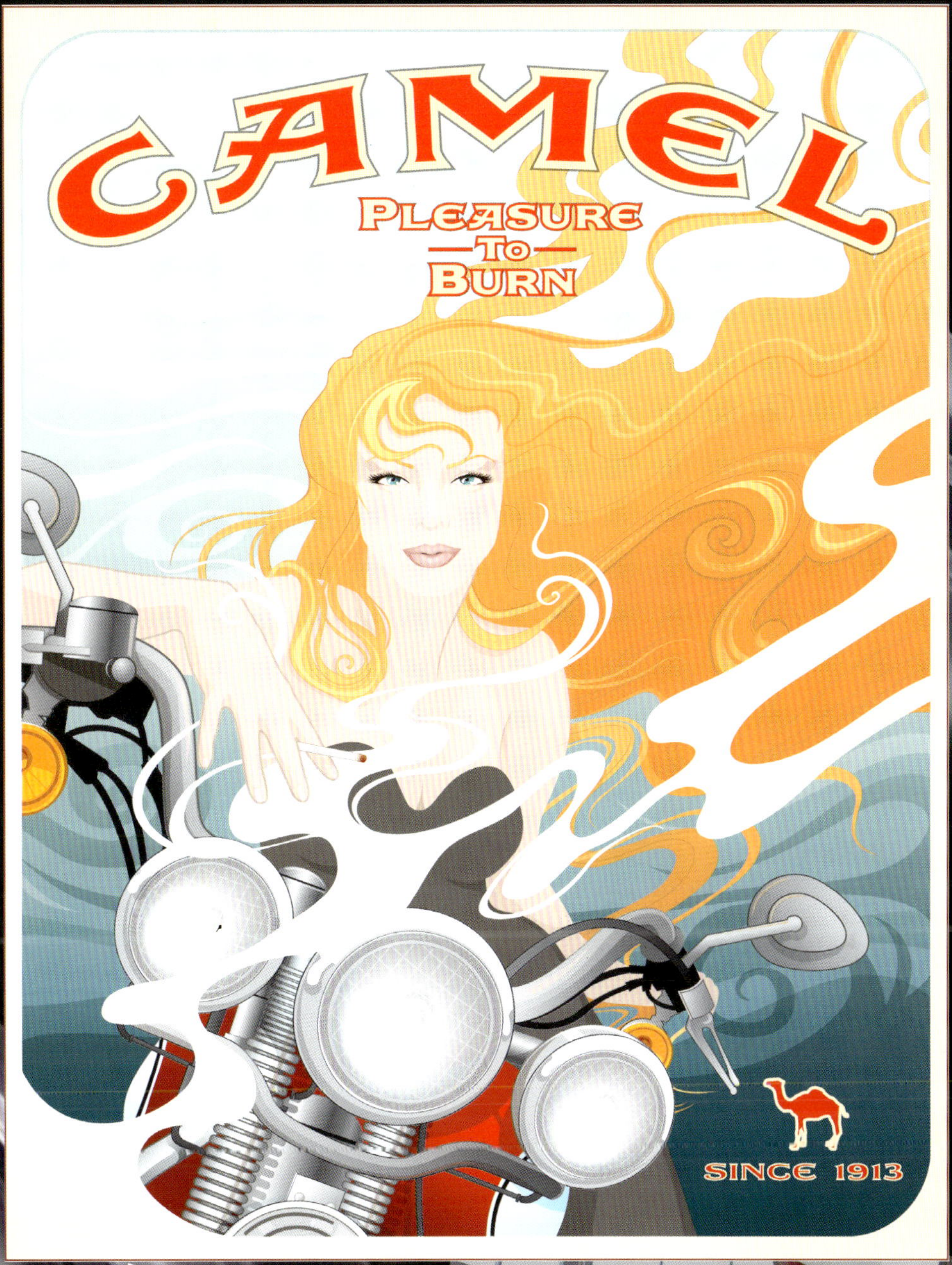

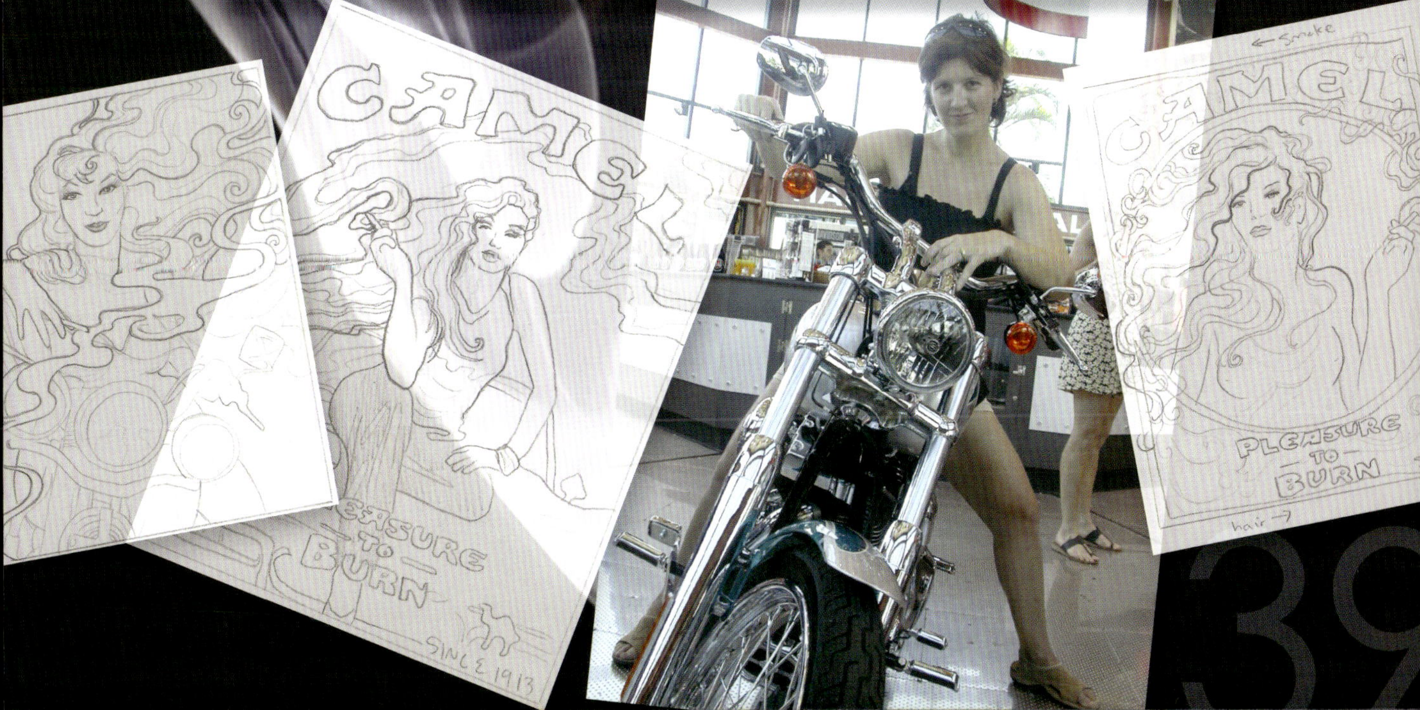

KEYSTONE LIGHT®

A SALUTE TO THE AMERICAN SOLDIER.

ALWAYS SMOOTH

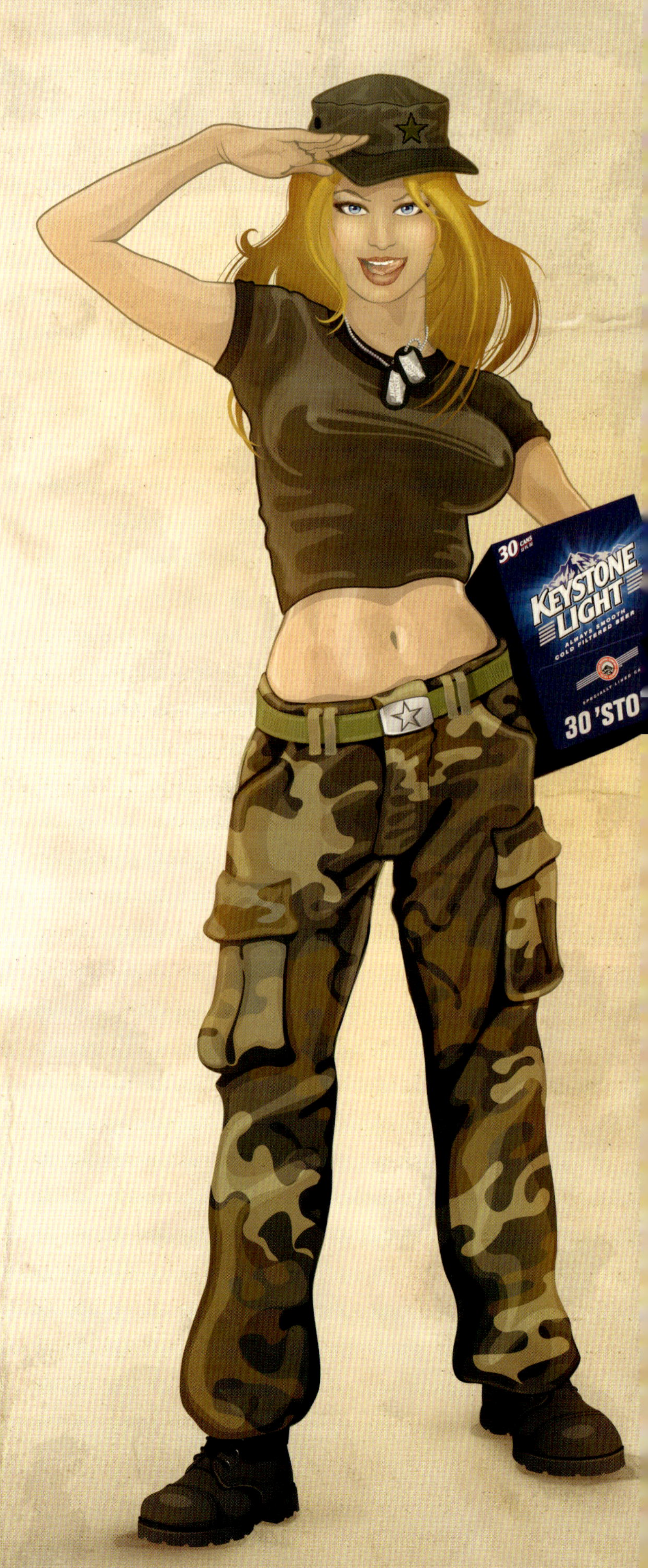

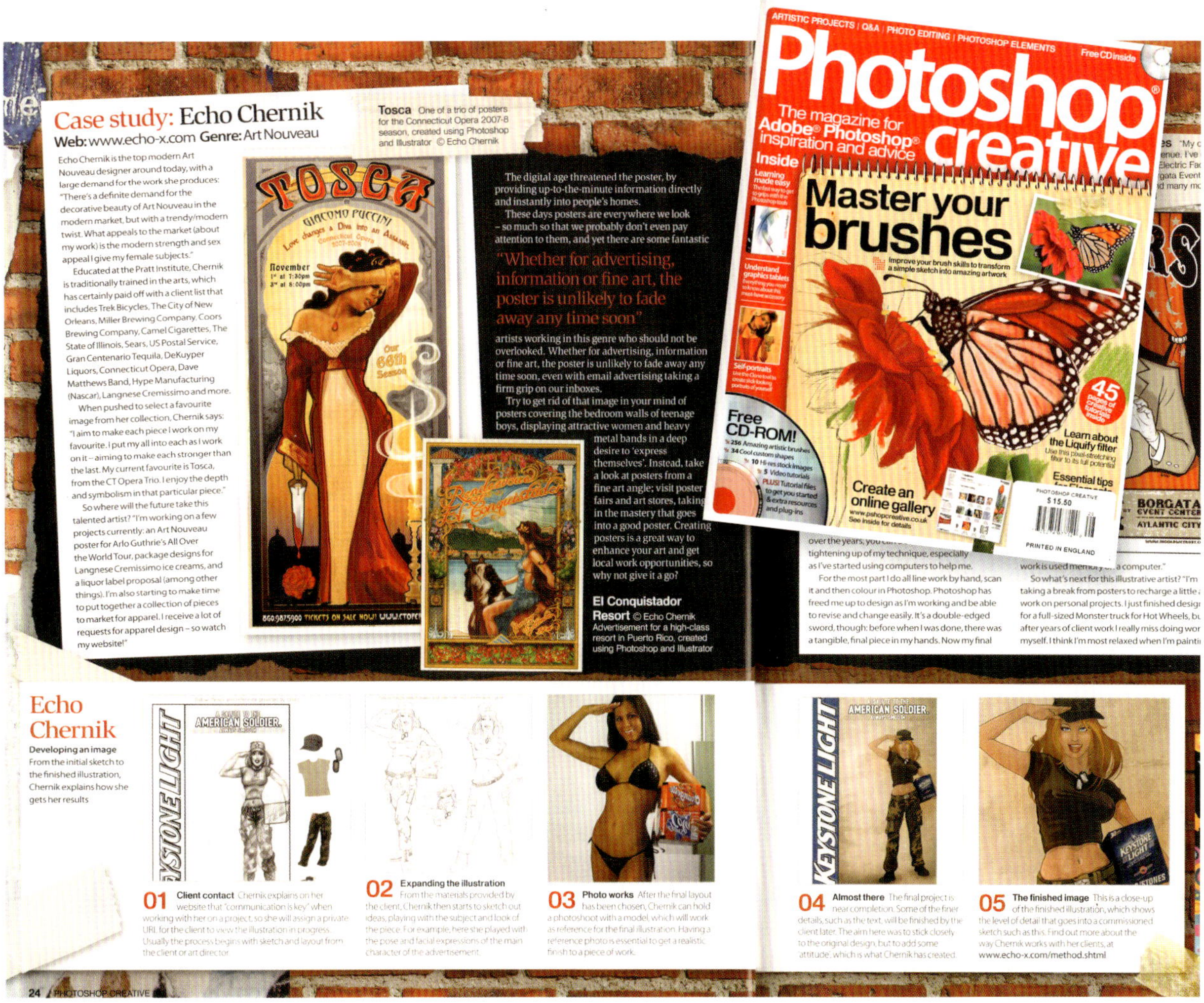

Case study: Echo Chernik

Web: www.echo-x.com **Genre:** Art Nouveau

Echo Chernik is the top modern Art Nouveau designer around today, with a large demand for the work she produces: "There's a definite demand for the decorative beauty of Art Nouveau in the modern market, but with a trendy/modern twist. What appeals to the market (about my work) is the modern strength and sex appeal I give my female subjects."

Educated at the Pratt Institute, Chernik is traditionally trained in the arts, which has certainly paid off with a client list that includes Trek Bicycles, The City of New Orleans, Miller Brewing Company, Coors Brewing Company, Camel Cigarettes, The State of Illinois, Sears, US Postal Service, Gran Centenario Tequila, DeKuyper Liquors, Connecticut Opera, Dave Matthews Band, Hype Manufacturing (Nascar), Langnese Cremissimo and more.

When pushed to select a favourite image from her collection, Chernik says: "I aim to make each piece I work on my favourite. I put my all into each as I work on it – aiming to make each stronger than the last. My current favourite is Tosca, from the CT Opera Trio. I enjoy the depth and symbolism in that particular piece."

So where will the future take this talented artist? "I'm working on a few projects currently: an Art Nouveau poster for Arlo Guthrie's All Over the World Tour, package designs for Langnese Cremissimo ice creams, and a liquor label proposal (among other things). I'm also starting to make time to put together a collection of pieces to market for apparel. I receive a lot of requests for apparel design – so watch my website!"

Tosca One of a trio of posters for the Connecticut Opera 2007-8 season, created using Photoshop and Illustrator © Echo Chernik

The digital age threatened the poster, by providing up-to-the-minute information directly and instantly into people's homes.

These days posters are everywhere we look – so much so that we probably don't even pay attention to them, and yet there are some fantastic artists working in this genre who should not be overlooked. Whether for advertising, information or fine art, the poster is unlikely to fade away any time soon, even with email advertising taking a firm grip on our inboxes.

> "Whether for advertising, information or fine art, the poster is unlikely to fade away any time soon"

Try to get rid of that image in your mind of posters covering the bedroom walls of teenage boys, displaying attractive women and heavy metal bands in a deep desire to 'express themselves'. Instead, take a look at posters from a fine art angle; visit poster fairs and art stores, taking in the mastery that goes into a good poster. Creating posters is a great way to enhance your art and get local work opportunities, so why not give it a go?

El Conquistador Resort © Echo Chernik Advertisement for a high-class resort in Puerto Rico, created using Photoshop and Illustrator

For the most part I do all line work by hand, scan it and then colour in Photoshop. Photoshop has freed me up to design as I'm working and be able to revise and change easily. It's a double-edged sword, though: before when I was done, there was a tangible, final piece in my hands. Now my final

So what's next for this illustrative artist? "I'm taking a break from posters to recharge a little ... work on personal projects. I just finished design for a full-sized Monster truck for Hot Wheels, bu... after years of client work I really miss doing wor... myself. I think I'm most relaxed when I'm painti...

Echo Chernik

Developing an image From the initial sketch to the finished illustration, Chernik explains how she gets her results

01 Client contact Chernik explains on her website that "communication is key" when working with her on a project, so she will assign a private URL for the client to view the illustration in progress. Usually the process begins with sketch and layout from the client or art director

02 Expanding the illustration From the materials provided by the client, Chernik then starts to sketch out ideas, playing with the subject and look of the piece. For example, here she played with the pose and facial expressions of the main character of the advertisement

03 Photo works After the final layout has been chosen, Chernik can hold a photoshoot with a model, which will work as reference for the final illustration. Having a reference photo is essential to get a realistic finish to a piece of work

04 Almost there The final project is near completion. Some of the finer details, such as the text, will be finished by the client later. The aim here was to stick closely to the original design, but to add some 'attitude', which is what Chernik has created

05 The finished image This is a close-up of the finished illustration, which shows the level of detail that goes into a commissioned sketch such as this. Find out more about the way Chernik works with her clients, at www.echo-x.com/method.shtml

24 PHOTOSHOP CREATIVE

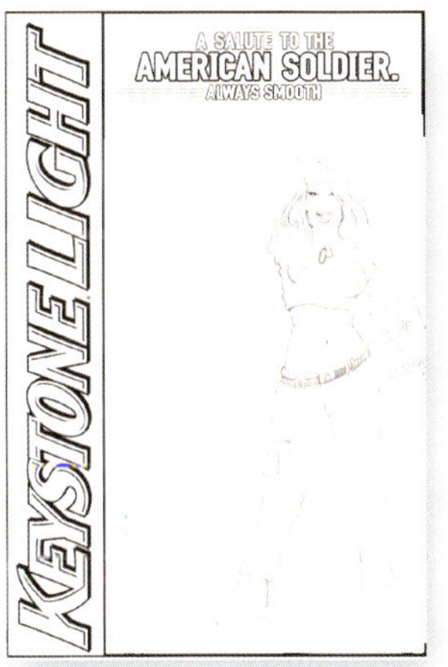

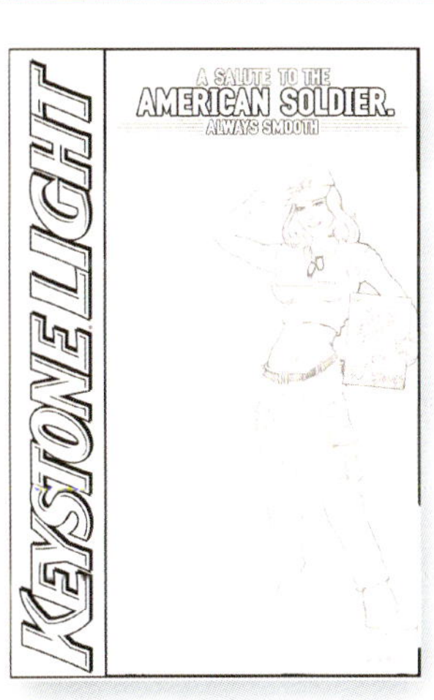

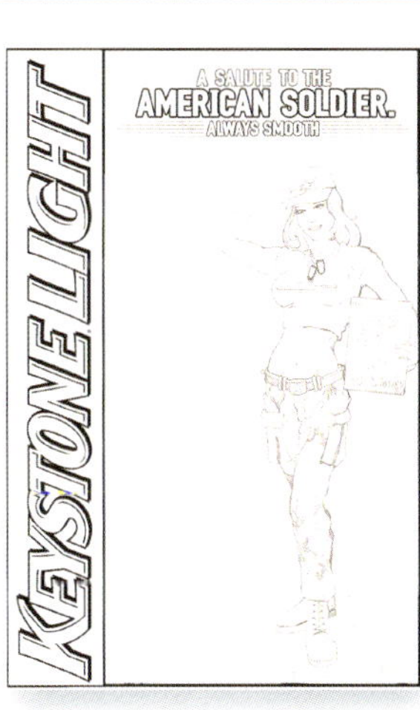

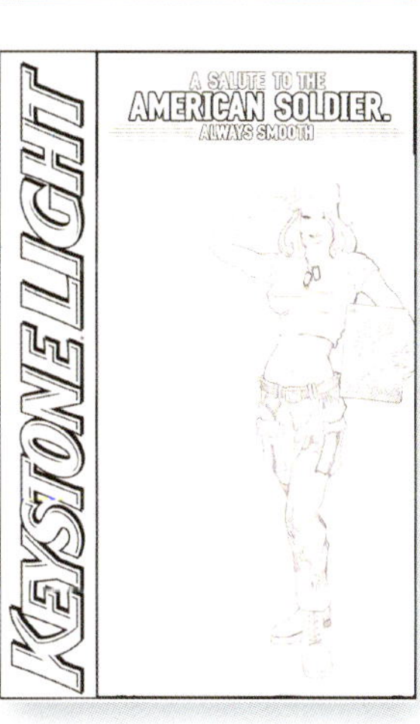

A Salute to the American Soldier
Client: Keystone Light
Agency: Integer Group
Year: 2006
Model: Christine LeMaster

I was chosen for this project for my ability to create a vector woman who looked sexy without being cartoonish. As the above article in Photoshop Creative Magazine (issue 28) demonstrates, I was supplied with a rough sketch, and clothing samples for the piece. This particular project had a pretty good idea of the direction that they wanted. The model shoot with swimsuit model Christine LeMaster went great, and you can see examples above of how I mock up props if I don't have exactly what I plan to draw. The client requested that I stick the army girls tongue out a bit. This is an example of a piece where the client went with a sketch that was my least personal favorite, but they were exceptionally pleased. And that's what matters.

Often the client will supply you with brand art to be incorporated in the piece. In this case, they sent me the Keystone Light flat art, which I illustrated onto the box that she is holding. This magazine advertisement ran as a salute to the military.

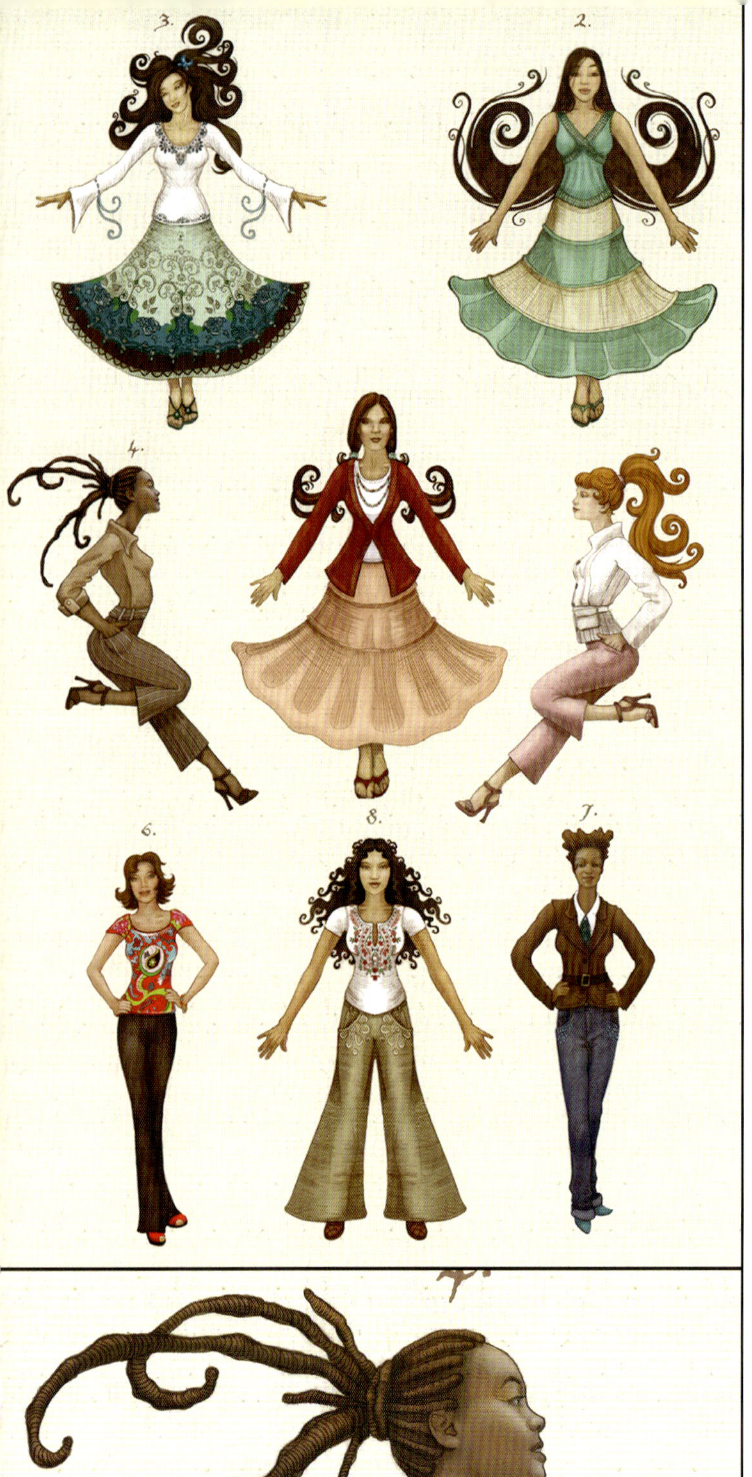

Fashion Butterflies
Client: Sears
Year: 2006
Models: References Provided

One of the stranger projects that I ever worked on was for a major retail client - Sears! The project was one of several pitches (from the advertising agency to their client - Sears). It is common for an advertising agency to approach their client with several different directions and let them choose. They may never be published. In this concept, teenage girls were put into the new Spring line of Sears clothes, but were illustrated to look like they were butterflies pinned down inside a display case... The concept seemed a little creepy to me at the time.

What is interesting about this piece - and what I want to stress - is that I was supplied with example artwork and a background texture that I was to simulate in terms of style. They specifically asked for this level of finish and execution. One of the ways successful commercial illustrators keep busy is to have the flexibility to simulate other styles and put aside their own "style" to meet the needs of the client. It's not something every artist can do, but it is an important trait to possess to remain consistently busy; and some of those pieces you may want to never see the light of day.

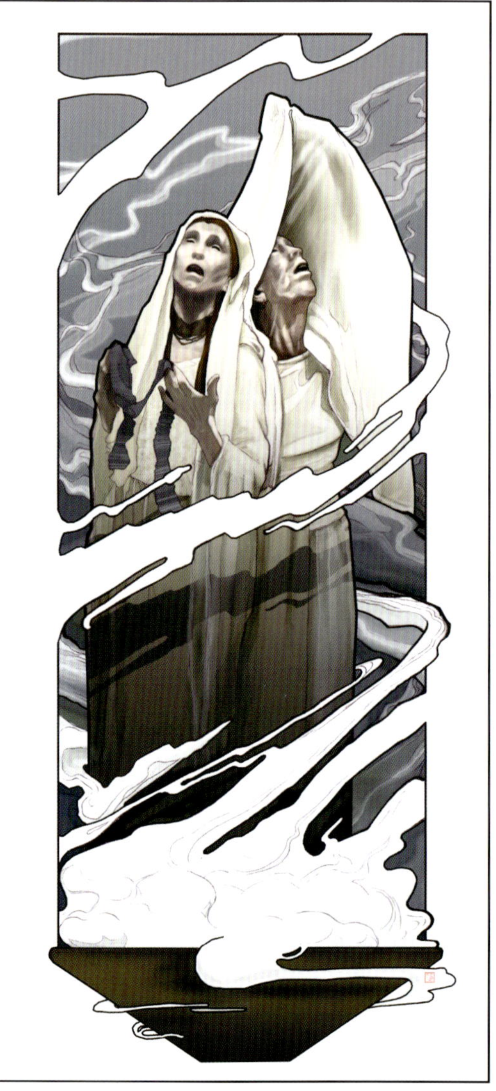

Dido and Aeneas
Client: Fordham University Opera
Year: 2003
Models: References Provided

This is a very early piece of mine - one of the first full color pieces executed in the art nouveau style. I would love to one day re-do this in the much more refined style that I have developed over the years, and still consider it a really strong composition. You can see the early use of smoke, and breaking the borders. It illustrates the feel of the play with both gesture and colors.

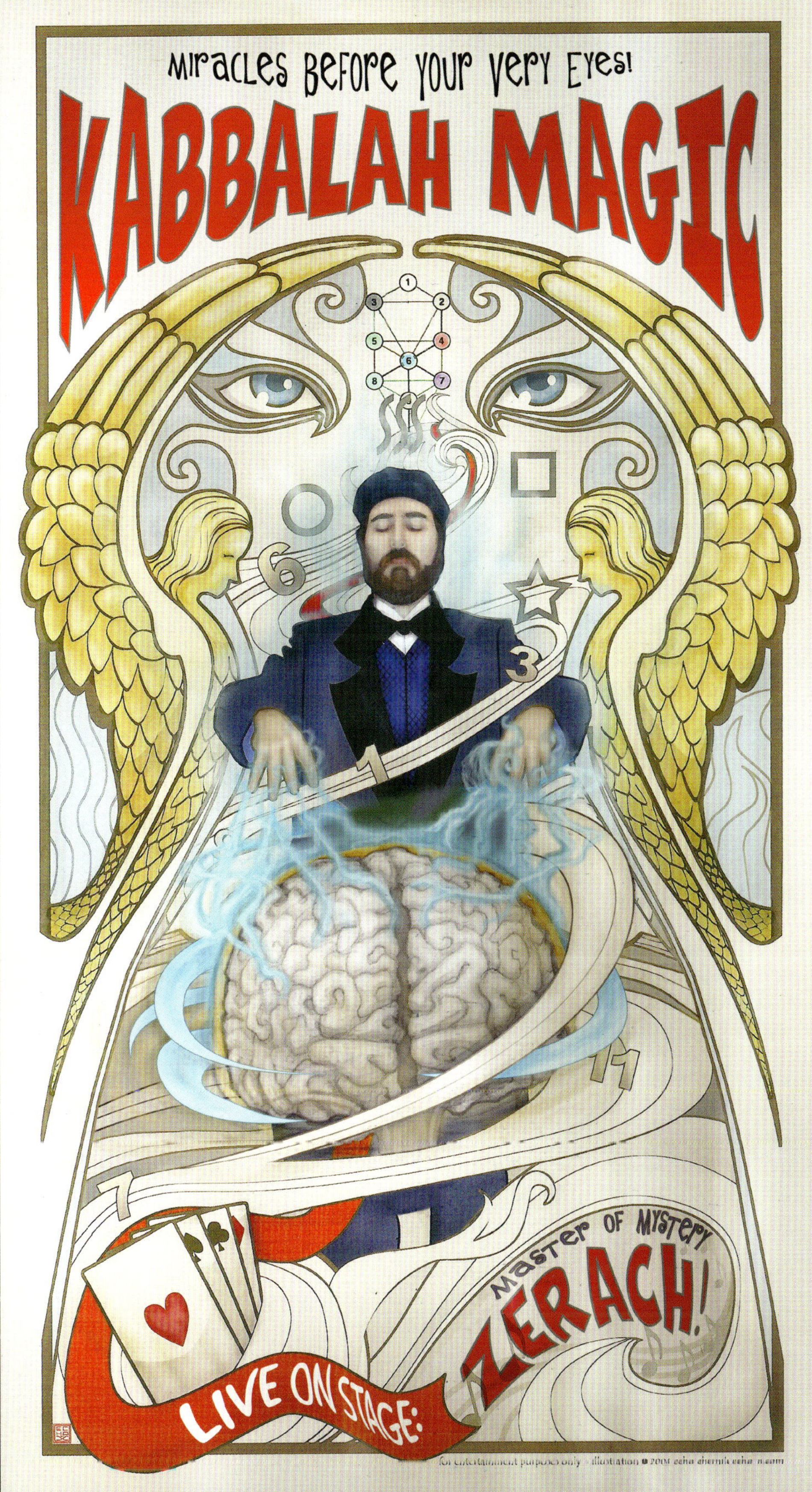

Kabbalah Magic
Client: Master of Mystery, ZERACH!
Year: 2004
Model: Master of Mystery, ZERACH!

My preferred style lends itself to recreating vintage-like products. The Master of Mystery: Zerach! was an orthodox Jewish magician who themed his performances with Kabbalah. He required the poster to be slightly antiqued and include very specific imagery his audience will understand and recognize, including the Seriphot and Arl of the Covenant. There are two versions of this poster: the one featured above, and one that replaced the brain with a levitating woman.

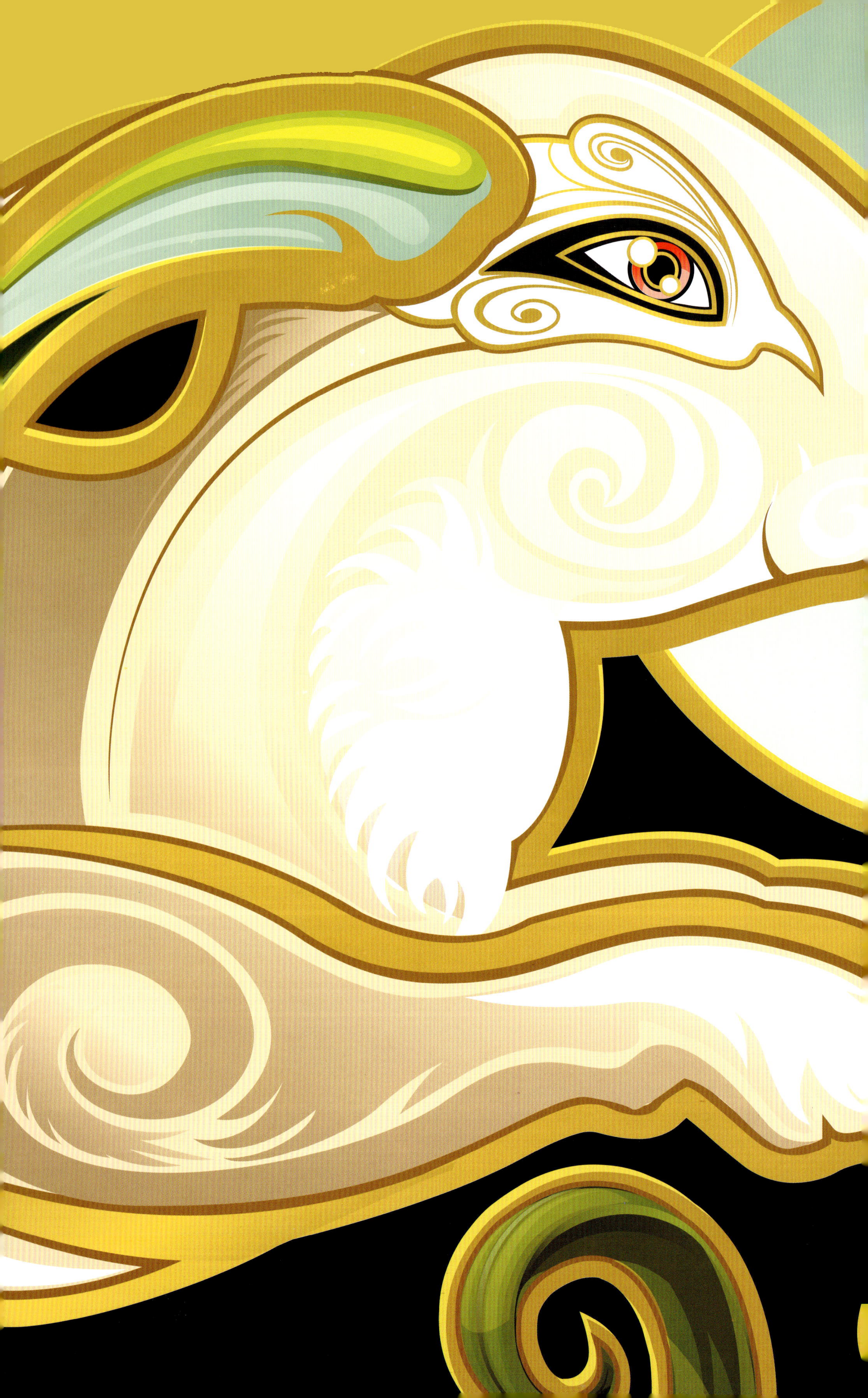

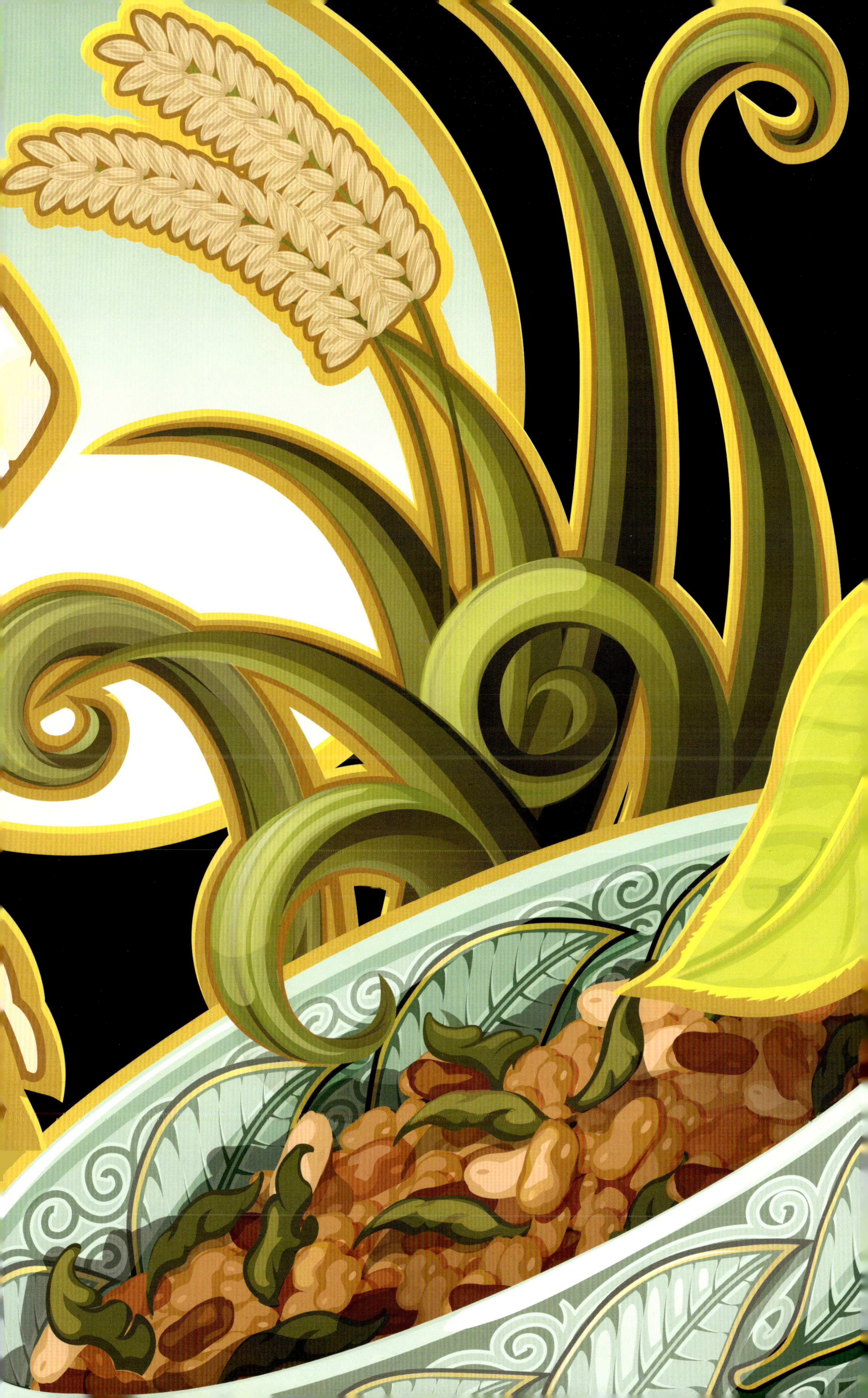

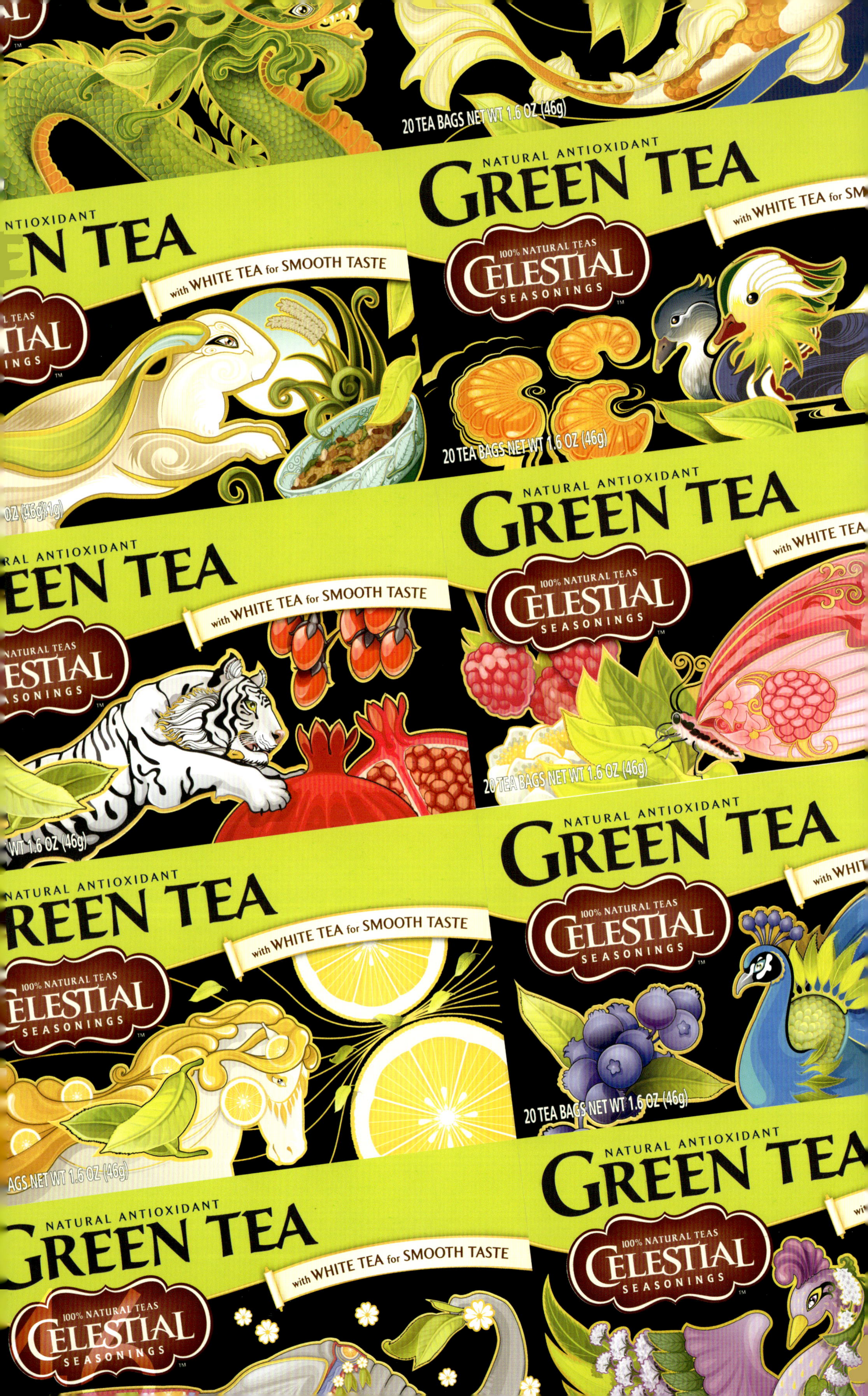

20 TEA BAGS NET WT 1.6 OZ (46g)
NTIOXIDANT
N TEA
with WHITE TEA for SMOOTH TASTE
L TEAS
TIAL
INGS
OZ (46g)
NATURAL ANTIOXIDANT
GREEN TEA
with WHITE TEA for SM
100% NATURAL TEAS
CELESTIAL
SEASONINGS
20 TEA BAGS NET WT 1.6 OZ (46g)
RAL ANTIOXIDANT
EEN TEA
with WHITE TEA for SMOOTH TASTE
NATURAL TEAS
ESTIAL
SONINGS
WT 1.6 OZ (46g)
NATURAL ANTIOXIDANT
GREEN TEA
with WHITE TEA
100% NATURAL TEAS
CELESTIAL
SEASONINGS
20 TEA BAGS NET WT 1.6 OZ (46g)
NATURAL ANTIOXIDANT
REEN TEA
with WHITE TEA for SMOOTH TASTE
100% NATURAL TEAS
ELESTIAL
SEASONINGS
AGS NET WT 1.6 OZ (46g)
NATURAL ANTIOXIDANT
GREEN TEA
with WHIT
100% NATURAL TEAS
CELESTIAL
SEASONINGS
20 TEA BAGS NET WT 1.6 OZ (46g)
NATURAL ANTIOXIDANT
GREEN TEA
with WHITE TEA for SMOOTH TASTE
100% NATURAL TEAS
CELESTIAL
SEASONINGS
NATURAL ANTIOXIDANT
GREEN TEA
100% NATURAL TEAS
CELESTIAL
SEASONINGS

Products & Packaging

I'll need some extra samples of that!

There are few things more rewarding than seeing your artwork on the shelves, and in the mainstream. Perhaps some illustrators get bored of it, but it never fails to give me happy little goosebumps each time I see it out there. To me, if I ever lose that feeling, it means that I've lost the love of being a commercial illustrator. So, here's hoping that day never comes.

Package design has it's own set of rules. The artwork is often not flat, but needs to encompass several sides of a box or package. Typography must be considered (and is often in development parallel to your artwork). Package design is usually committee decided and must conform to an existing or developing brand. You are also much more likely to be called on to consider printing elements such as spot varnishes and die cuts, and handed a mechanical or template to work within. It's a different animal, but certainly one of my personal favorites!

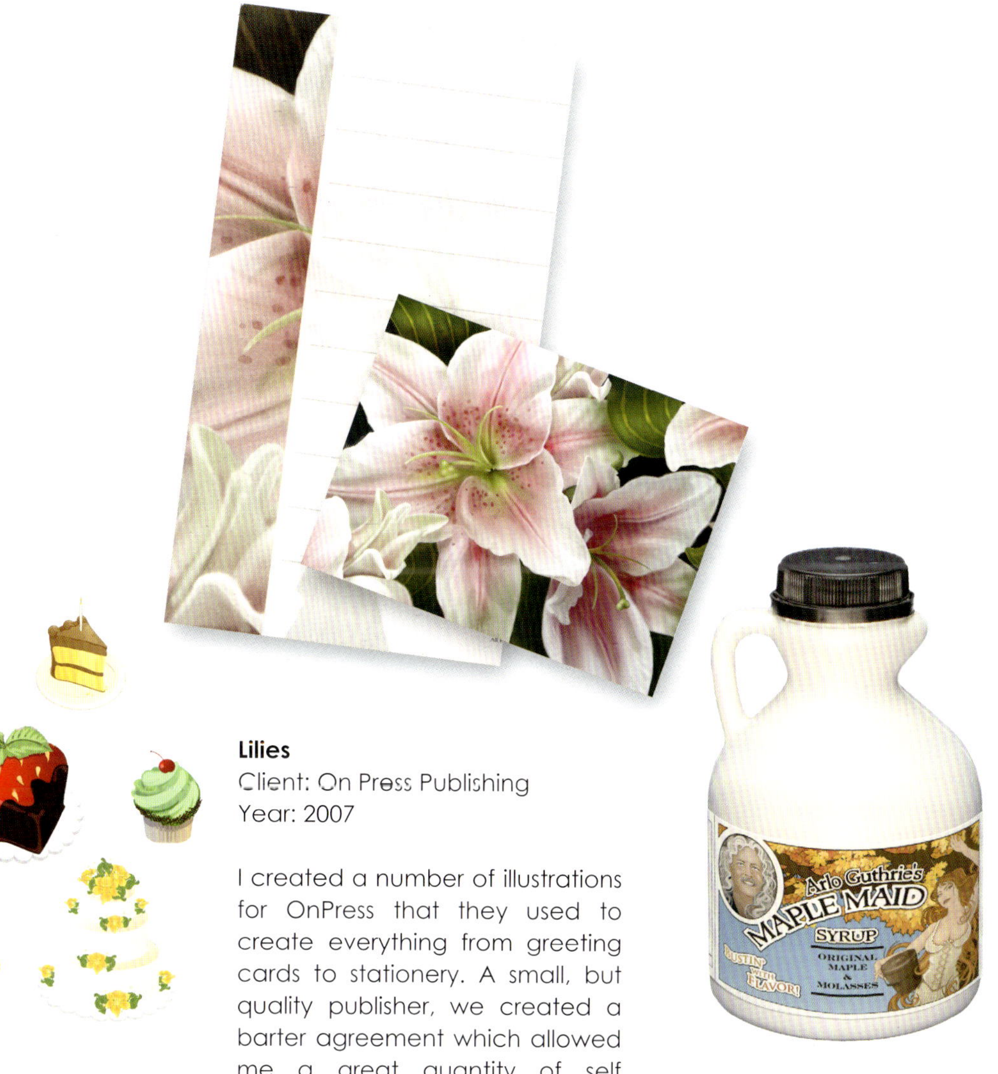

34 Vector Cakes
Client: Withheld
Year: 2006

Remember, versatility!

Lilies
Client: On Press Publishing
Year: 2007

I created a number of illustrations for OnPress that they used to create everything from greeting cards to stationery. A small, but quality publisher, we created a barter agreement which allowed me a great quantity of self promotional items and greeting cards featuring my artwork. Barter can be a wonderful, selectively used tool to create a win-win situation.

Maple Maid Syrup
Client: Arlo Guthrie
Year: 2006

Molasses & Maple Syrup. Yum!

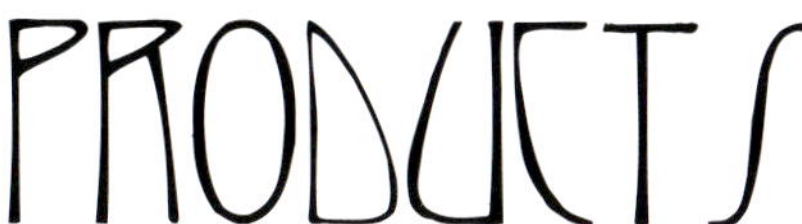

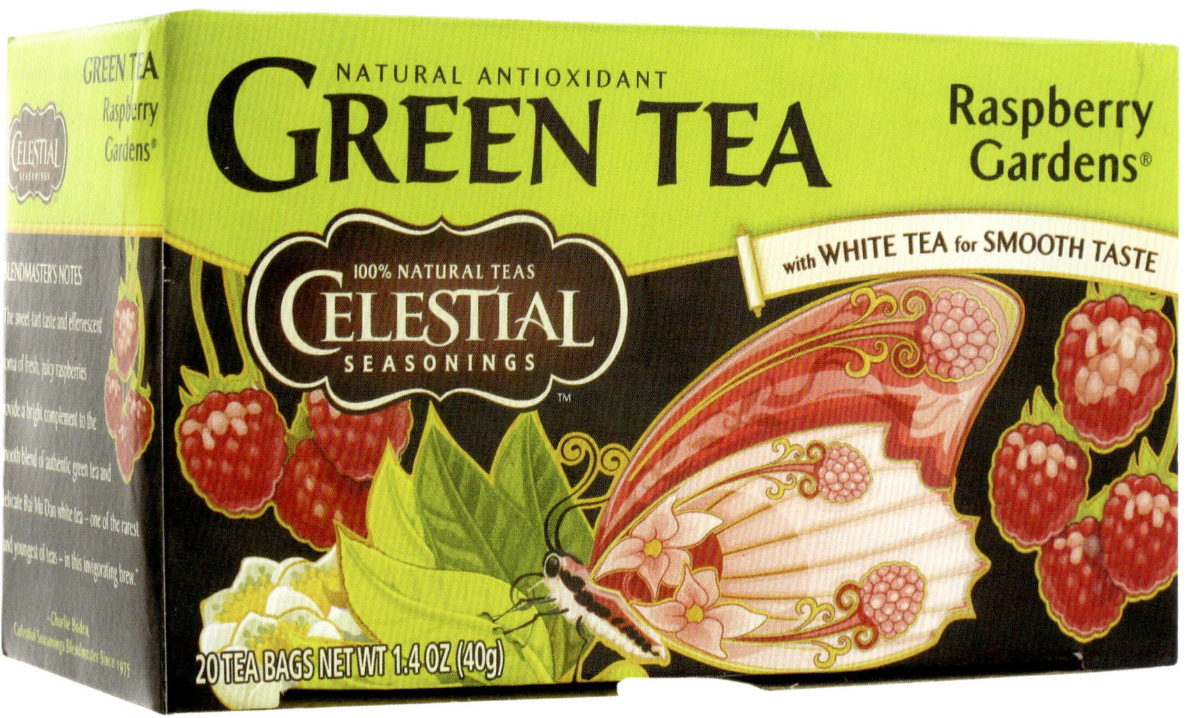

Green Tea Zodiac
Client: The Hain Celestial Group
Agency: Internal
Year: 2008-2010

The largest and most prestigious project I worked on during this period were my eleven boxes of green teas for Celestial Seasonings. It was very communicative and sketch-heavy art direction, and the collaborative process was key. My usual inclination is to overkill with details, and they reigned me in many times, urging me to be more simple and more clear. The decaffeinated Koi was one of the first, and after completing a fully rendered and 3-dimensional looking fish, I spent a week stripping away detail until it resembled the cloisonné (ceramic decoration) style the client desired. In some cases, it took us several rounds of 'finishes' before they approved the result. The raspberry Butterfly, for example, was completed and scrapped almost 5 times; but the whole team wanted these to be perfect as did I, and the results speak for themselves. The client was trying a new direction, with the dark boxes and unique cloisonné imagery, and had their own challenges getting internal approval on the direction. Their innovative concept was well received! The first set of nine boxes were completed in 2008-9. Later in 2009 they used another illustrator to integrate their official Sleepytime Bear™ within the brand using some vector elements from my illustrations. In 2010, I illustrated a tenth box, the Hare. At the time of this writing in 2011, I am working my eleventh box for the series.

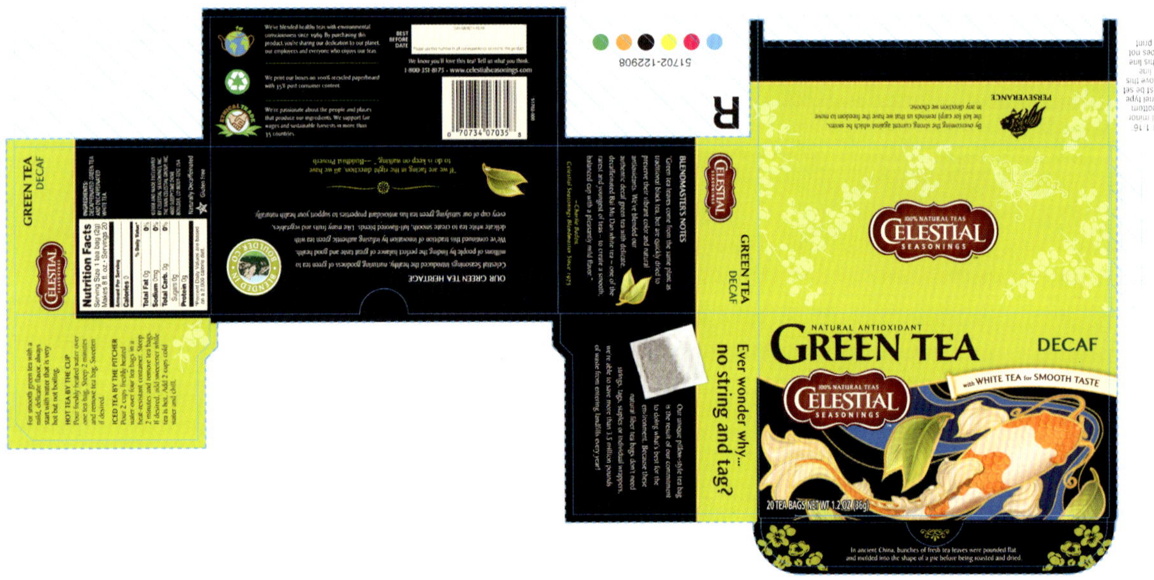

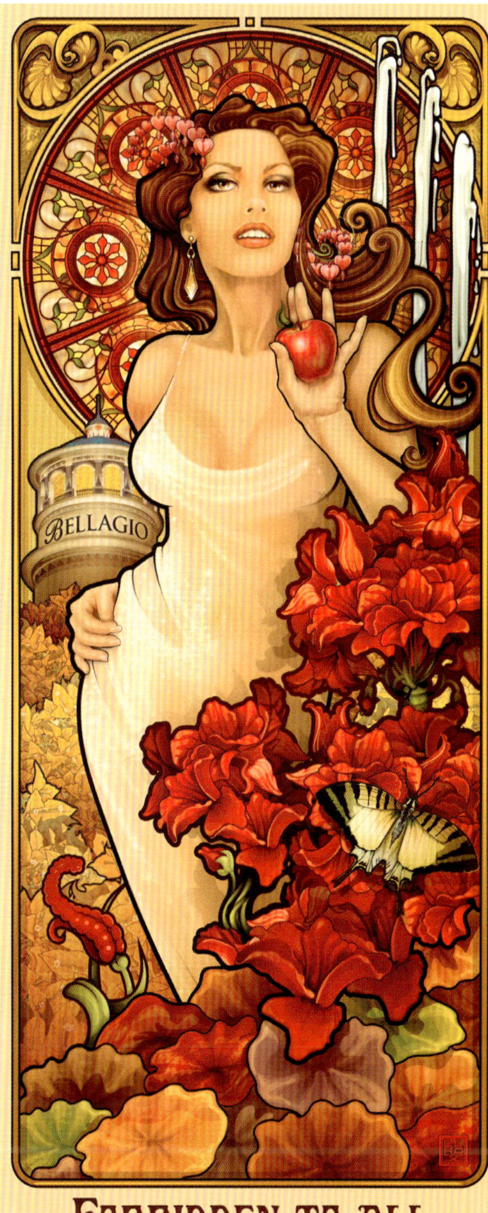

Bellagio's Eve
Client: Bellagio Resort & Casino, Las Vegas
Project: New Year's Eve Invitation
Year: 2006
Model: Meghan Perkins

I was approached by the advertising agency with a mocked up Mucha lithograph of a woman with an apple pasted into her hand. "We would like to present to our client something like this - a super high art nouveau invitation personifying Eve for their New Years Eve party. We wanted you wanted to bid on it and know what you suggest to make it better?" I thought the concept was great, and pitched that we re-illustrate it incorporating elements from the Casino. So, I included the rose window in the background from the Bellagio, the tower, and even the corner flourishes and Chihuly flowers can be found on location.

I also was called upon to illustrate the plexiglass window (below) that went on the front of the tri-fold illustration. The entire thing was bound in leather and arrived in a box. Only 3500 were made for this very exclusive event.

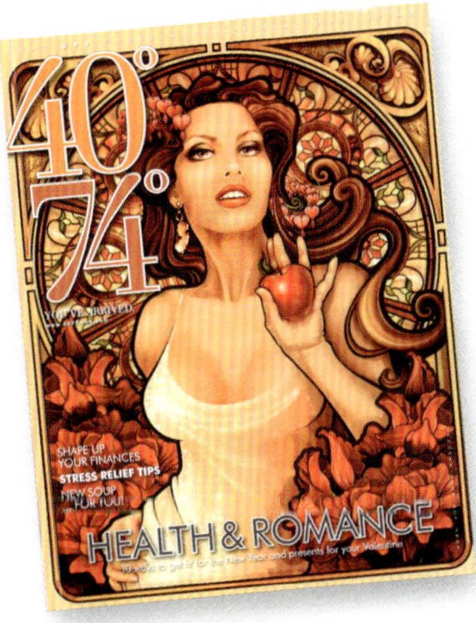

One of the nice things about copyright control is that I can resell the same or modified illustration for use by someone else. Here Eve was used as a magazine cover.

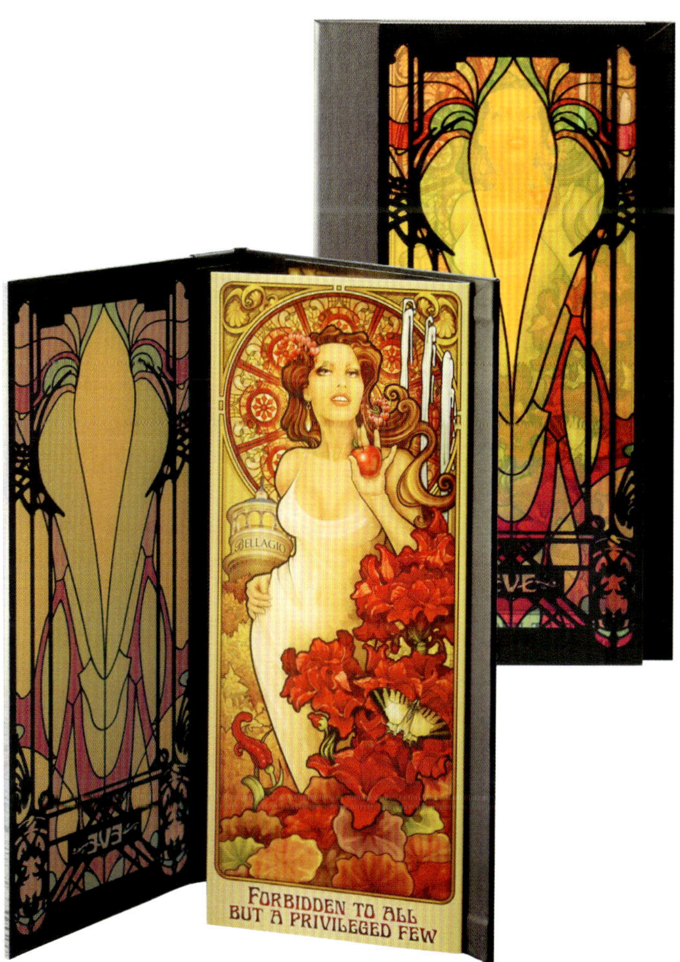

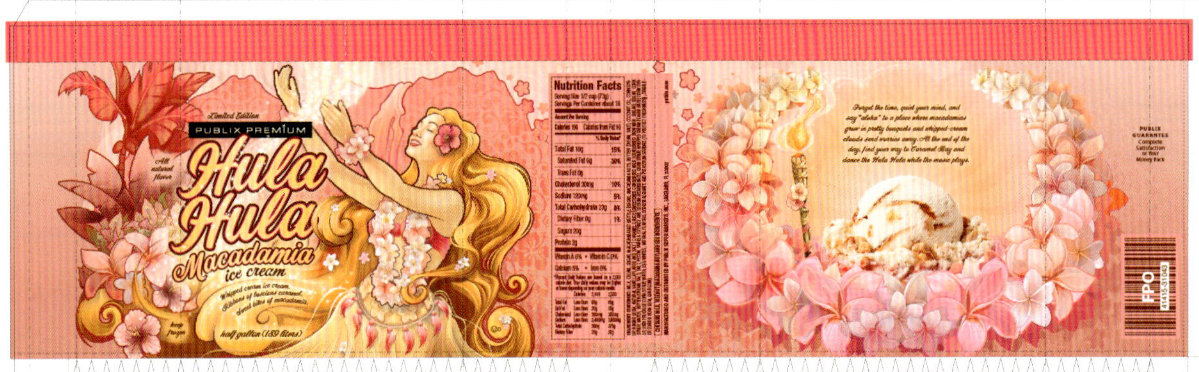

Hula Hula Macadamia
Client: Publix
Year: 2009

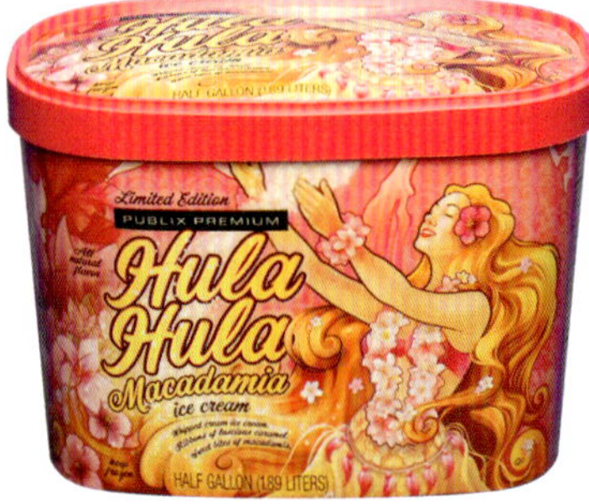

In the Southeastern United States, primarily in Florida, Publix is a chain of supermarkets with an incredible reputation for quality. I know - it's been my local store since moving from New York. Publix is an employee owned business, where every person in the company has a vested interest in the success of the business. Their custom-labelled products reflect that concern for quality and reputation. Local gourmets actually prefer a lot of their products to brand names and not just because they cost less.

FedEx shows up at my door one day, and I open the box to a rush of dry ice smoke. The art director sent me, for inspiration, five unmarked, in development stage, half-gallons of their test-recipes for inspiration! The women in my family are obsessed with ice cream - born and raised on it being an essential meal of the day. In fact, it is not uncommon, when we gather in groups, to replace a meal (such as breakfast) with a trip to the ice cream parlor. So, to say I got paid (partly) in ice cream is one of the great coups of my career.

Cremissimo
Client: Langnese (Germany)
Agency: Ropelius
Year: 2009-10

Langnese is the German Heartbrand subsidiary of the Anglo-Dutch company Unilever. They offer a large line of readily available products spanning every kind of frozen treat. Think of them as the Good Humor of Germany - but with a reputation for high quality desserts. Some products I reillustrated and others are brand new. I would love to try this ice cream someday, it looks scrumptious.

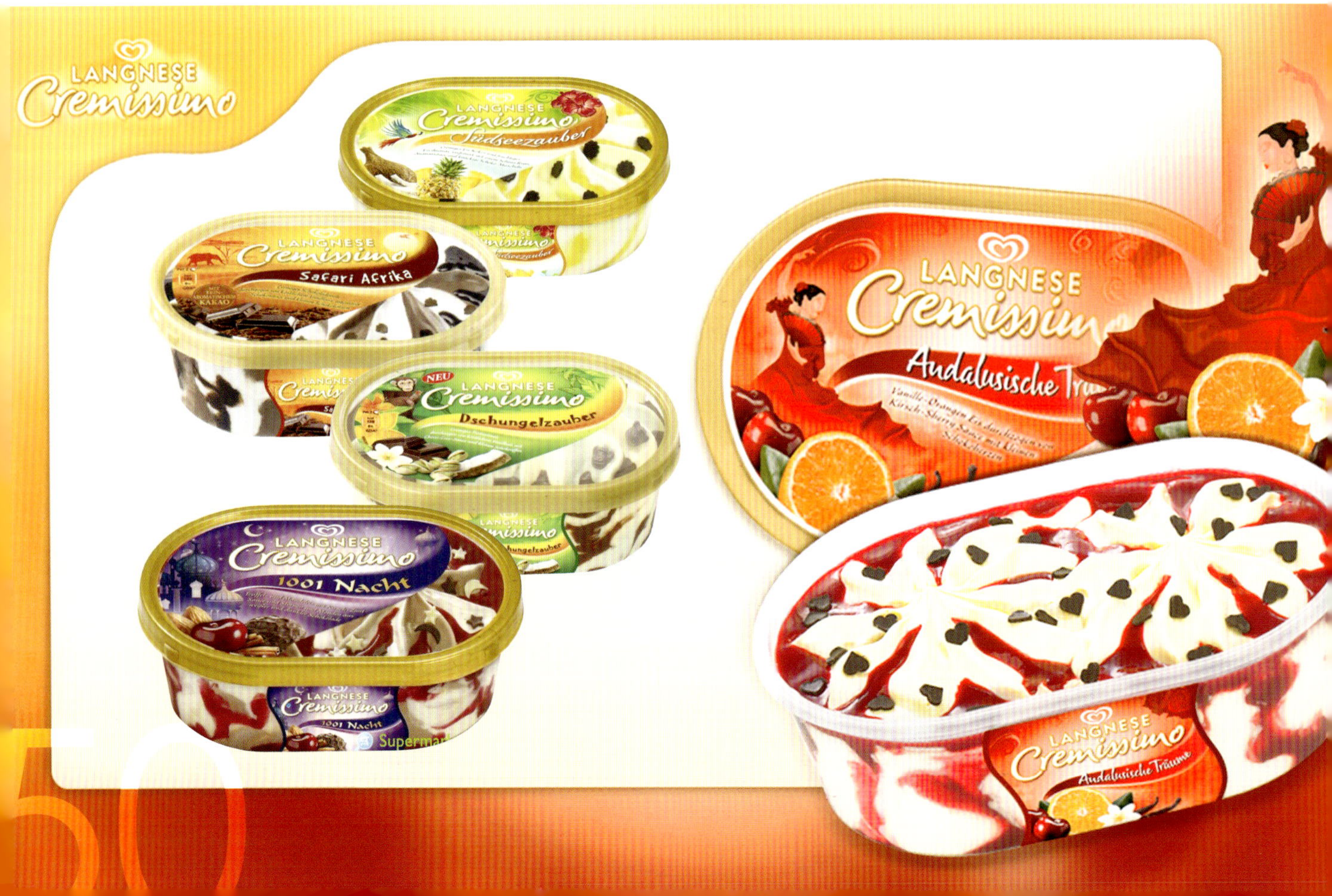

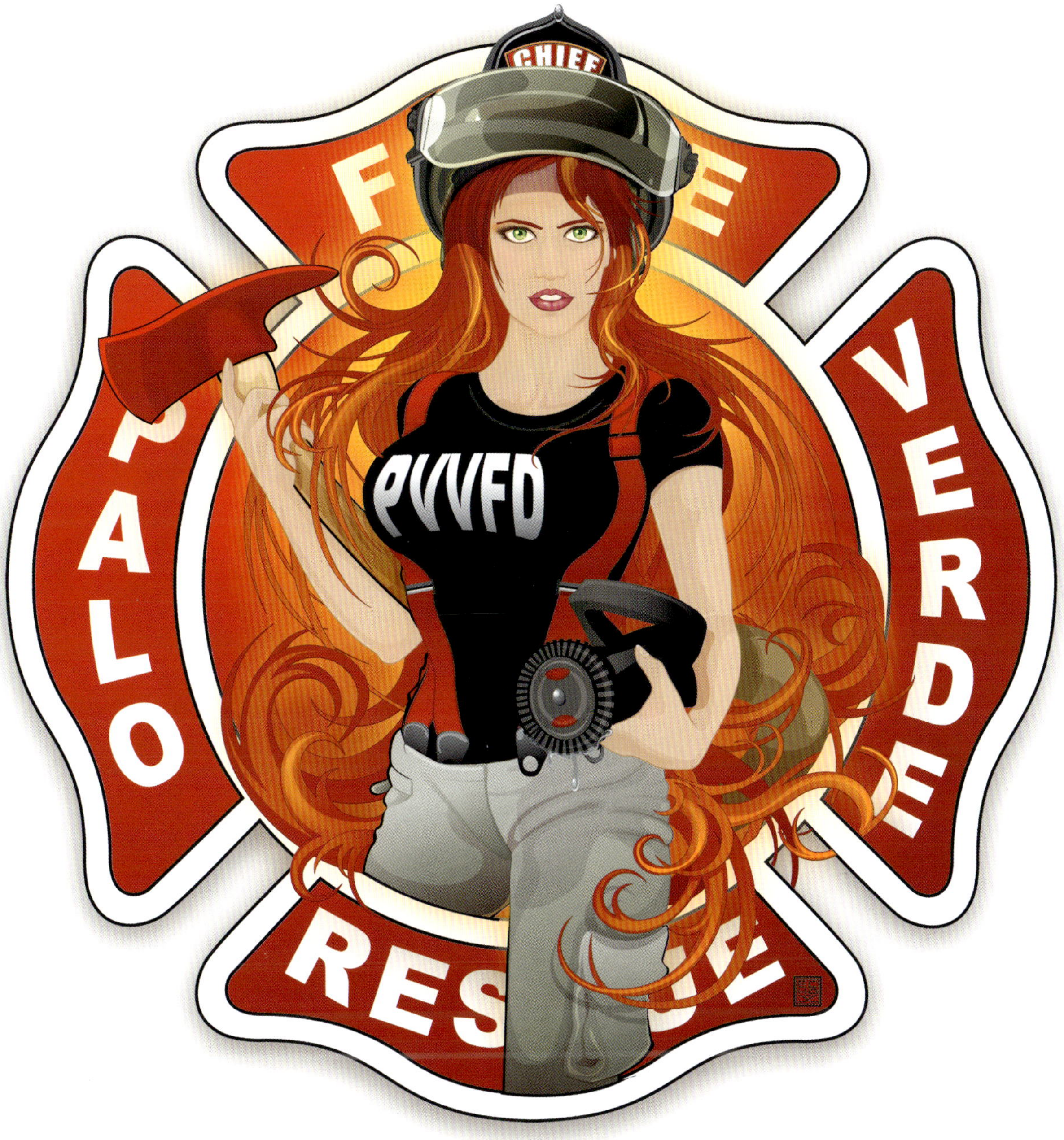

Fire Girl
Client: Palo Verde Volunteer Fire & Rescue
Year: 2003
Model: Echo Chernik

Illustrators sometimes require the strangest props. You can rent costumes and props, and we develop quite an eclectic collection cluttering our studios. My studio is full of skulls, gasmasks, swords, garments, drapes, artillery, and duct tape to hold it all in place. But occasionally you don't have what you need handy. So, you can either purchase it (and bill it to the client), or strap on your cutest smile and go ask permission. I have walked into a curio shop and asked them if I could take some shots of Lazarus wearing their antique Indian headdress, trekked on down to Trek bikes and asked to borrow one of their bikes, took shots on motorcycles in the Harley Davidson showroom. As for this project, I showed up at our local fire department and asked to don the chief's gear. People are usually quite helpful if they find it entertaining to watch.

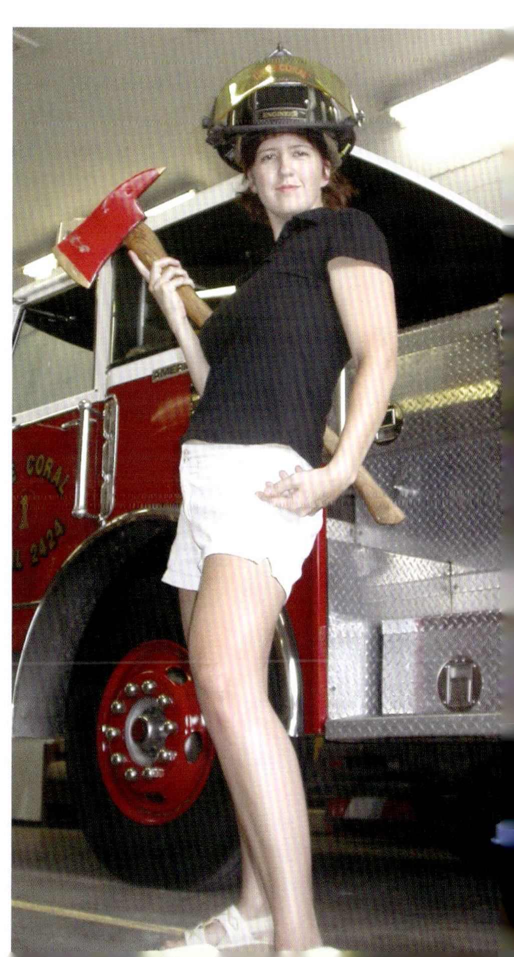

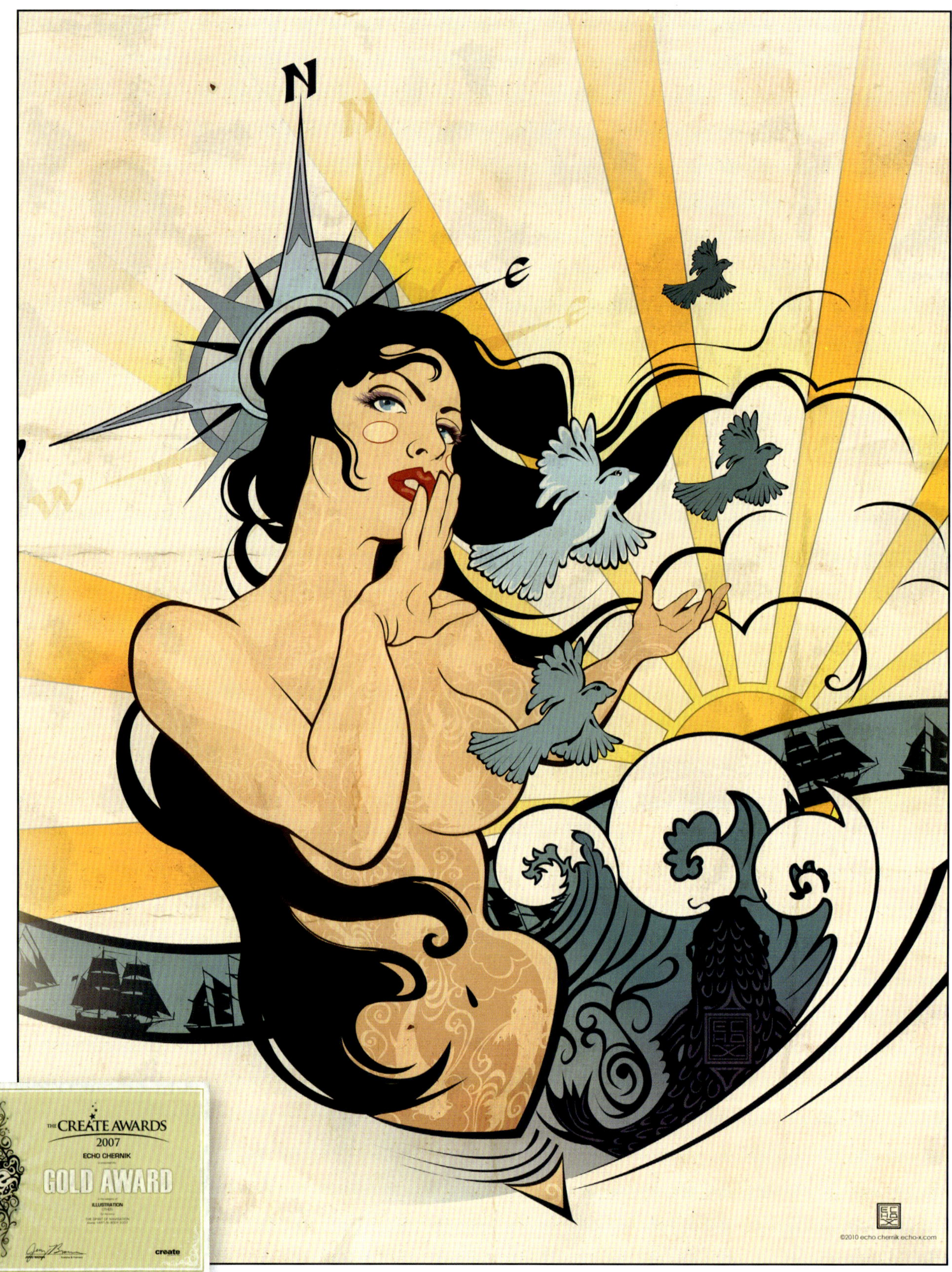

The Spirit of Navigation
Client: Art-n-Body
Agency: Internal
Year: 2007
Model: Meghan Perkins

When Art-n-Body approached me with some tattoo inspired apparel to produce, their budget was very limited - but the creative outlet to do something out of my comfort zone was really enticing. The only art direction on this piece was "to do something Nautical." Sometimes wide open art direction is really great. The Spirit of Navigation is a personification of finding your way at sea. I read once that sailors are able to determine their proximity to shore based on the type of birds they see. Birds can only fly a certain distance from the safety of shore. It was while drawing this piece that I first fell in love with Meghan as a model and muse. Those lips are all hers.

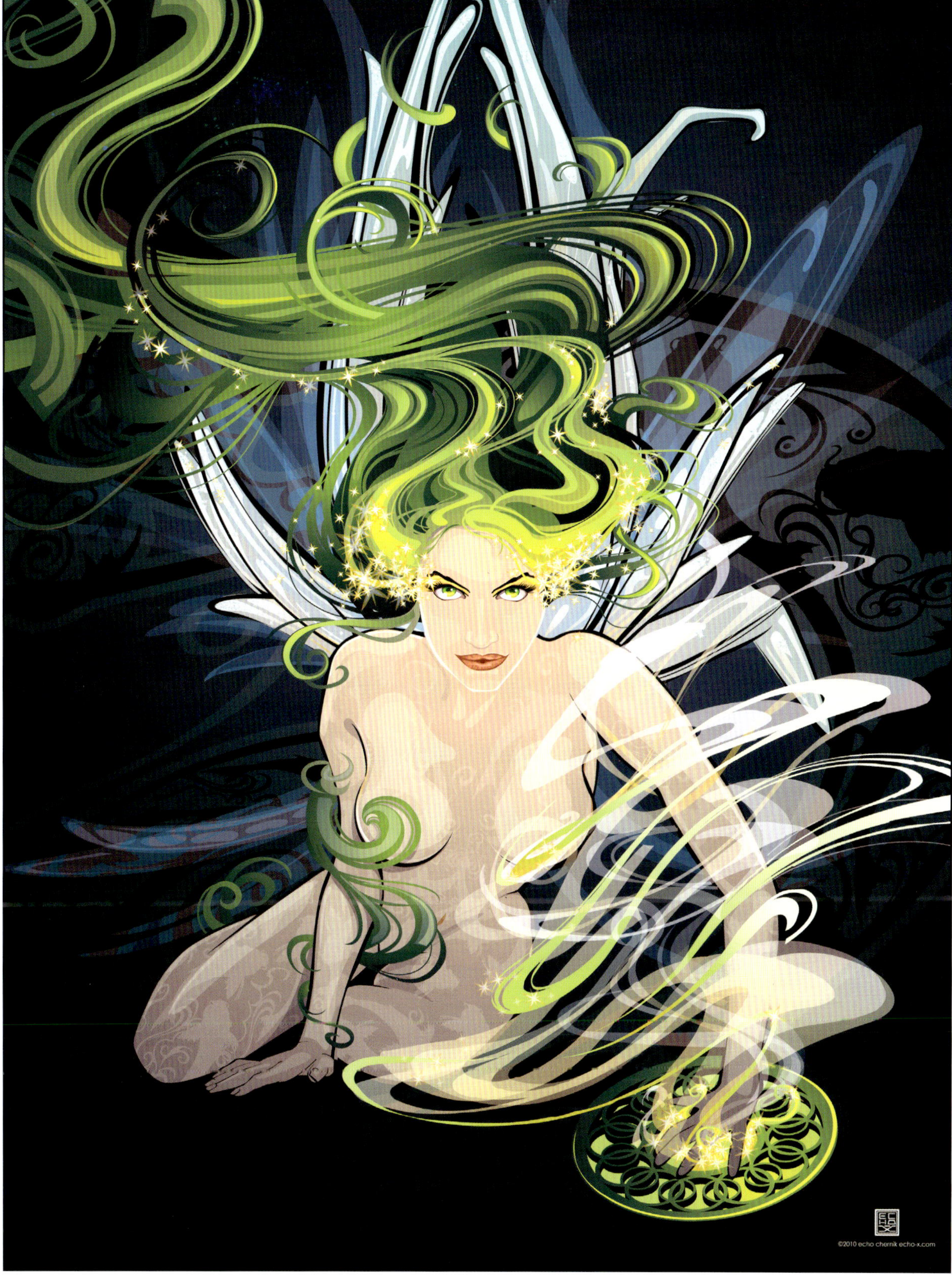

Absinthe Fairy
Client: Hot Topic (Proposal)
Agency: The Fairy Society
Year: 2006
Model: Meghan Perkins

Years ago, I joined the art licensing group The Fairy Society who represents many of the biggest name illustrators of fairies in the country. Honestly, aside from my preferred style having beautiful women I'm not that fairy-friendly. A few months in, the Society called me asking for art that they could pitch to Hot Topic for clothes. They were bringing art from many of their illustrators to the meeting and they wanted me included - but I didn't have any 'true' fairies in my portfolio ready to sell. I spent about a week on this piece before sending it in. Hot Topic chose to go in a cute and whimsical direction that year. In 2009, a famous Chicago speak-easy converted into an absinthe bar, and licensed it for their brand.

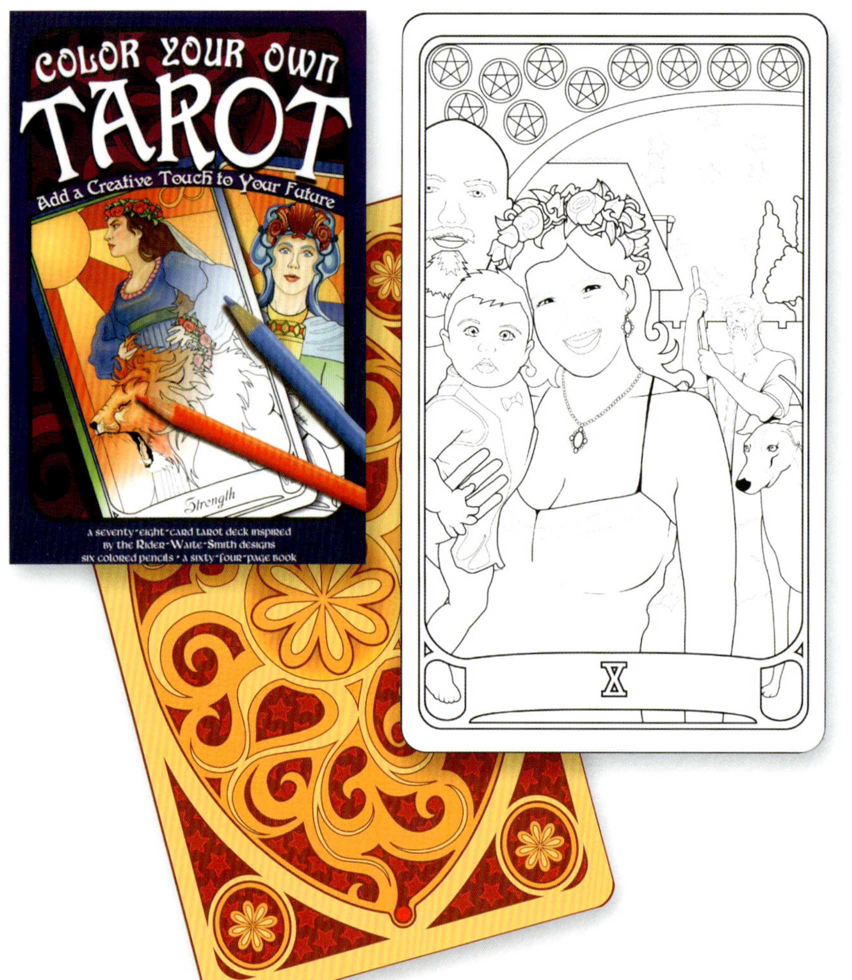

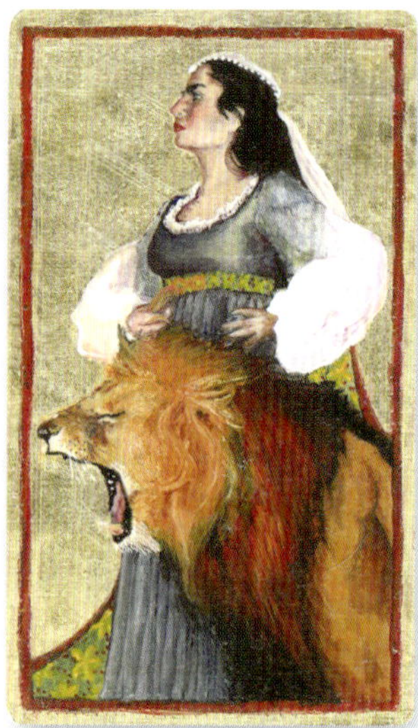

Which came first? Actually, the oil-painted and gold-leafed version was done ten years earlier. As many artists do, I thought a tarot deck of my own would be really neat - so I started it. But then my obsession for details took over. I wanted every one to be an oil painting and gold leafed. I never finished it. When this project came along, I repurposed some of my original drawings.

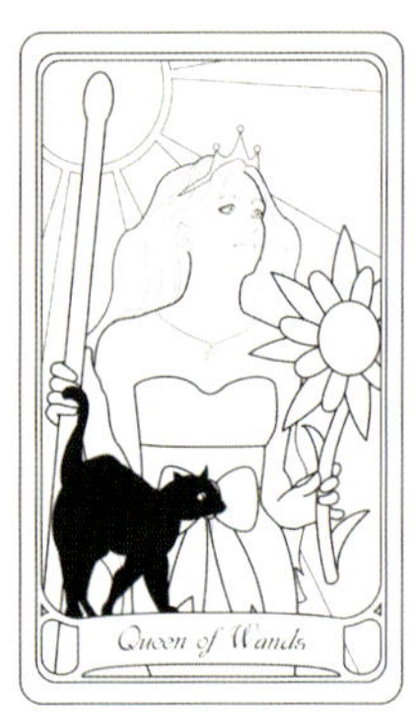

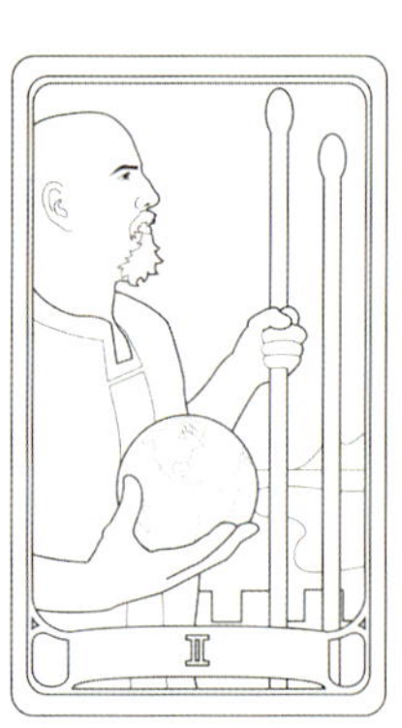

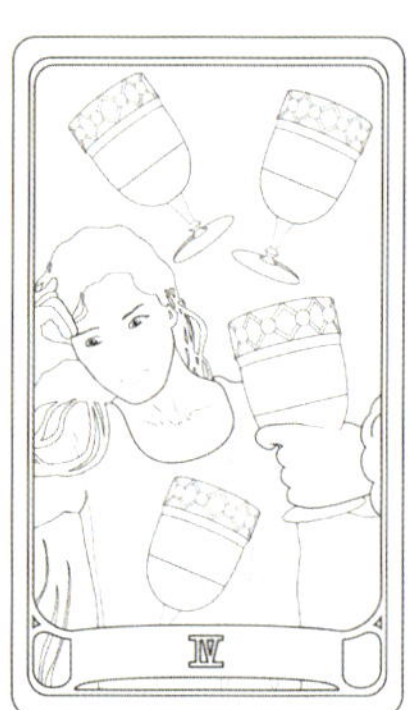

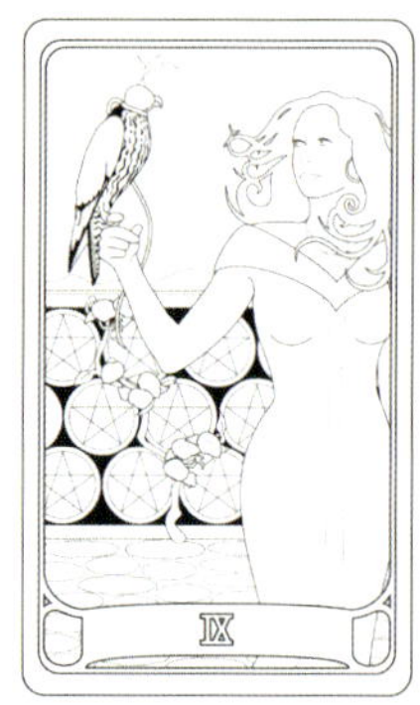

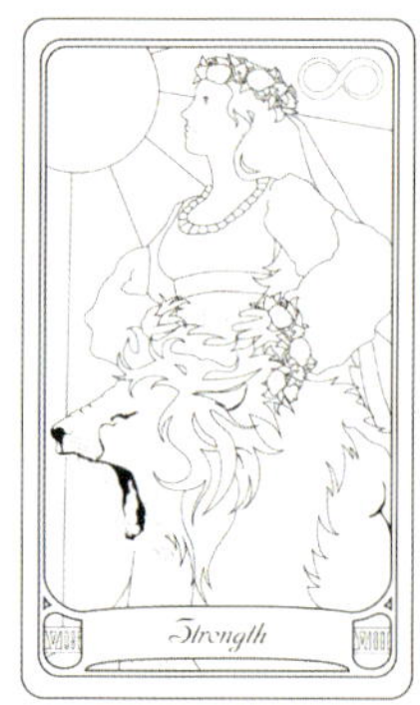

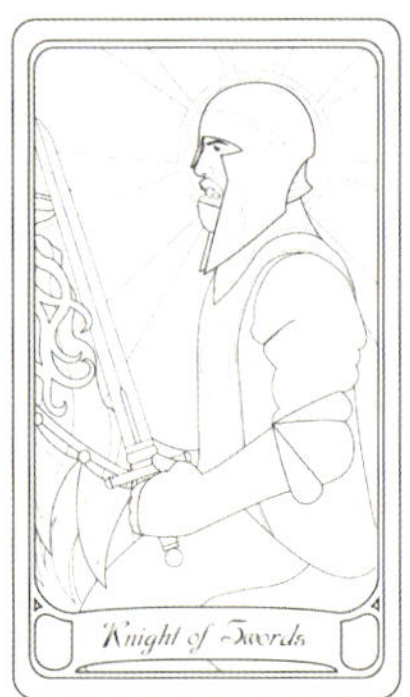

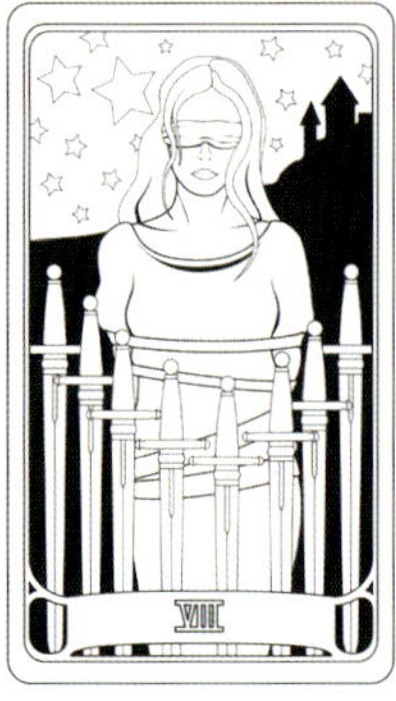

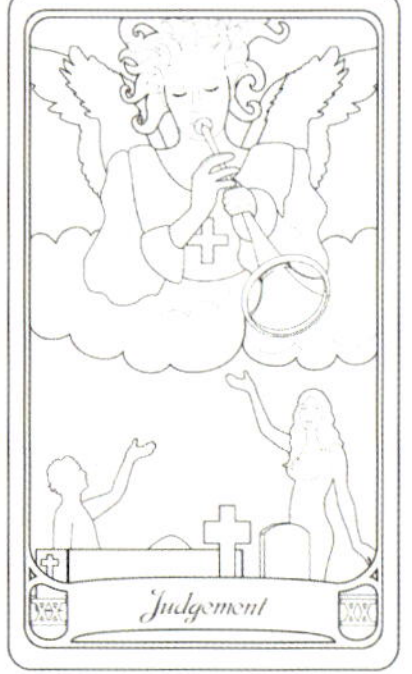

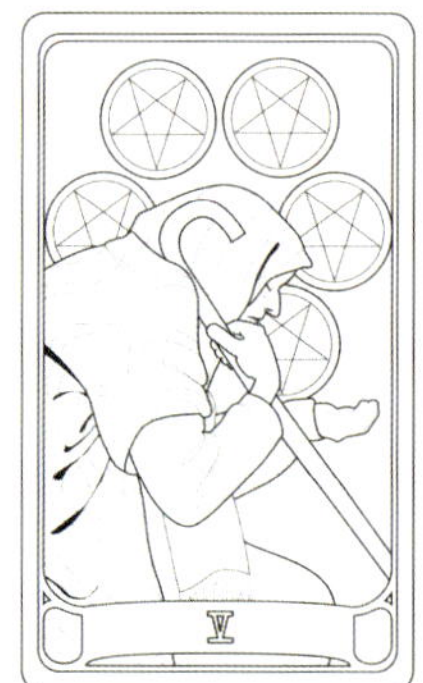

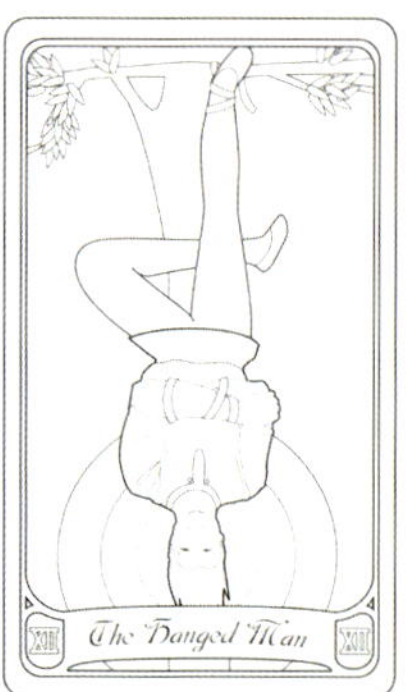

Color Your Own Tarot
ISBN-10: 1-59609-170-3
Client: Penguin Group (USA)
Publisher: Chamberlain Bros.
Author: Doria Columbia
Year: 2006

Models: Echo Chernik, Lazarus Chernik, Runa Chernik, Katheryn Chernik, Robert McKinney, Holly McKinney, Tim McKinney, and others.

It's not the Tarot deck that everyone is asking for - but it is a tarot deck. It was voted by fans online as the best of its type because it is very easy to color, which I took into account when illustrating it.

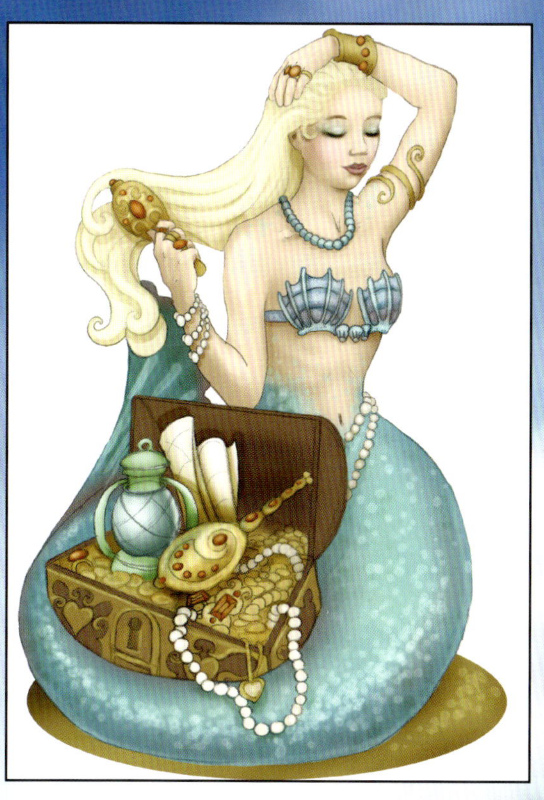

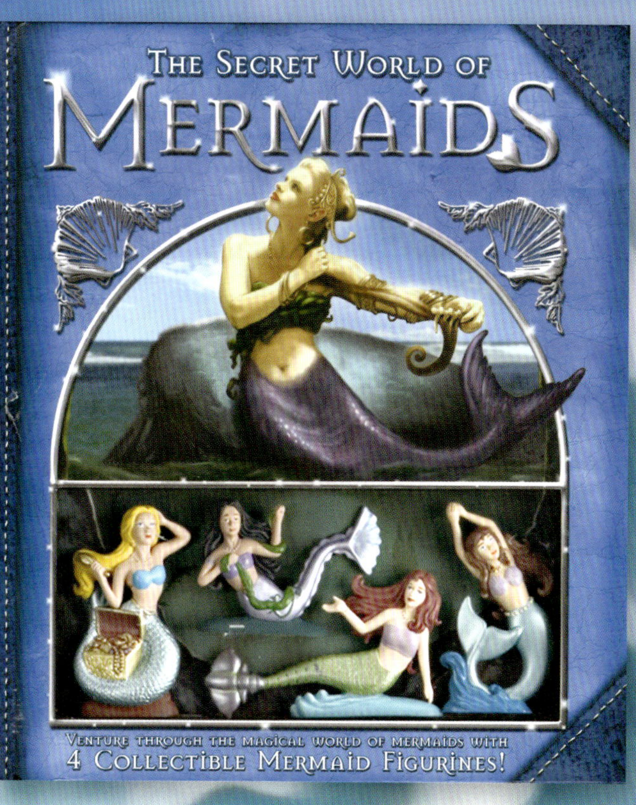

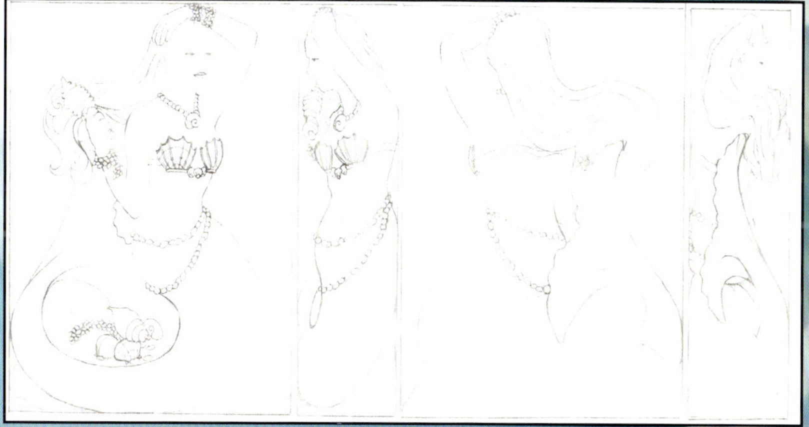

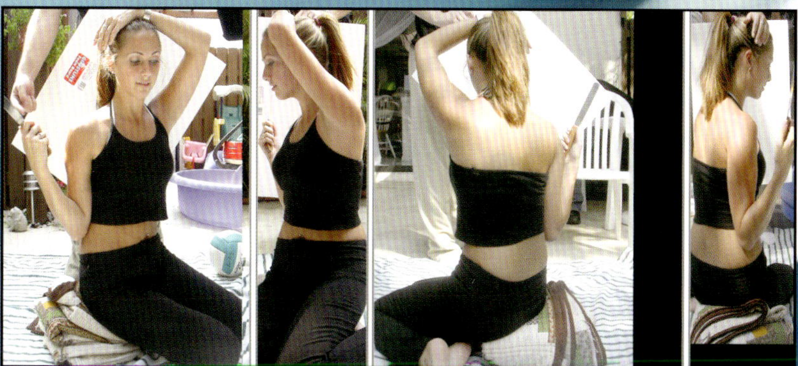

Secret World of Mermaids Figurines
ISBN-10: 1-59223-368-6
Client: Becker & Mayer
Publisher: Silver Dolphin
Author: Francine Rose
Year: 2006

This project was more of a toy than a book. Dozens of illustrators contributed to it but I designed the figurines packaged with the book. It was the first time I designed for sculptors. My usual level of detail was inappropriate because the toy sculptor could only approximate my drawings. My final deliverables were sixteen drawings and four color studies of four figurines, and art direction was pretty specific.

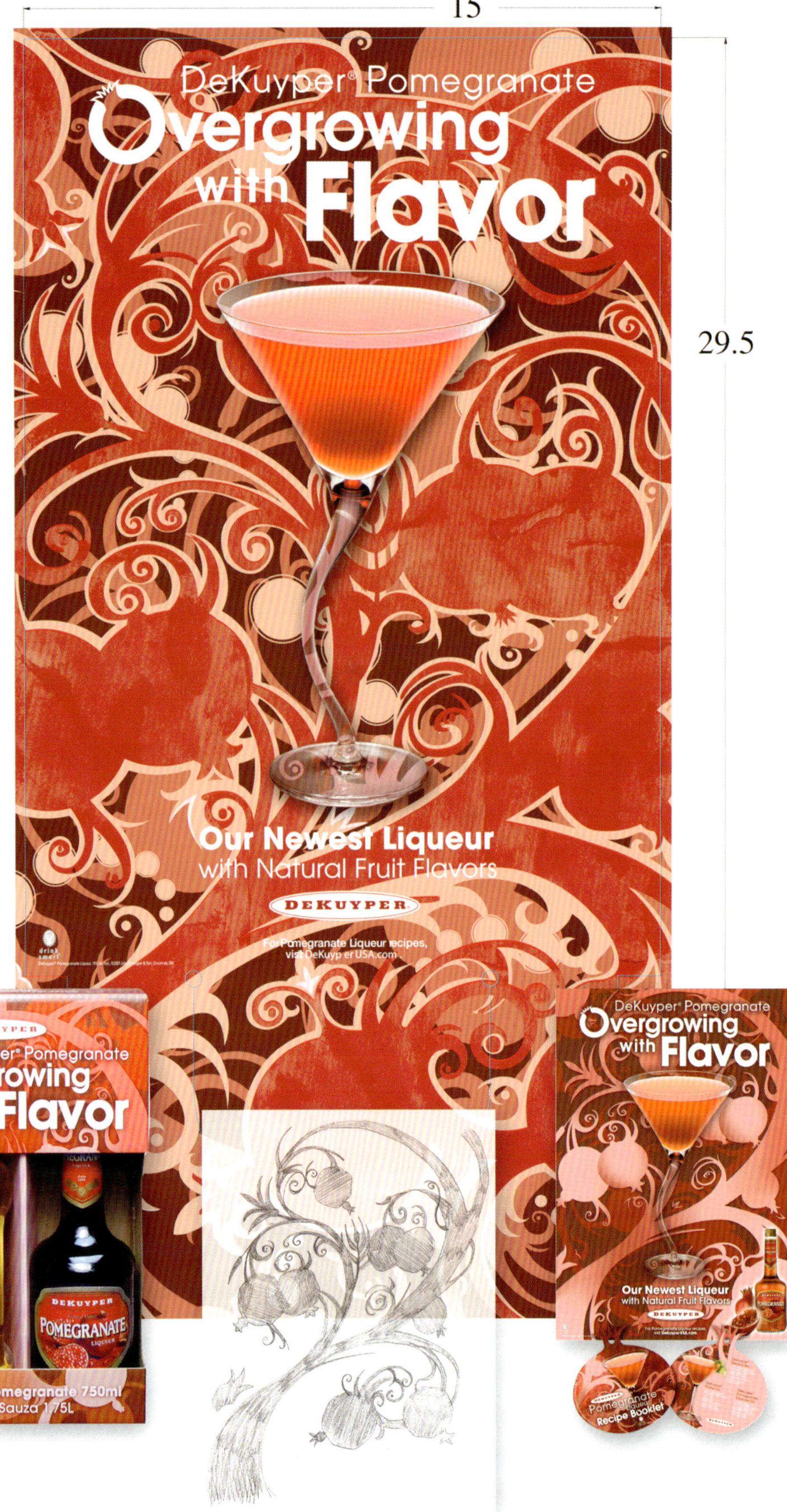

Pomegranate Background
Client: DeKuyper Liqueurs
Agency: Zipatone
Year: 2006

Sometimes all I do for a project is a background or border that becomes an integral part of a brand. I illustrated two backgrounds for DeKuyper Liqueurs that the agency used for everything from package designs, displays, hang-tags, collateral material, giveaways and probably more. There is also a tropical version (not shown).

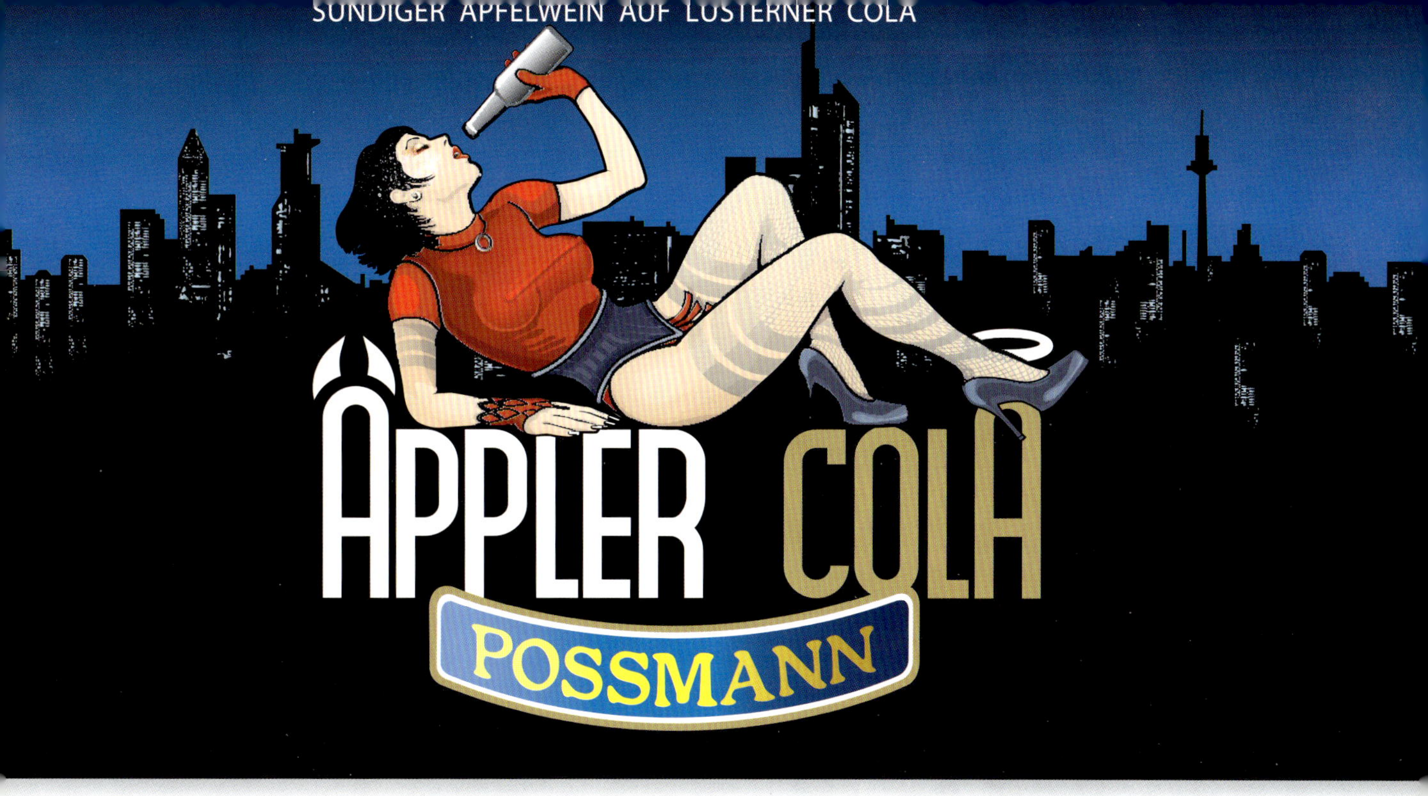

Appler Cola Girls
Client: Possman
Agency: Internal
Year: 2008
Model: Christine LeMaster

My German clients are often pretty kinky (see page 69 for more on this). Among my more visible projects was a hard-cider and cola mix produced by a large and respected orchard named Possman. They do not produce anything else like it and this particular brand is way out of the ordinary for them. It took me a few tries to satisfy their German aesthetic. They had particular tastes in mind for the women, in particular their hair and costumes. They also wanted the women to be less idealized than my U.S. clients want, and the rendering to be stark and minimalistic in palette. Three labels were designed and produced to be used alternately on bottles and cases so that consumers could collect them all. Available in Germany.

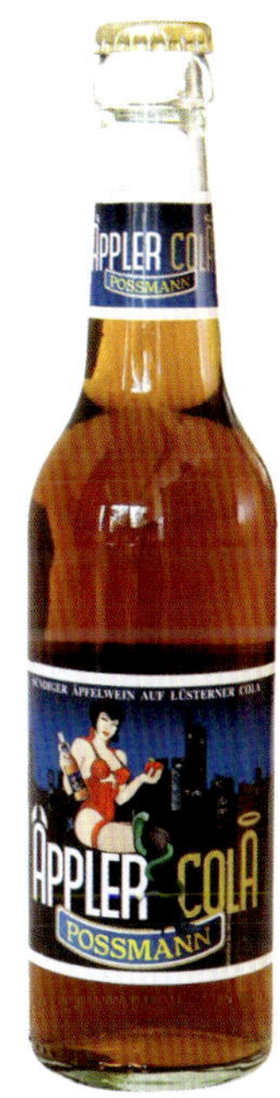

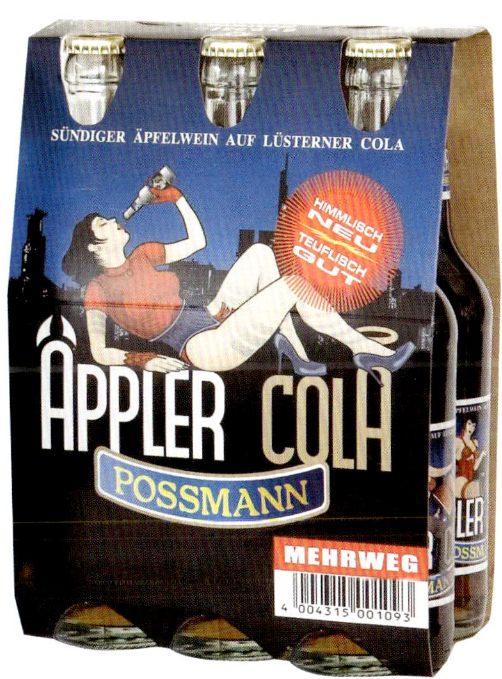

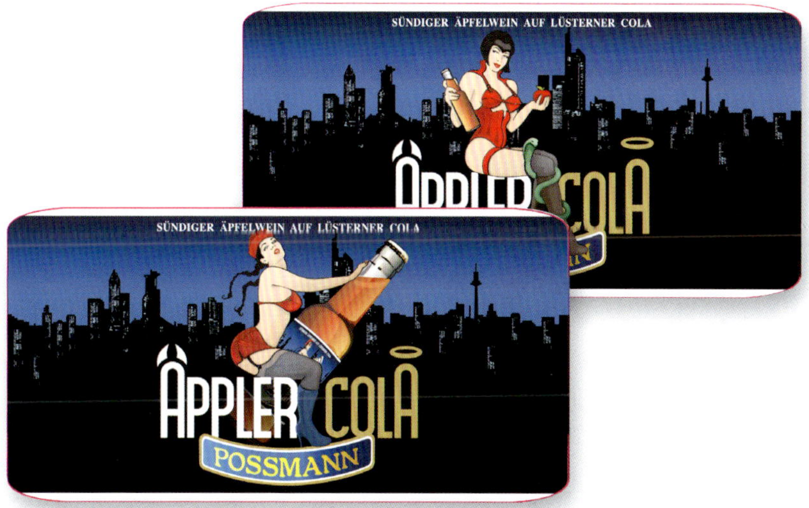

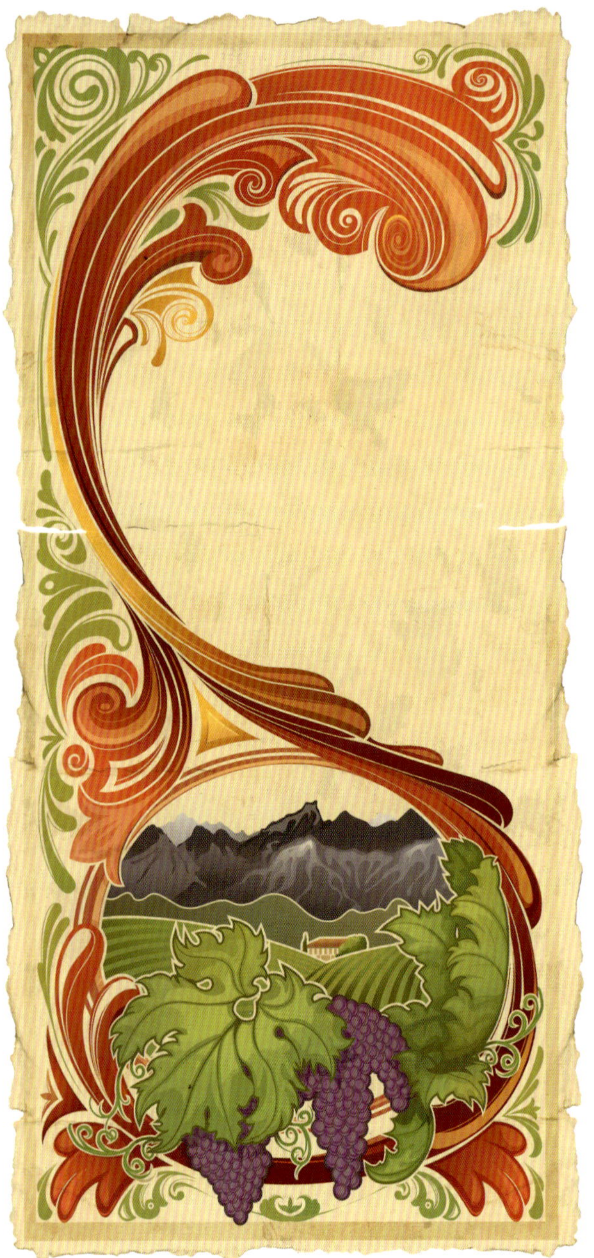

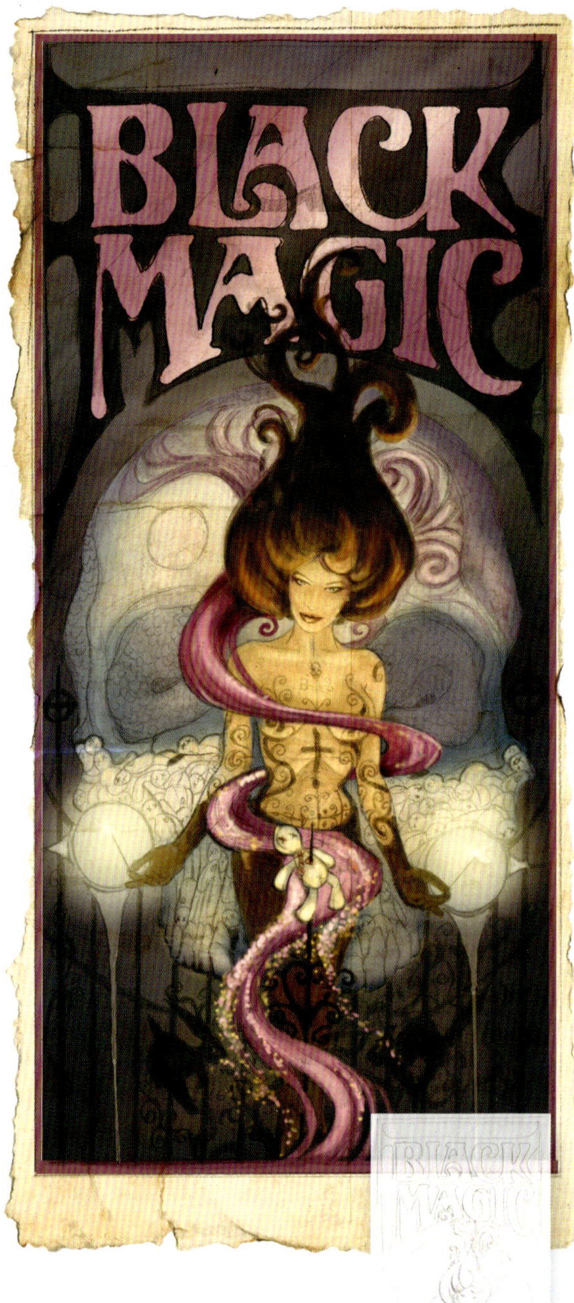

Argentinean Wine Label
Client: not disclosed
Agency: Timothy Harris Design
Year: 2009

I get a lot of bid requests for wine labels, but many wineries are so small, that my style is cost-prohibitive. Timothy Harris Design is a specialty firm focused on the Wine industry and I felt very proud that they asked me to produce the label for their client. At the time, the name of the brand hadn't been decided on and the label was going to be used for multiple varieties of Argentinean wine. The agency was to add the typography after submission. I never found out what the final wine name was, nor where I could purchase a bottle (or a case).

Black Magic Wine Label
Client: not disclosed
Agency: confidential
Year: 2007
Model: Meghan Perkins

This is one of those projects that could have been great. It is always rare for a client to approach me with a really great idea. The wine brand was Black Magic and they wanted an art nouveau inspired witch or voodoo priestess. They loved every sketch and I started on the color compositions to flesh out the feel of the piece... and then they killed the project. I have a feeling that some higher authority pulled the plug fearful of a public backlash against the brand - but I will never know.

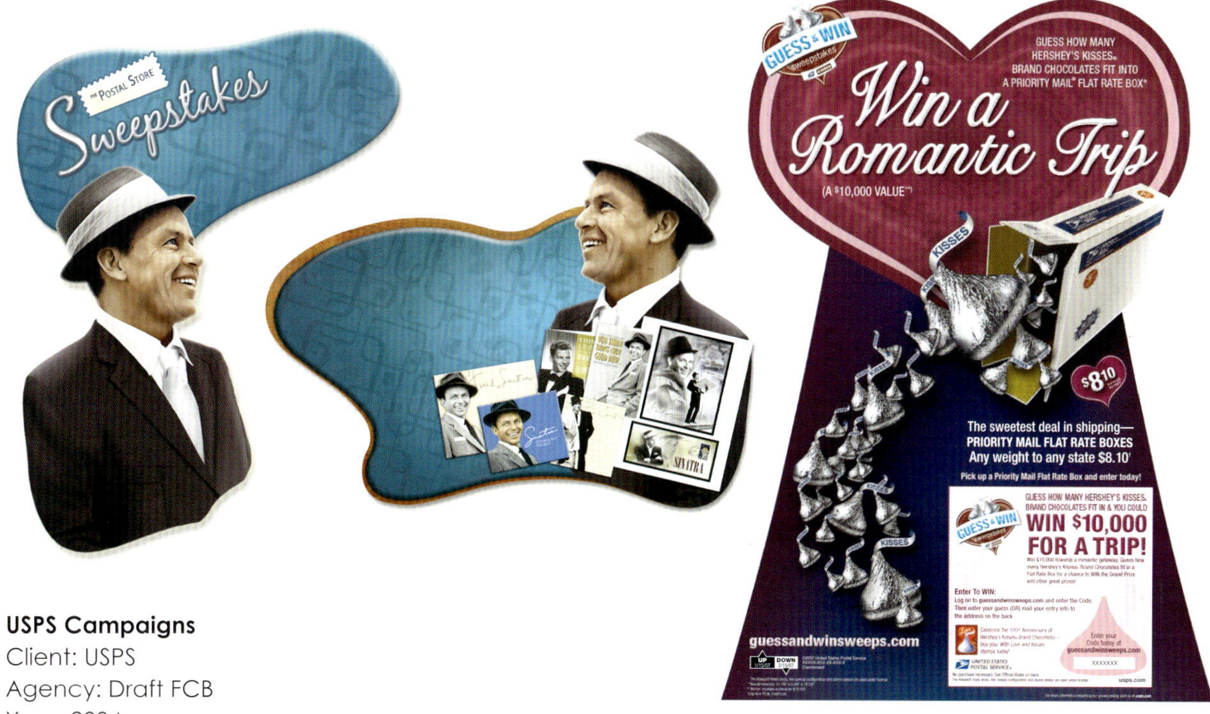

USPS Campaigns
Client: USPS
Agency: Draft FCB
Year: 2004

I was hired by Draft to do production illustrations for two projects for the United States Post Office. Production illustrations are done to the exact specifications of the client as if they did it themselves. The first was for their Valentines Day POP (point-of-purchase) displays. A year later, I created all of the backgrounds, and various other design elements for the Sinatra campaign. The Sinatra photo that they wanted to use was too small, so they had me paint it (overnight) at a much larger print-ready size. Both campaigns won MarCom awards.

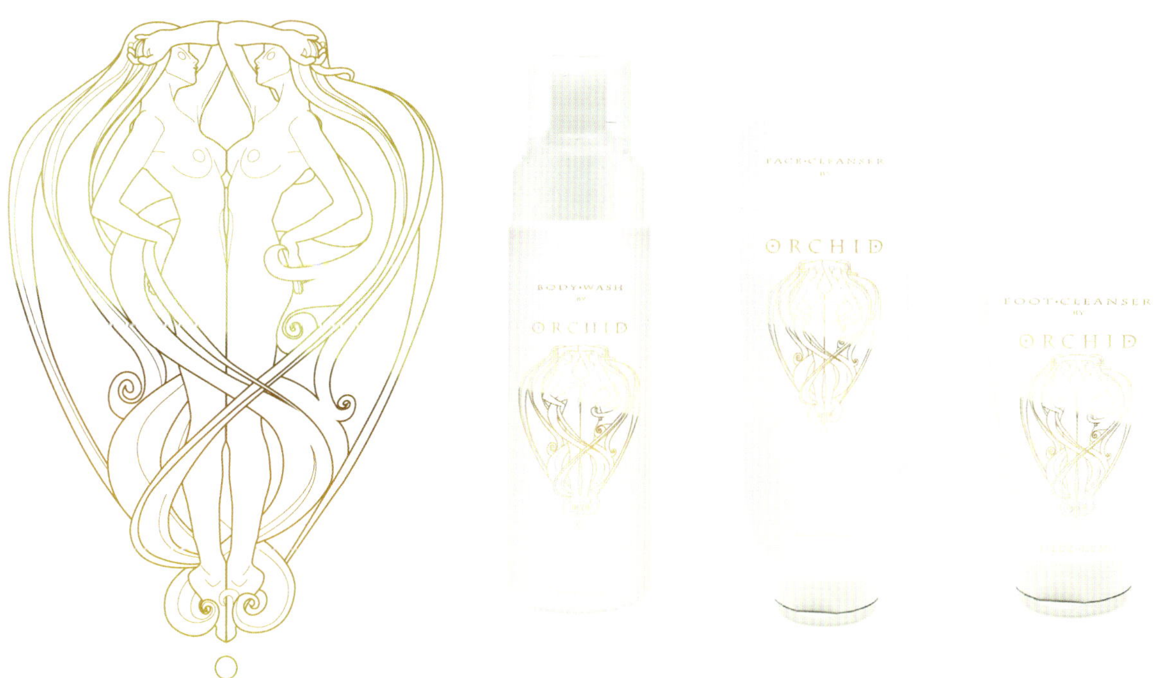

Orchid Girls
Client: Confidential
Agency: Confidential
Year: 2004
Model: Withheld

This was one of the few projects I worked on in collaboration with Lazarus. We were hired to contribute designs to a pitch for developing a luxury brand of soaps, lotions and body cleansers. We were given a creative brief with references to the biggest brand names and most luxurious brands in the cosmetics industry. Among the designs, Lazarus sketched out an art nouveau logo of Gemini, intended to be imprinted in gold foil. I finished it and Lazarus mocked up bottles for presentation of various sizes.

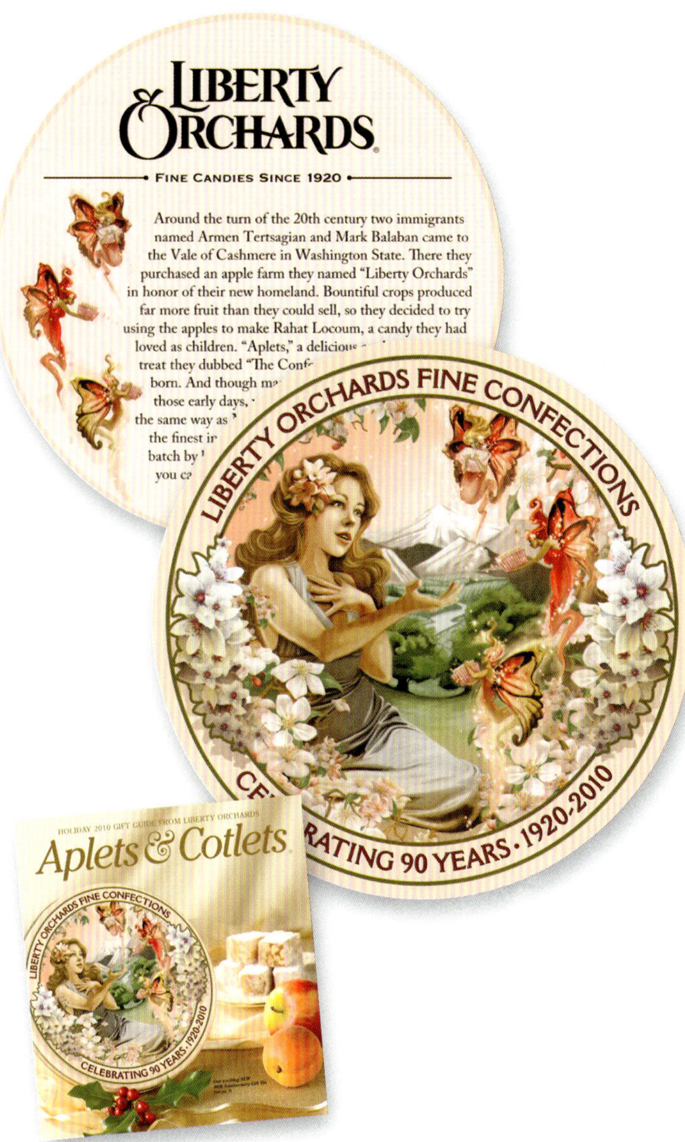

Liberty Orchard Faerie Garden
Client: Liberty Orchard
Agency: Internal
Year: 2010

Projects on a deadline can be interesting when completed in transit. 2010 was a dramatic year for me. I had just started exploring my own pieces and we were embarking on our second summer tour of art shows and conventions selling prints and Giclees. Just as the tour began, Liberty Orchard called and dropped this beautiful confection tin in my lap... while I was on the road... travelling in an RV... with only three days to spare between shows... using only a tablet and a laptop... a broken laptop. It goes to show that great art can be created anywhere, and with anything. Then a surprise. It turned out the Art Director was travelling to one of my shows: San Diego Comic Con. One day he simply walked up to my booth and handed me proofs of the label and they were 50% larger than I designed. It seems that the orchard loved it so much that they redesigned the tin to showcase the art-work better.

This project's short deadline was the result of another illustrator dropping the ball. I stress two things to those of you who want to be illustrators: Make your deadlines, and be prepared to pick up someone else's slack, usually on very, very short notice. Rush jobs and short deadlines are part of the excitement of this profession.

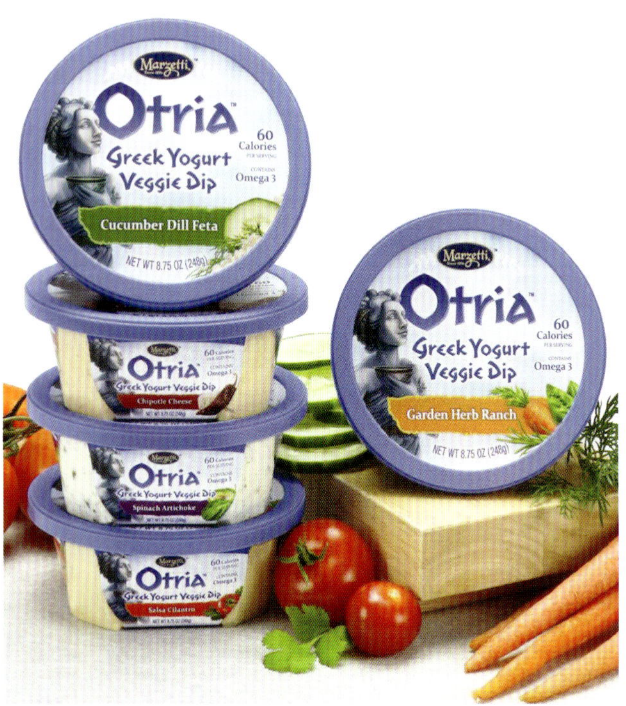

Otria
Client: Marzetti
Agency: Tailford Mitchell
Year: 2010

I had just finished a grueling show in NYC, and was preparing to drive my grandparents from Connecticut to Florida in three days. So, **of course**, my agent calls me up with this fun job. Ten hours of driving, four hours of drawing, ten hours of driving, four hours of second round approvals and a painting completed over Easter weekend. One thing you can expect in this industry is that if it's a holiday weekend, there will be a deadline. Nothing makes you look better than meeting that insane deadline and making the agency look good.

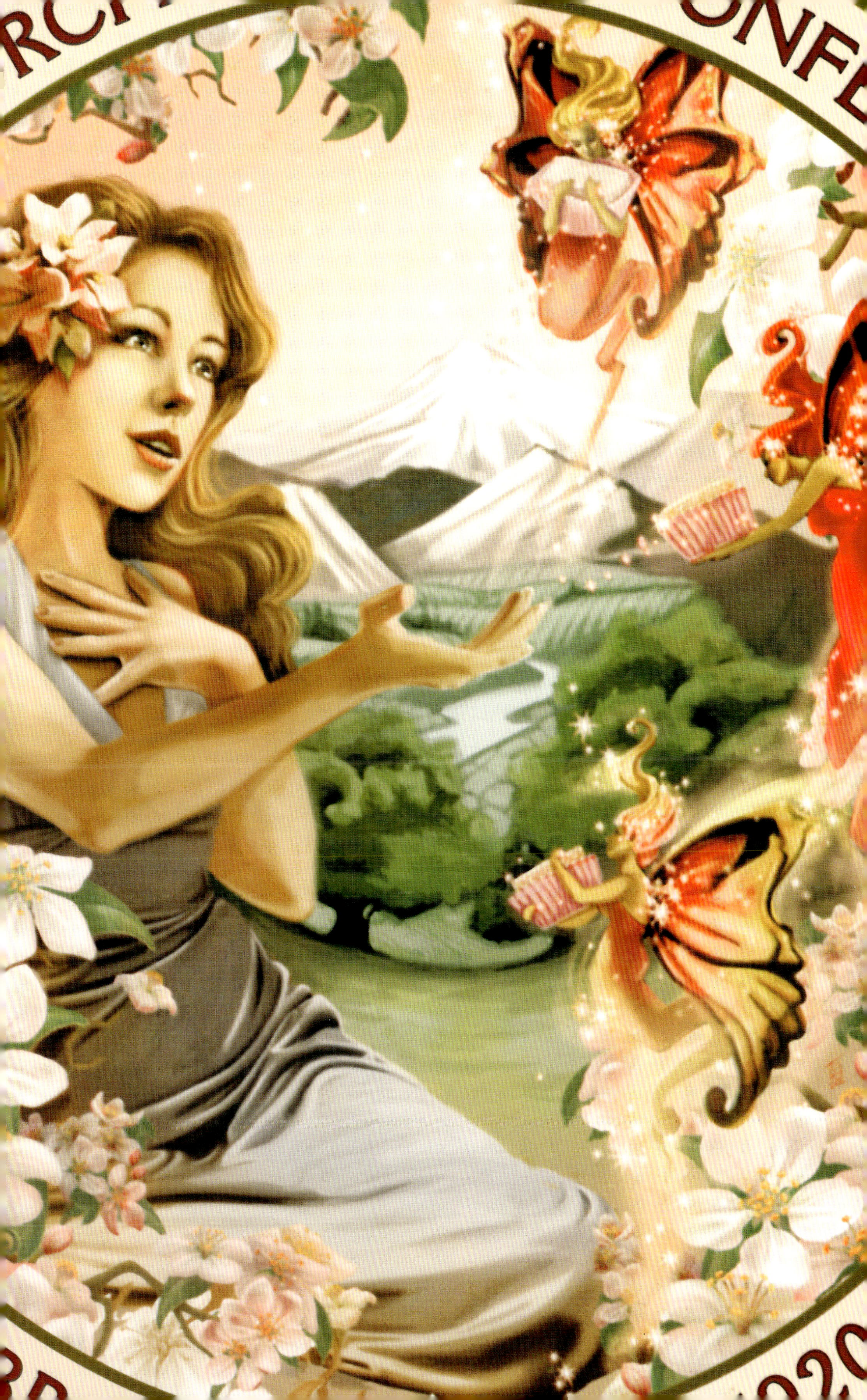

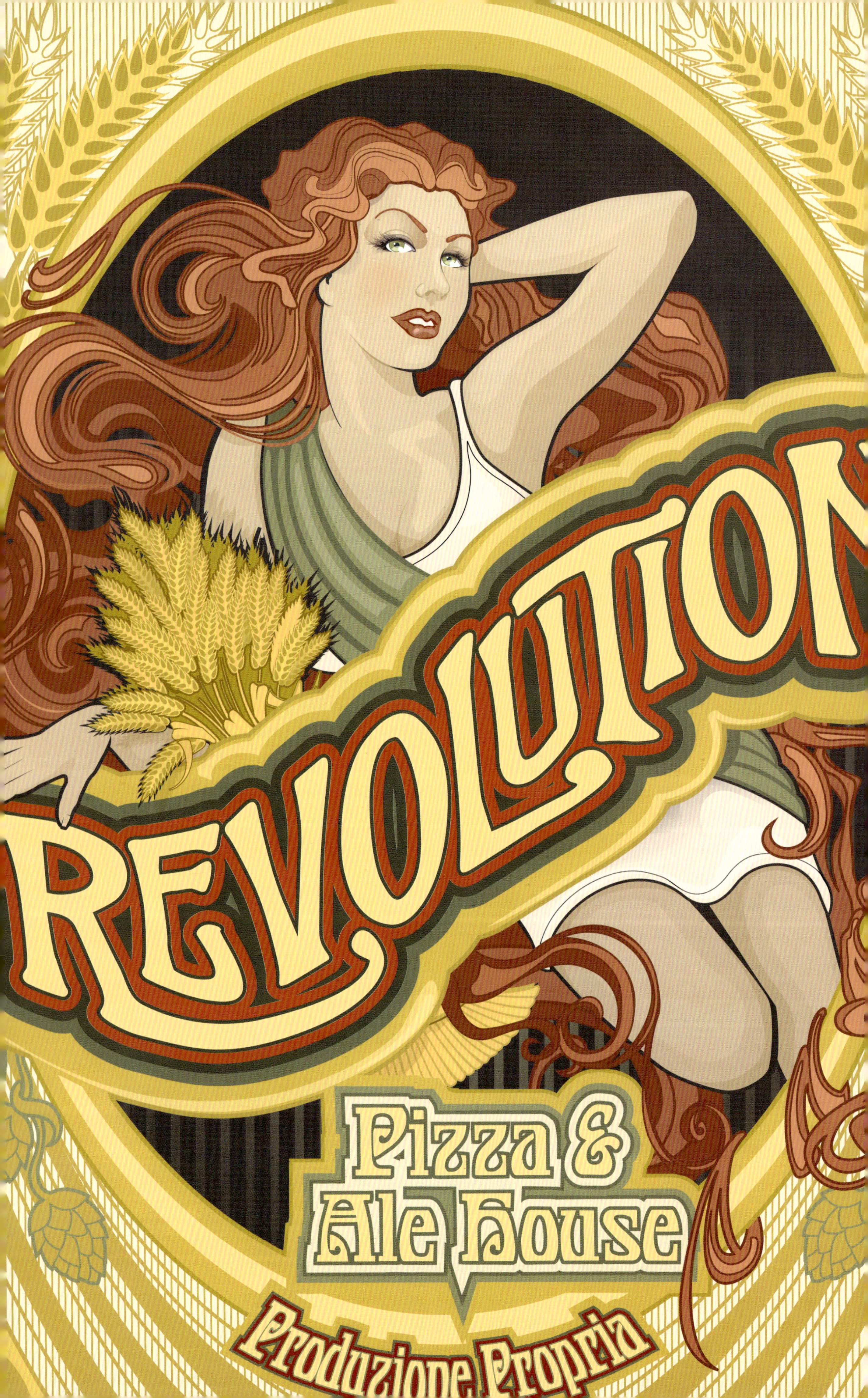
REVOLUTION
Pizza &
Ale House
Produzione Propria

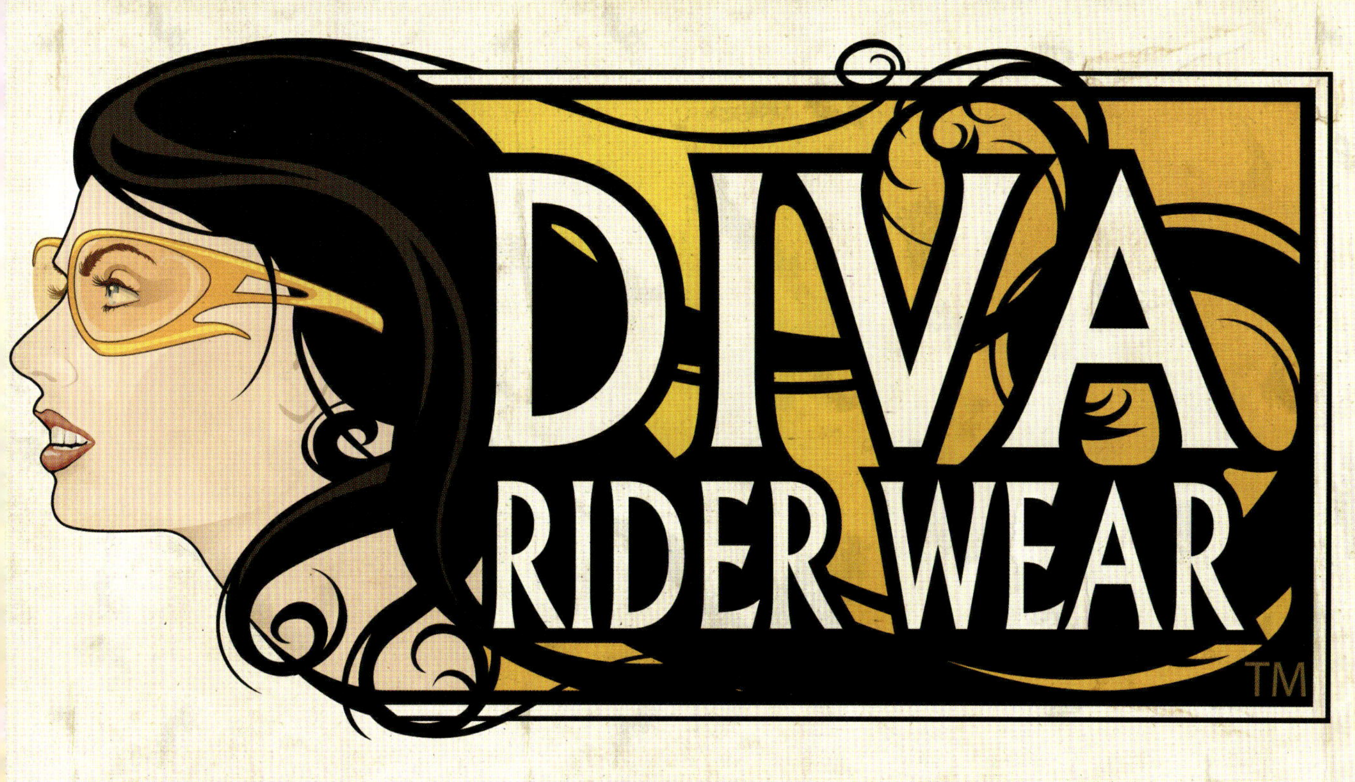

Diva Rider Wear
Year: 2010

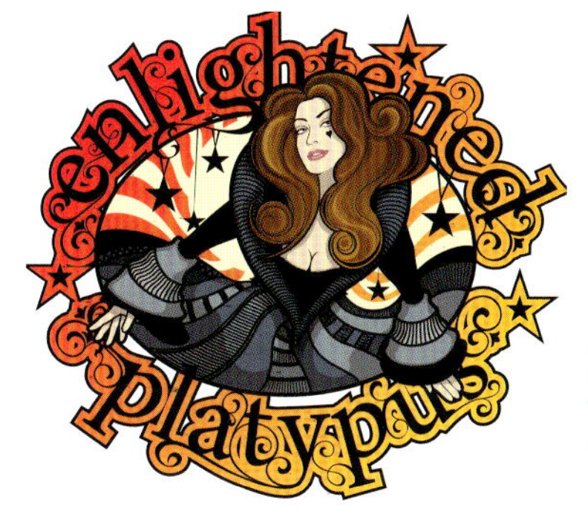

Enlightened Platypus
Year: 2010

Spirit of Mardi Gras
Client: City of New Orleans
Agency: MediaBuys
Year: 2006

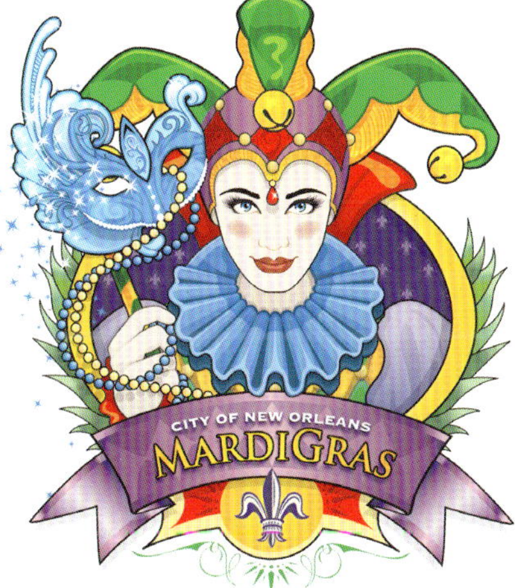

Sock Dreams
Year: 2008

Island Girl Records
Year: 2007

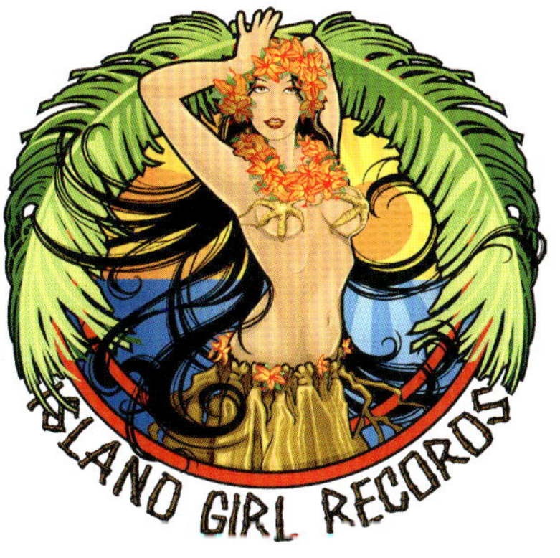

FACING PAGE
Revolution Pizza & Ale House
Year: 2008

Logos are specifically designed to be eye-catching and memorable - but are usually much less ornamental than my style. Still, there are projects that need me. The first ever official logo for Mardi Gras was a pro-bono project to assist the government revitalize the city. It brings back personal memories of Katrina. Everyone remembers it hitting New Orleans - but it made landfall at my studio in Florida a few days prior.

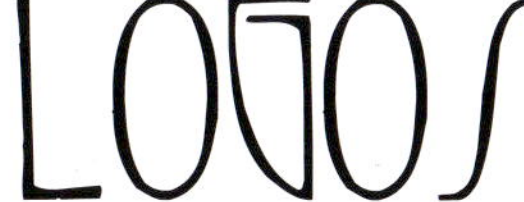

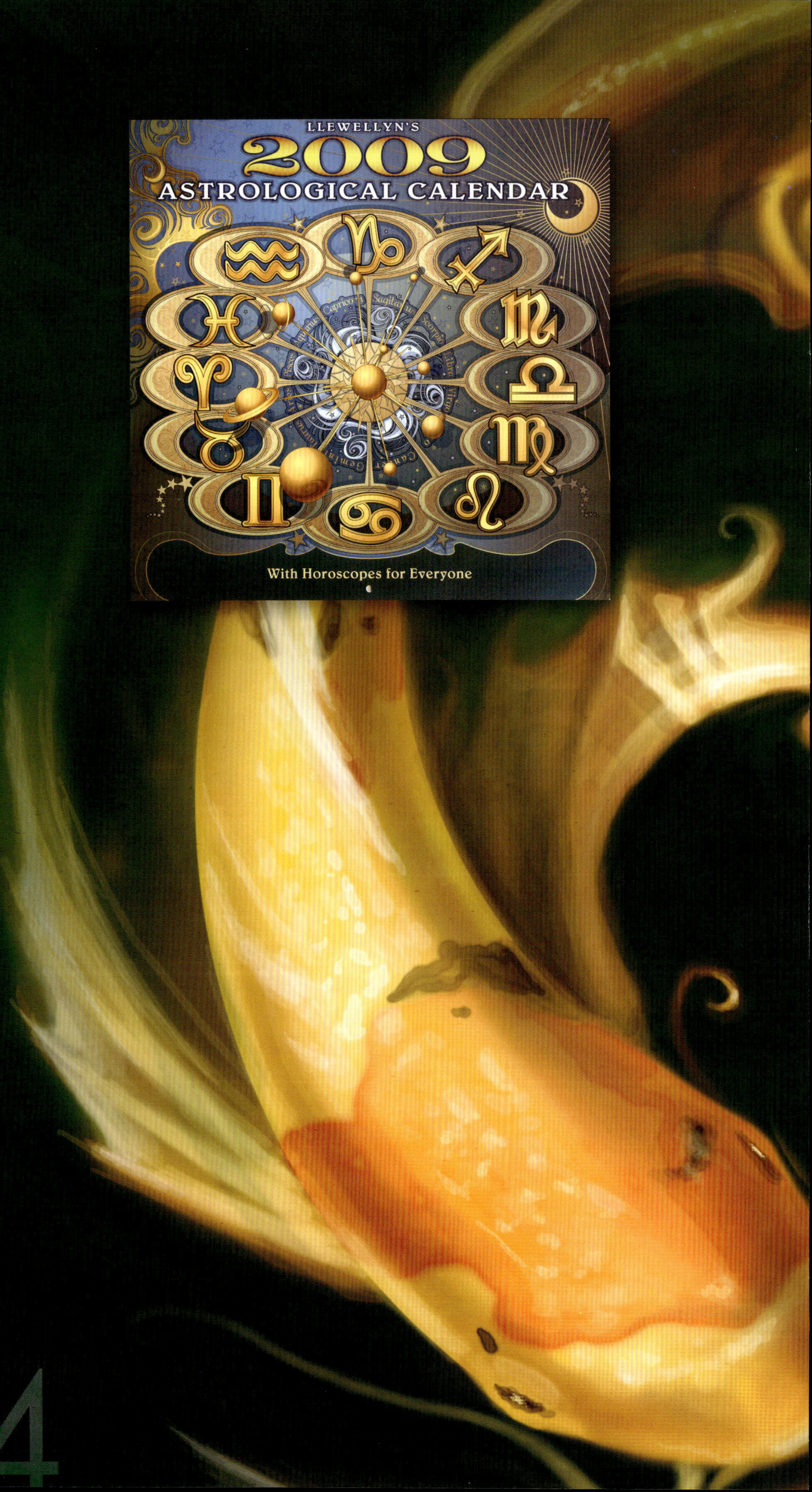

LLEWELLYN'S

2009

ASTROLOGICAL CALENDAR

With Horoscopes for Everyone

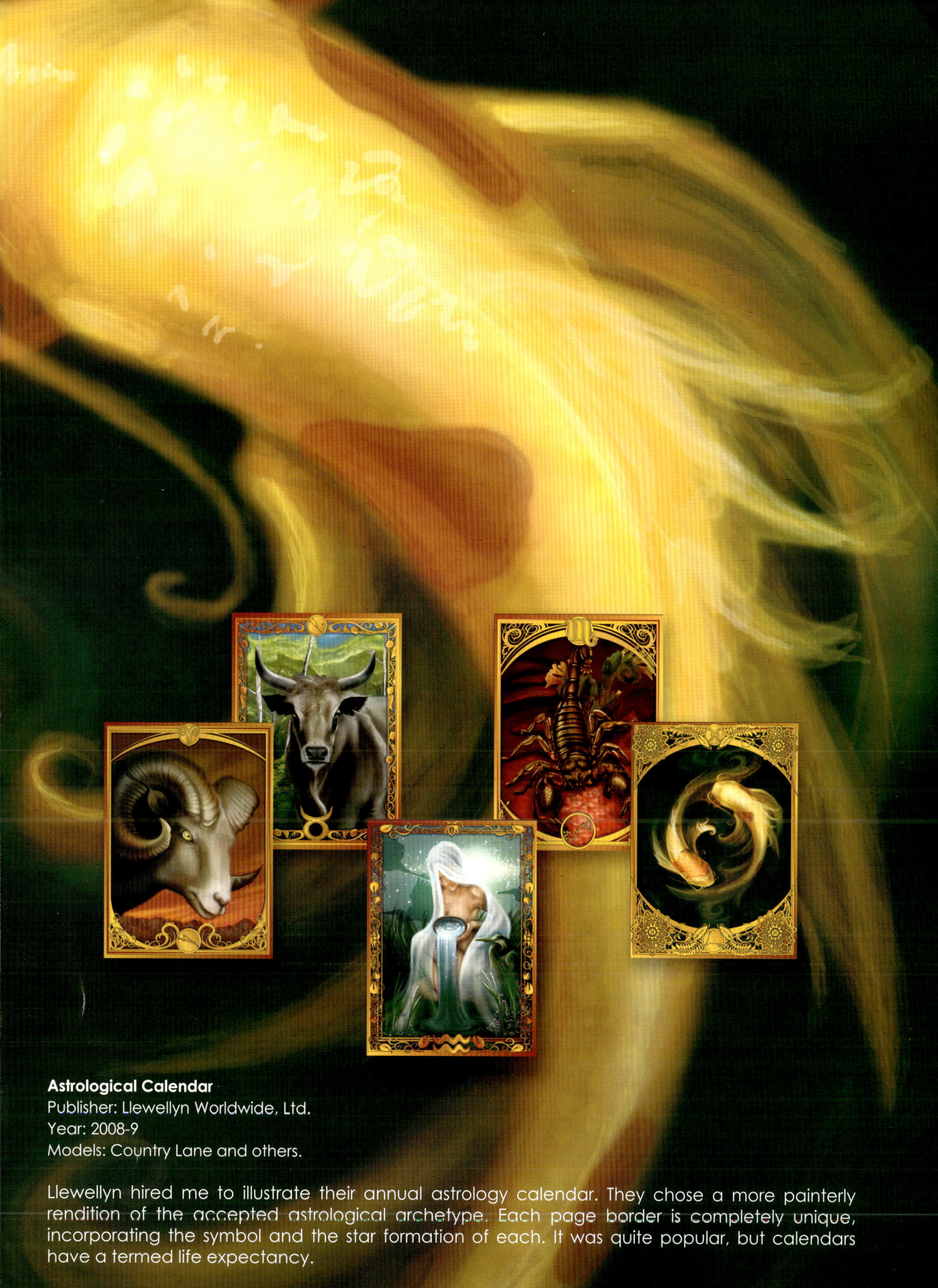

Astrological Calendar
Publisher: Llewellyn Worldwide, Ltd.
Year: 2008-9
Models: Country Lane and others.

Llewellyn hired me to illustrate their annual astrology calendar. They chose a more painterly rendition of the accepted astrological archetype. Each page border is completely unique, incorporating the symbol and the star formation of each. It was quite popular, but calendars have a termed life expectancy.

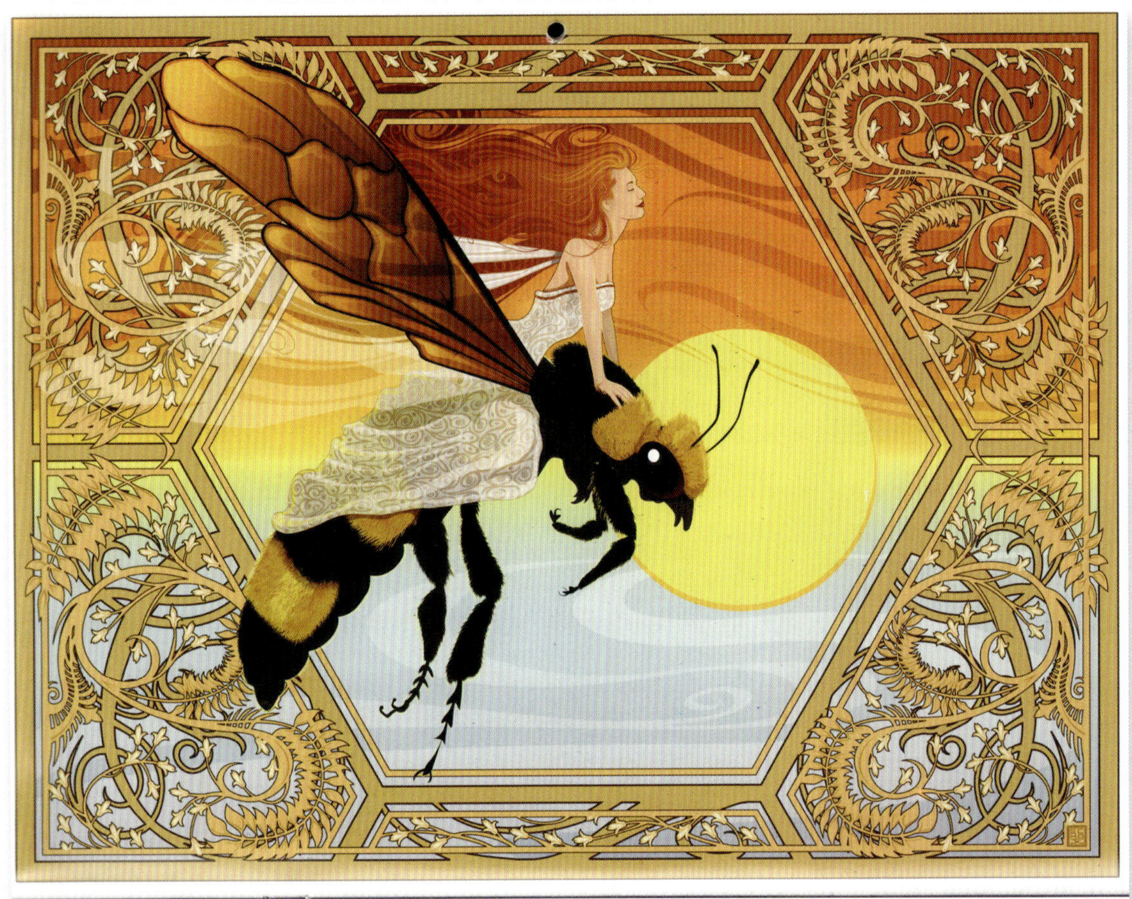

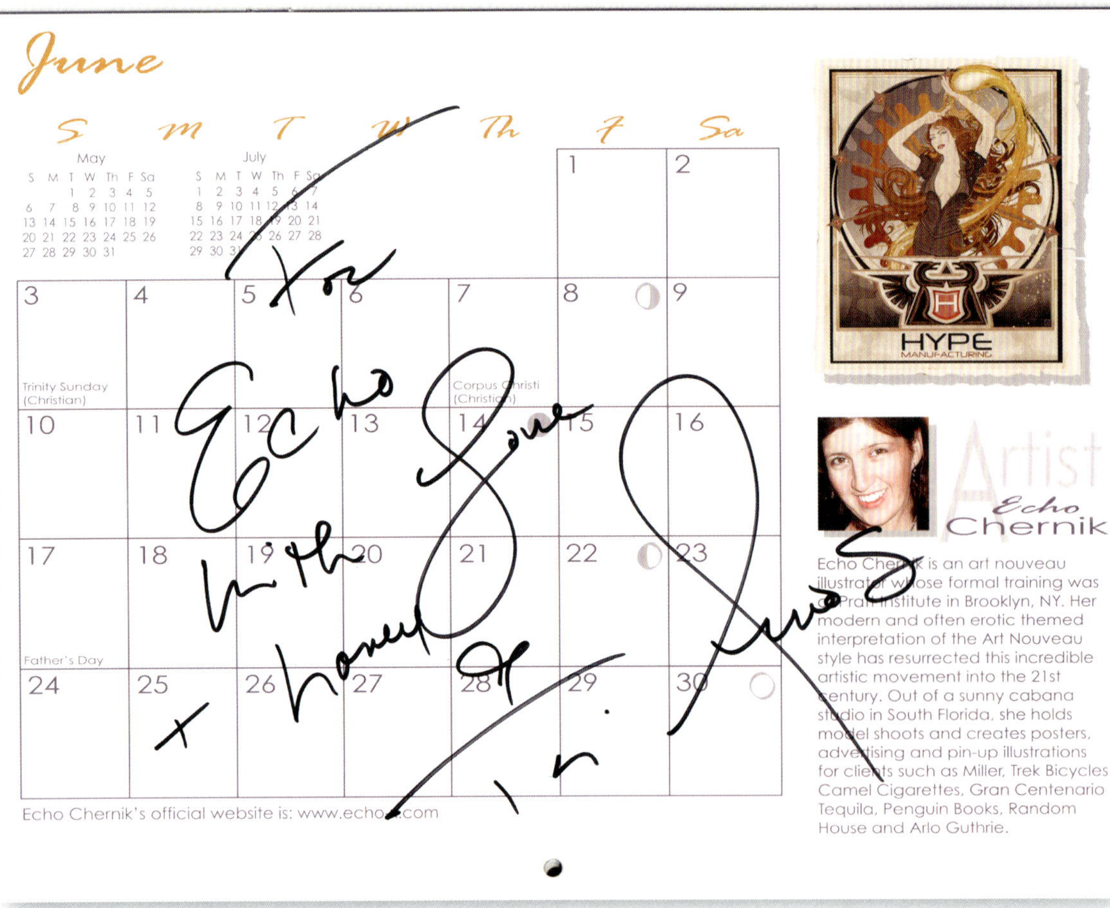

Tori Amos' RAINN Calendar 2007
Client: RAINN.org
Year: 2007
Model: Tori Amos

Every year, Tori Amos' RAINN foundation puts out a benefit calendar to raise money and awareness for victims of Rape, Abuse and Incest. I was proud to be selected to be a part of the 2007 calendar, and Tori was kind enough to write a little thank you to me.

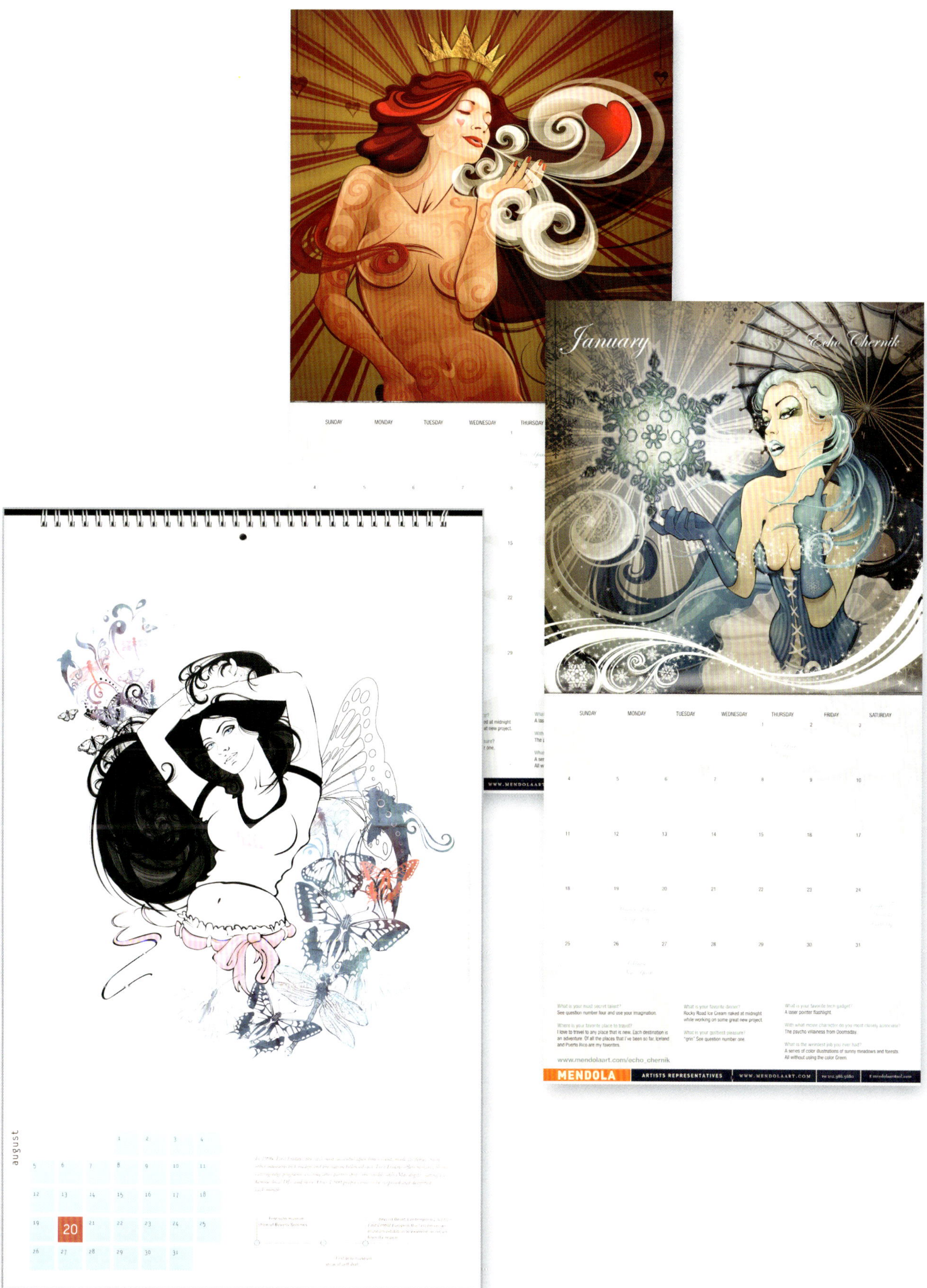

"Museum of Contemporary Art"
Client: Museum of Contemporary Art Chicago
Agency: Munro Campagna Artist Representatives
Model: Meghan Perkins

Mendola Artists 2008
Mendola Artists 2009
Client: Mendola Artists Artist Representatives
Models: Country Lane, Tara Ryze

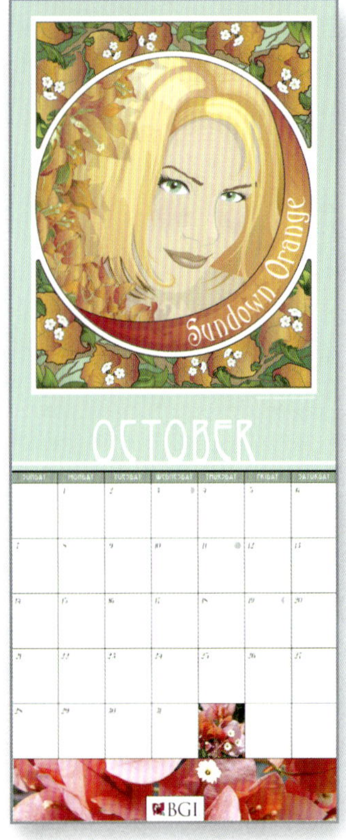

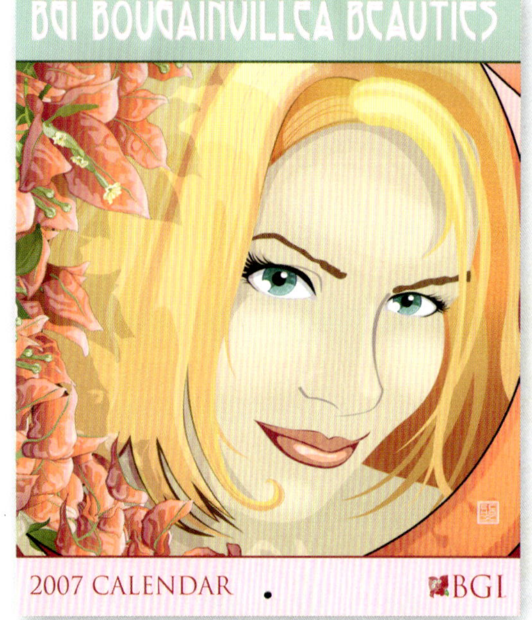

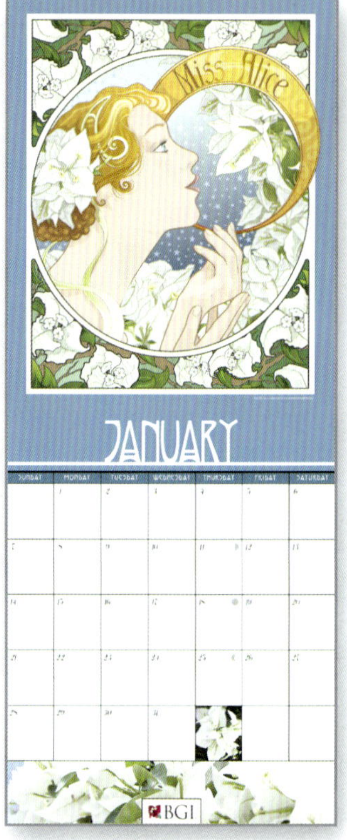

SEASON'S GREETINGS

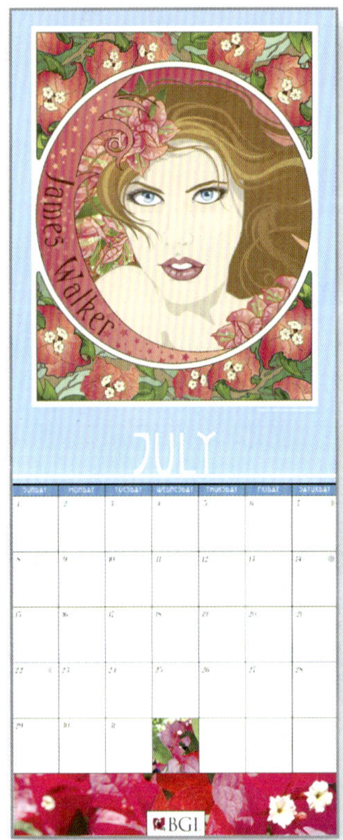

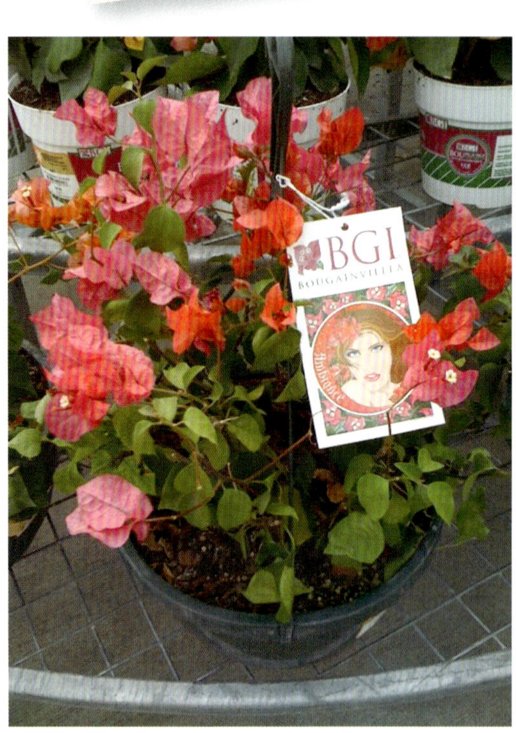

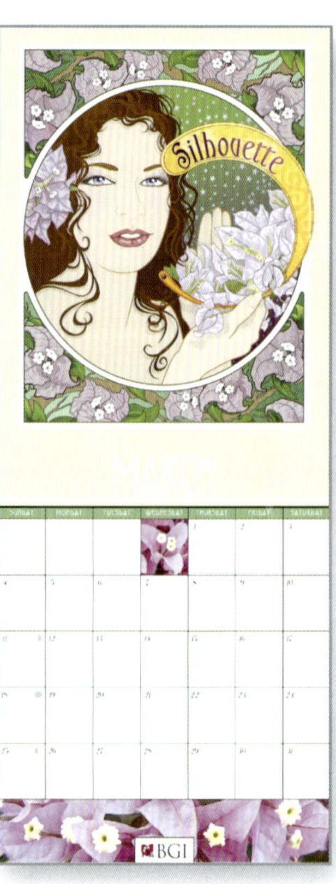

Bougainvillea
Client: Bougainvillea Growers International
Year: 2006-7
Models: various incl. employees of BGI

My first calendar was for a national Bougainvillea grower. Every month featured one of the varieties of Bougainvillea they grew. The illustrations bore the names of each variety and the colors had to match perfectly because they were also used as hangtags for the plants at resellers like Home Depot.

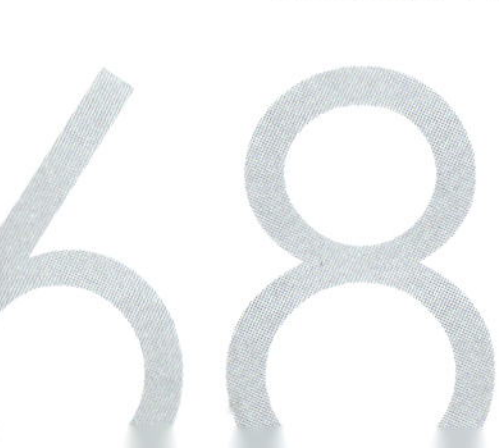

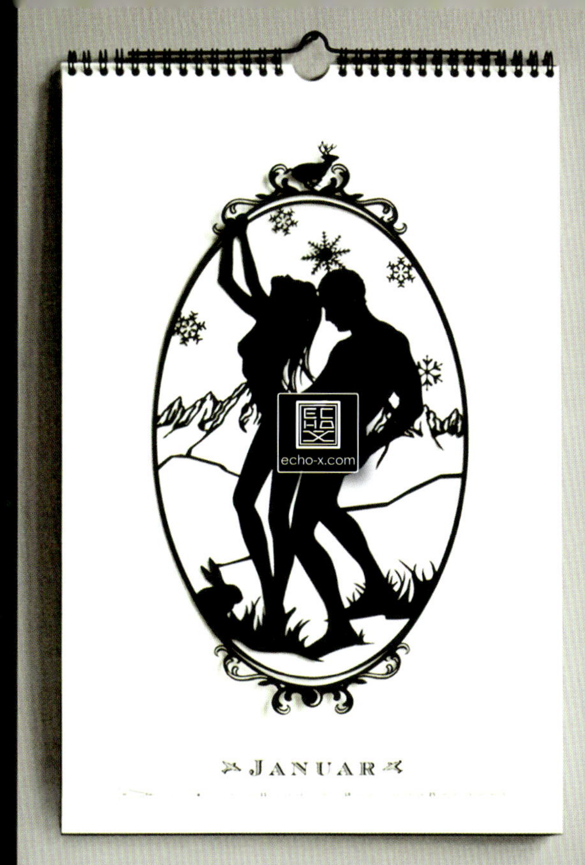

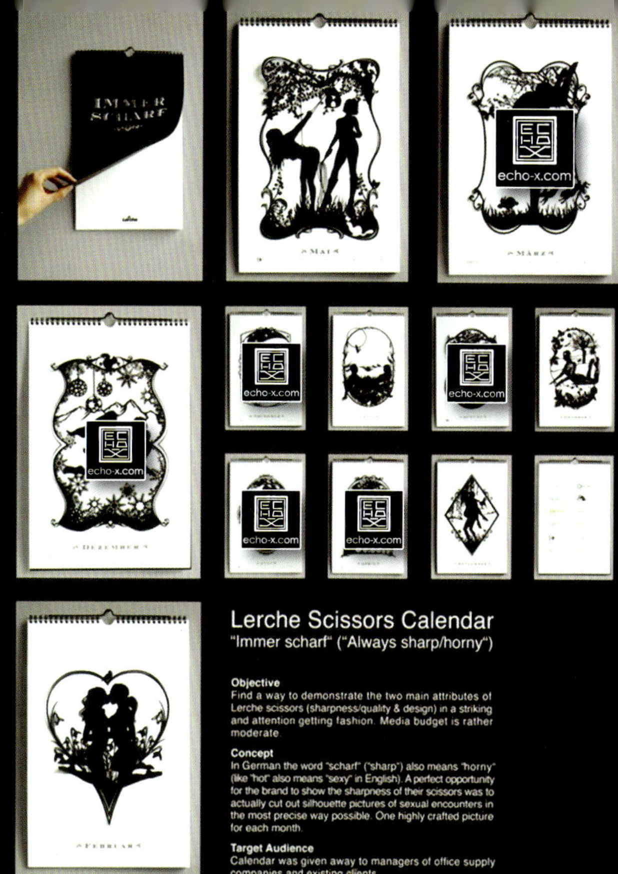

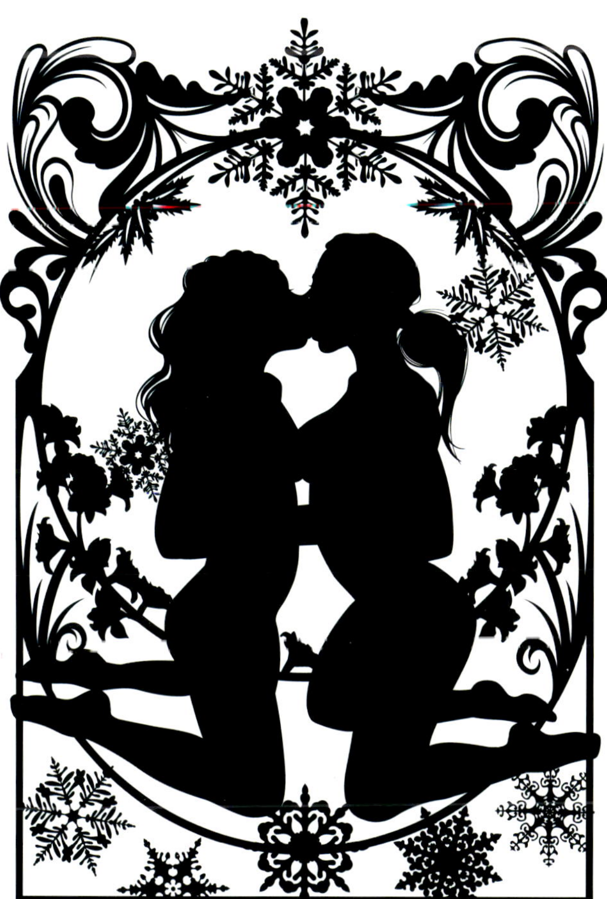

Lerche Scissors "Be Sharp" Promotion
Client: Lerche Scissors (Germany)
Agency: Scholz & Friends
Year: 2008-9
Models: Various

Sometimes what sounds like a really fun project on paper can turn tedious as a result of art direction. The concept for this calendar was as follows: The word for Sharp in German means not only sharp like a knife, but also means horny. The agency wanted to produce a calendar for a German scissor company, playing on the double entendre, and executed in a "scissor-cut silhouette" style. Really awesome and fun concept. They sent me a list of specific sexual positions and reference shots to use. The art director approved it to near-completion and then suddenly changed direction, reversing many approvals. Some art directors are a dream to work with, but it takes a really resolute artist (and good negotiator) to survive a tedious one. It's important to agree upfront how many iterations an illustration will go through. Sometimes its not the art or the art director - if a project has to go through committee, things can get rough without controls.

This calendar went on to win several international awards.

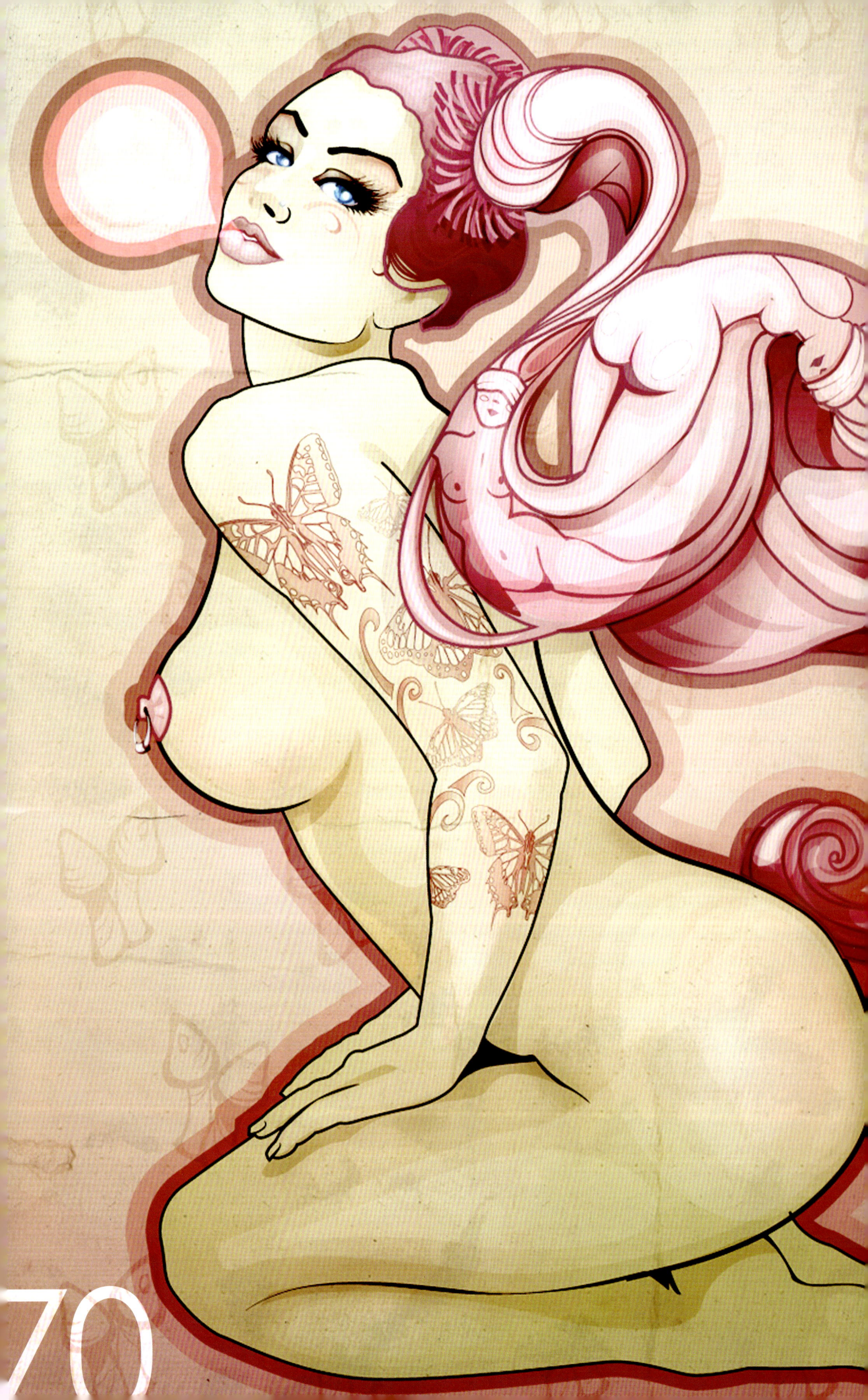

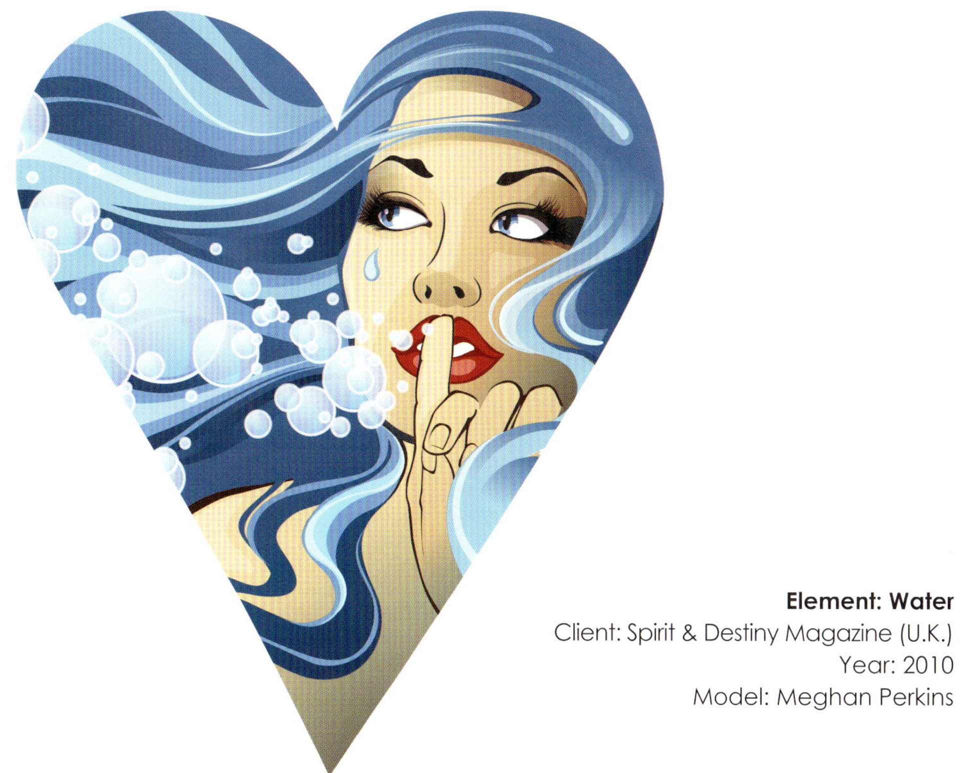

Element: Water
Client: Spirit & Destiny Magazine (U.K.)
Year: 2010
Model: Meghan Perkins

Bookcovers, Interiors and Editorial Illustration

There are trends in publishing illustration, just like in fashion. If you pay attention, you'll notice the gentle coming and going of these popular stylizations. People often ask me what I feel about the current trends in illustration, and where do I think they are going? I like to pay attention to trends, and perhaps let a little influence creep into my work, but I don't re-develop my portfolio. I receive frequent requests from clients to bend my style towards what's popular, or incorporate influences from other genres (50's pinup, fileatado, tattoo, stained-glass, etc.). I treat these as fun challenges to expand and explore my personal style - but I don't change my style completely. I'd rather lead trends than follow them.

My personal style is very complicated. Therefore, I receive a lot of calls from agencies who tried to emulate me with another illustrator, and gave up because it was too tedious.

All in all, good art is good art. An illustrator with great drawing skills will always find what they need to survive, regardless of the current trends.

FACING PAGE
Alt Porn
Client: Condé Nast Publications, Ltd. (U.K.)
Year: 2005
Model: Christine LeMaster

Alt Porn was one of two illustrations I created for a magazine article on Alternative Culture Pornography, which they defined as porn involving people from 'alternative lifestyles'. Oddly, this was not meant to suggest homosexual or fetish oriented pornography but was more of a fashion statement such as goth or cosplay. I'm still not sure why people with tattoos and/or piercings are considered 'alternative' anymore.

LAURELL K. HAMILTON

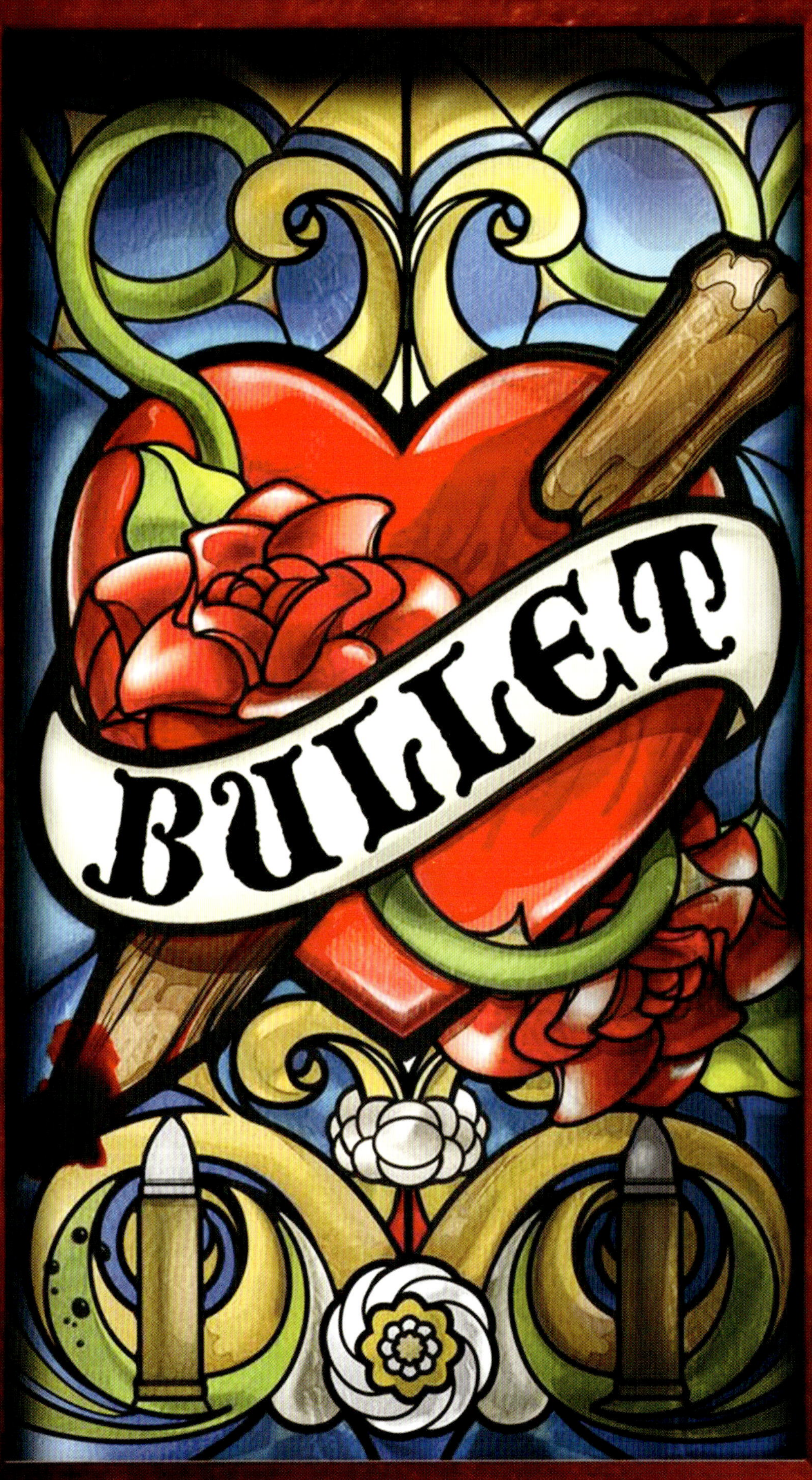

AN ANITA BLAKE,
VAMPIRE HUNTER, NOVEL

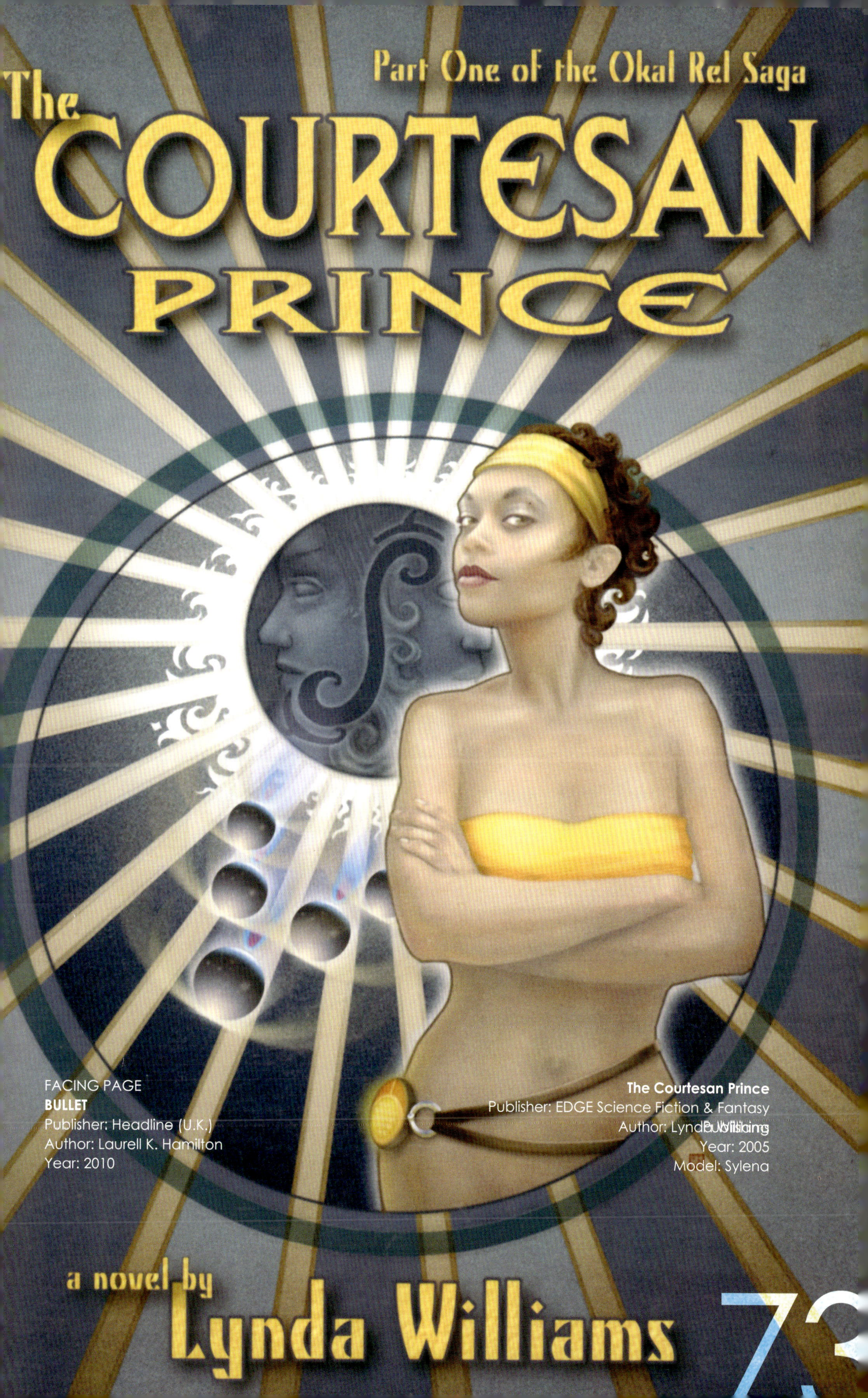

Part One of the Okal Rel Saga

The COURTESAN PRINCE

a novel by

Lynda Williams

FACING PAGE
BULLET
Publisher: Headline (U.K.)
Author: Laurell K. Hamilton
Year: 2010

The Courtesan Prince
Publisher: EDGE Science Fiction & Fantasy Publishing
Author: Lynda Williams
Year: 2005
Model: Sylena

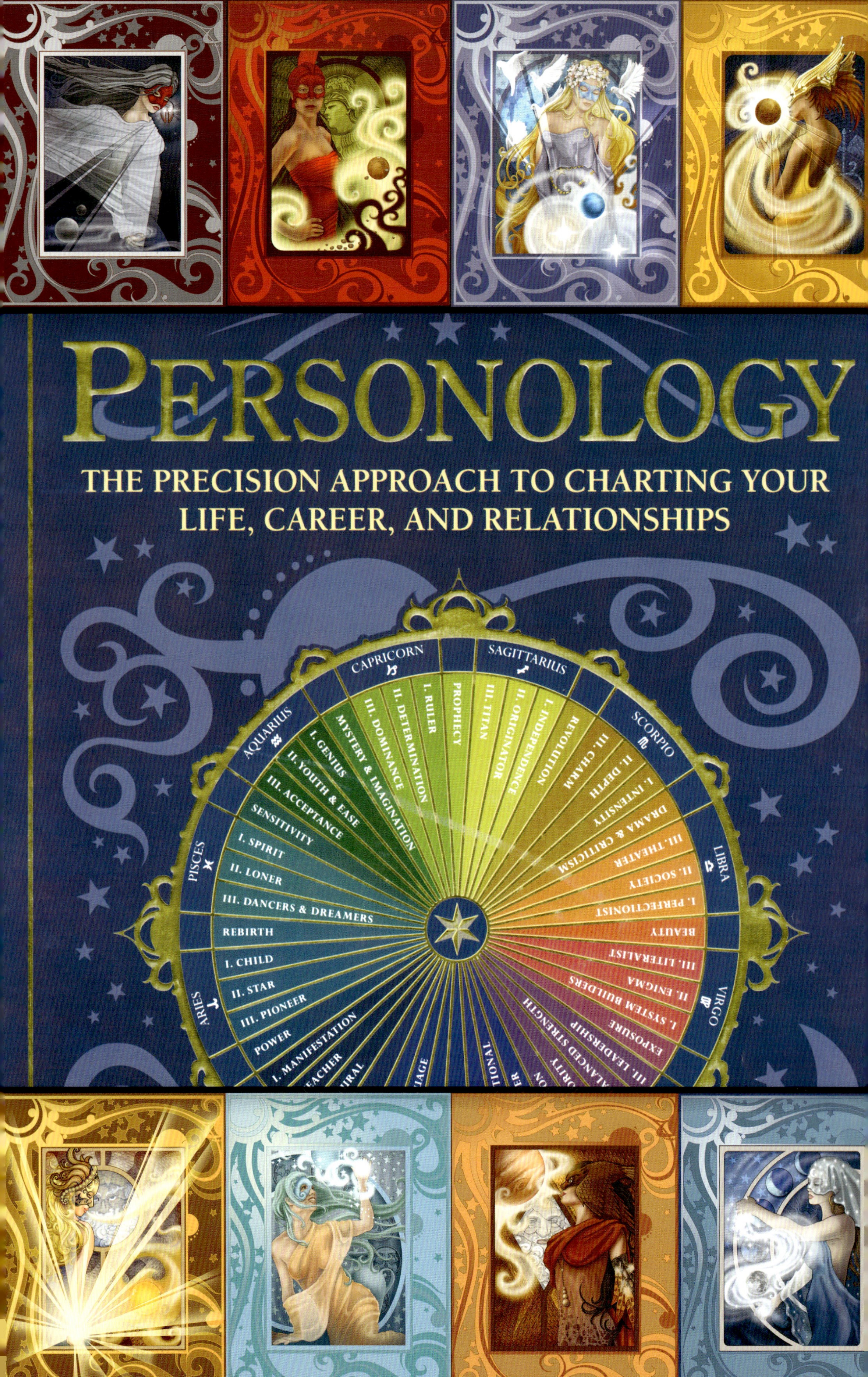
PERSONOLOGY
THE PRECISION APPROACH TO CHARTING YOUR LIFE, CAREER, AND RELATIONSHIPS
CAPRICORN
SAGITTARIUS
SCORPIO
LIBRA
VIRGO
ARIES
PISCES
AQUARIUS
I. GENIUS
II. YOUTH & EASE
III. ACCEPTANCE
SENSITIVITY
I. SPIRIT
II. LONER
III. DANCERS & DREAMERS
REBIRTH
I. CHILD
II. STAR
III. PIONEER
POWER
I. MANIFESTATION
MYSTERY & IMAGINATION
III. DOMINANCE
II. DETERMINATION
I. RULER
PROPHECY
III. TITAN
II. ORIGINATOR
I. INDEPENDENCE
REVOLUTION
III. CHARM
II. DEPTH
I. INTENSITY
DRAMA & CRITICISM
III. THEATER
II. SOCIETY
I. PERFECTIONIST
BEAUTY
III. LITERALIST
II. ENIGMA
I. SYSTEM BUILDERS
EXPOSURE

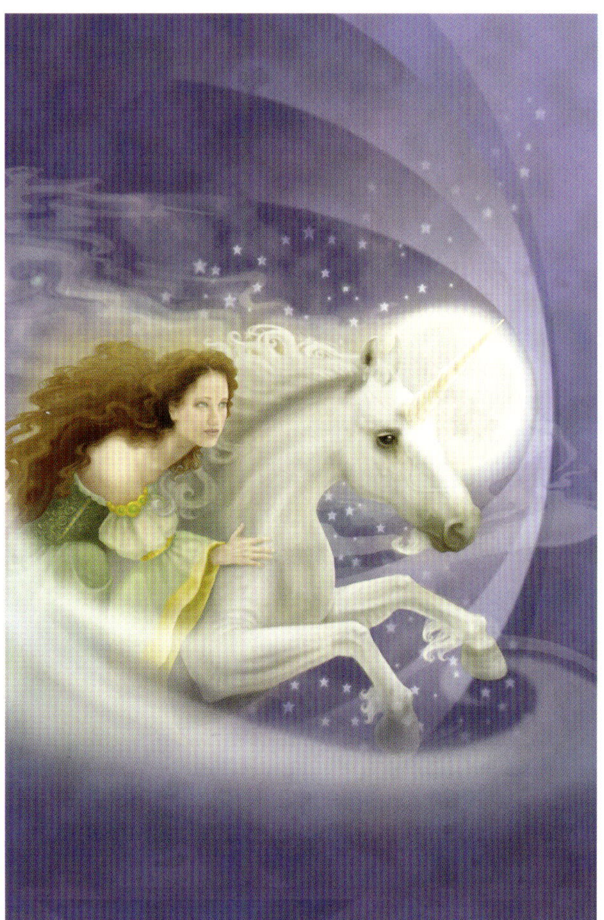

The Unicorn Treasury
Client: Magic Carpet Books
Author: Bruce Coville
Year: 2004
Model: Withheld

Yes, I paint some fantasy book covers. I am still proud of this one because of how well the unicorn itself came out. The entire piece is very dream-like, but it took a good half dozen sketches to get there. The art director consistently removed every art nouveau element I tried to put in. I was not well established for Art Nouveau at the time (2004) and I am sure if they selected me today for the job, the piece would have turned out more Art Nouveau.

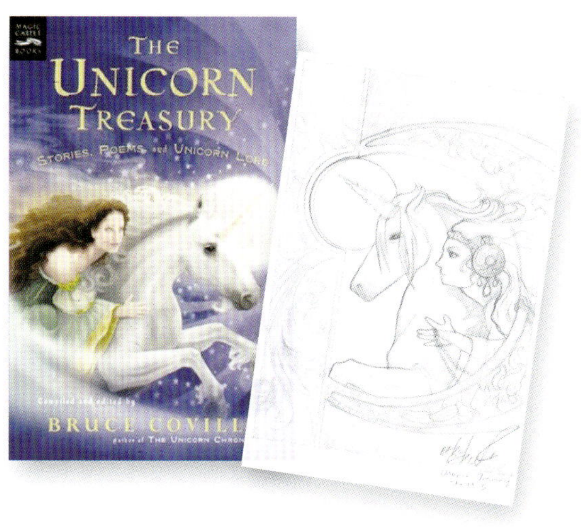

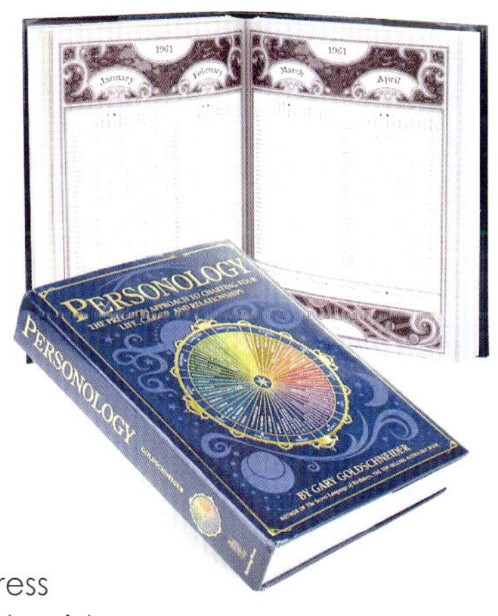

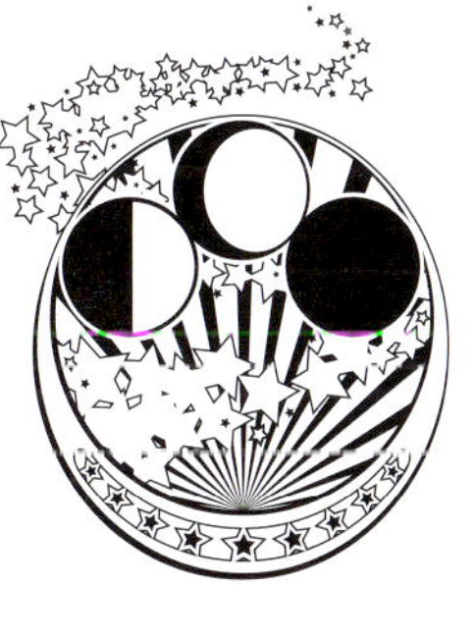

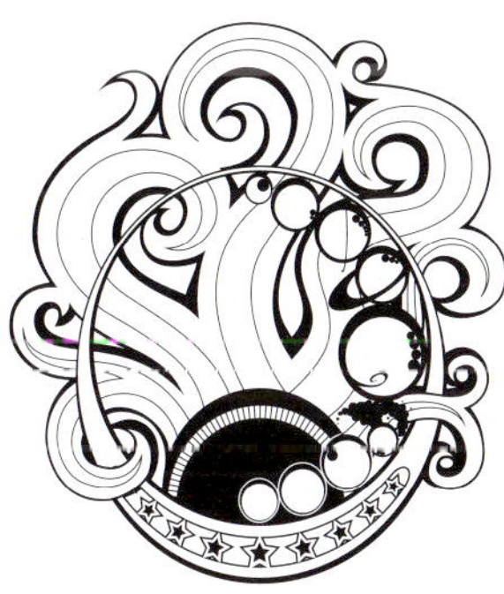

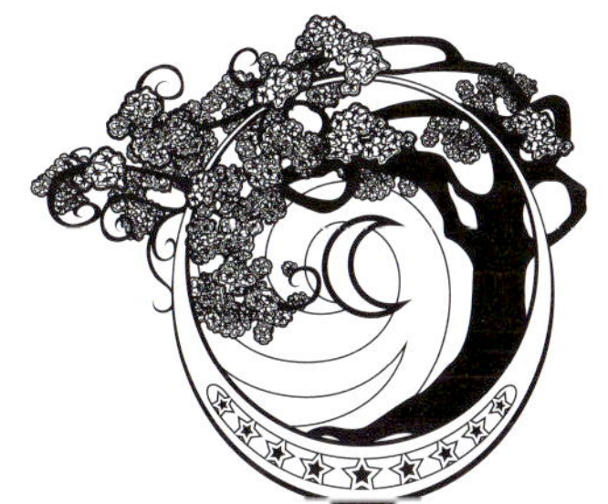

Personology
Publisher: Running Press
Author: Gary Goldschneider
Year: 2005
Models: Darla Squeo and others.

It is one thing to design and illustrate a cover but it's an entirely different project to illustrate an entire book. Personology is a book of astrological tables - over 500 of them! Of course, to break it up every so often they include text and one or more of my illustrations. I illustrated the entire jacket (front, spine and back), ten full pages representing the planets (and sun and moon), three exquisite spot illustrations {right], many icons and a chart template that was used on every one of the 500+ pages of tables. Whew.

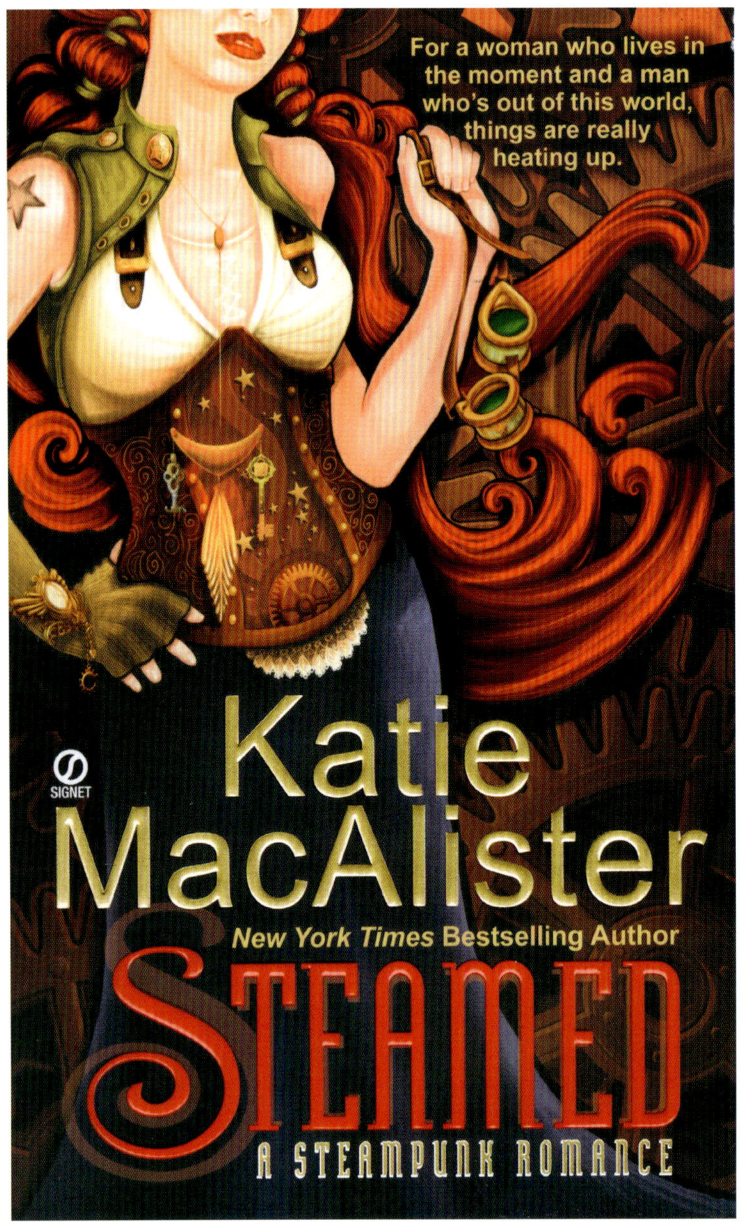

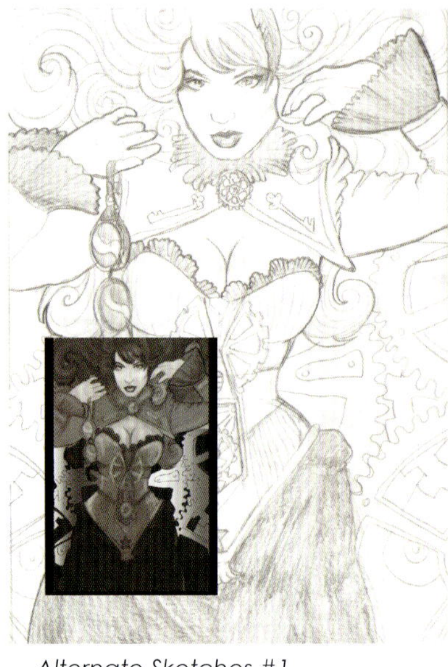

Alternate Sketches #1

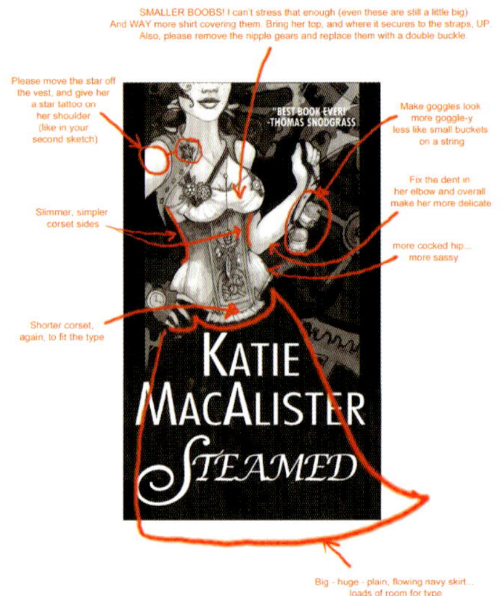

Art direction notes.

Steamed
Publisher: Penguin
Author: Kate MacAlister
Year: 2010

The process between a project's art director and the illustrator is always collaborative. Every illustrator's favorite words are "You're the artist, tell us what you recommend" or the rare bird "Do whatever you would like on this one." Much more often it is a collaborative effort of meetings, notes and sketches, back and forth. Sometimes, you receive a project with strict art notes and very little wiggle room - which can be a positive or a negative. Sometimes it takes all the guesswork out of the job and makes it easy.

The art director for Steamed knew exactly what she wanted, initially providing precise photo reference for pose, costume and accessories, and the finished project didn't deviate from her notes. When an art director suggests a direction, I supply what they ask for, but also like to supply alternates. Half the time, they love the new concept and change course, or extract elements to form a blend. You are the professional consultant, they value your artistic experience and vision. I always suggest presenting alternatives.

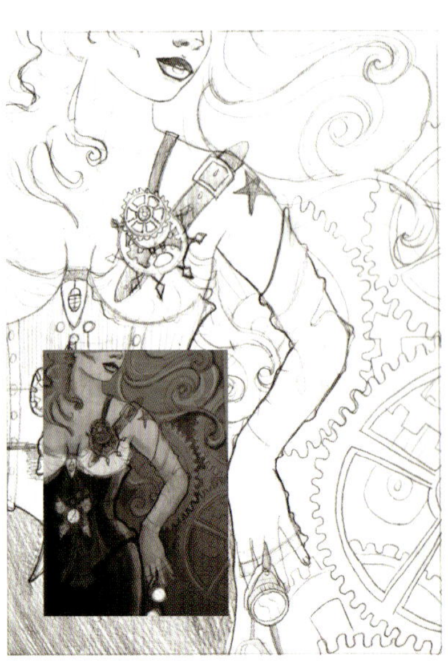

Alternate Sketches #2

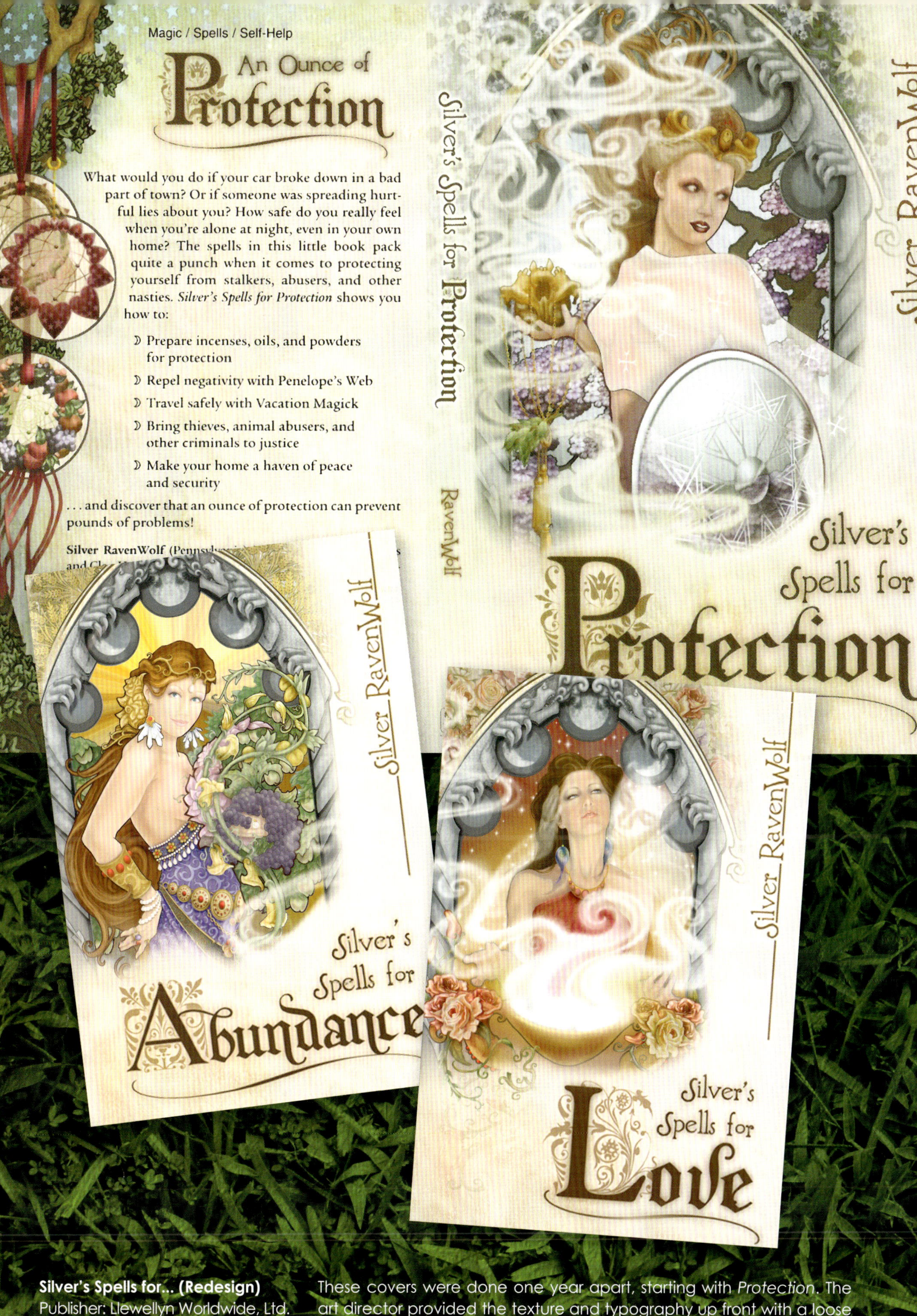

Silver's Spells for... (Redesign)
Publisher: Llewellyn Worldwide, Ltd.
Year: 2003, 2004, and 2005
Models: Darla Squeo, Echo Chernik and others.

These covers were done one year apart, starting with *Protection*. The art director provided the texture and typography up front with a loose pencil sketch of what she wanted and where she wanted it. Originally, Protection was envisioned to have a Helenic Goddess bearing a shield within a Roman archway. I offered my version with Darla holding a brazier (from a seal skull) and she loved it instantly. She gave me complete freedom on the next two.

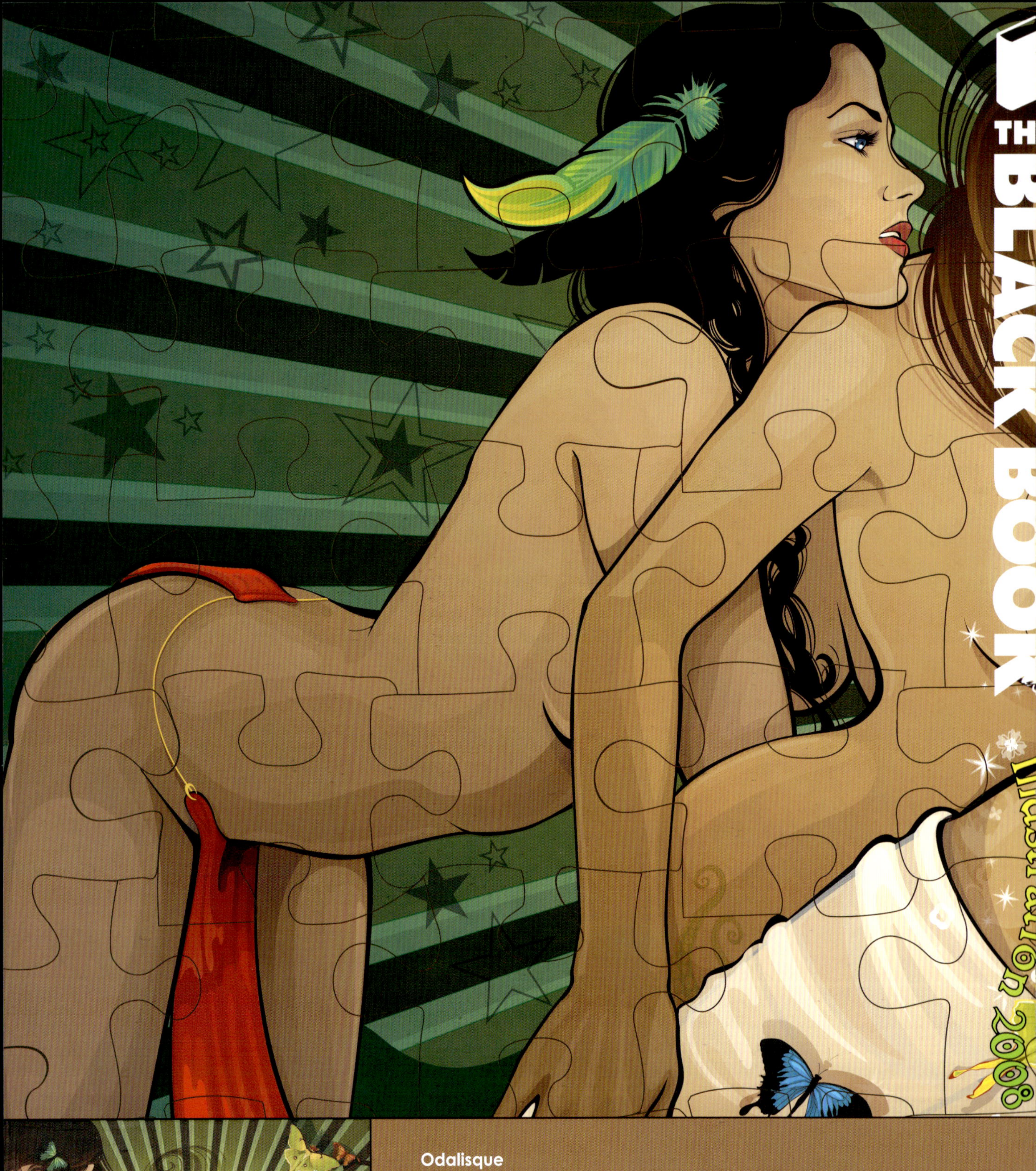

Odalisque
Client: The Black Book
Year: 2009
Models: Christine LeMaster

This project was not a commission. It was much more. The Black Book is an illustrious compilation of illustrators and photographers portfolios distributed to creative art departments looking for new talent. Creative Directors were polled to select their favorite advertising artist. The top ten were invited to submit completed illustrations for their cover. The only direction we had was that a puzzle piece would be cut out from the illustration and a scavenger hunt would be held to win one. The illustration had to seize the viewer and force them to viscerally NEED that puzzle piece in order to complete the art. It took all of three seconds to visualize exactly what I wanted to do. The puzzle piece line art was printed in spot varnish on the cover.

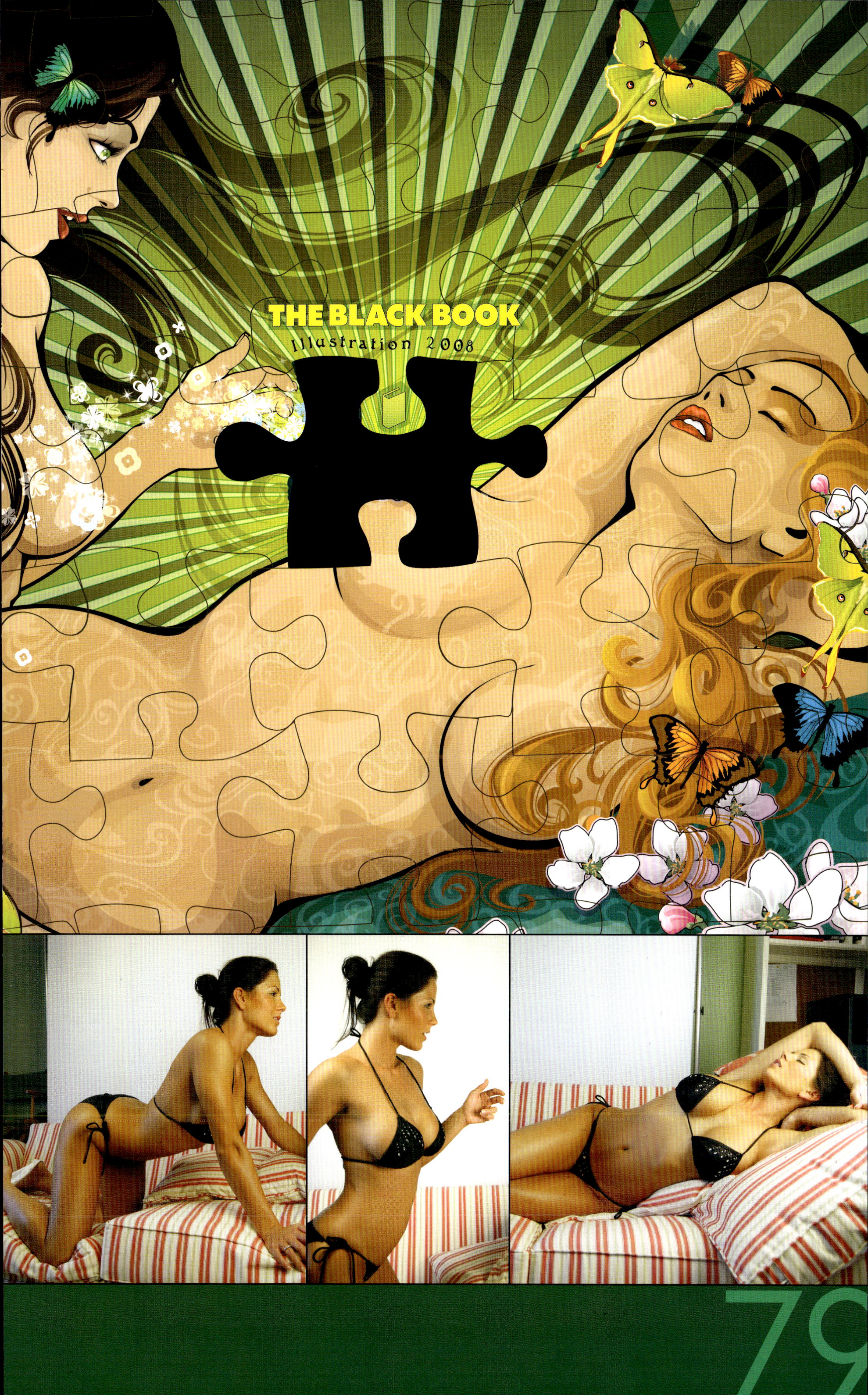
THE BLACK BOOK
Illustration 2008

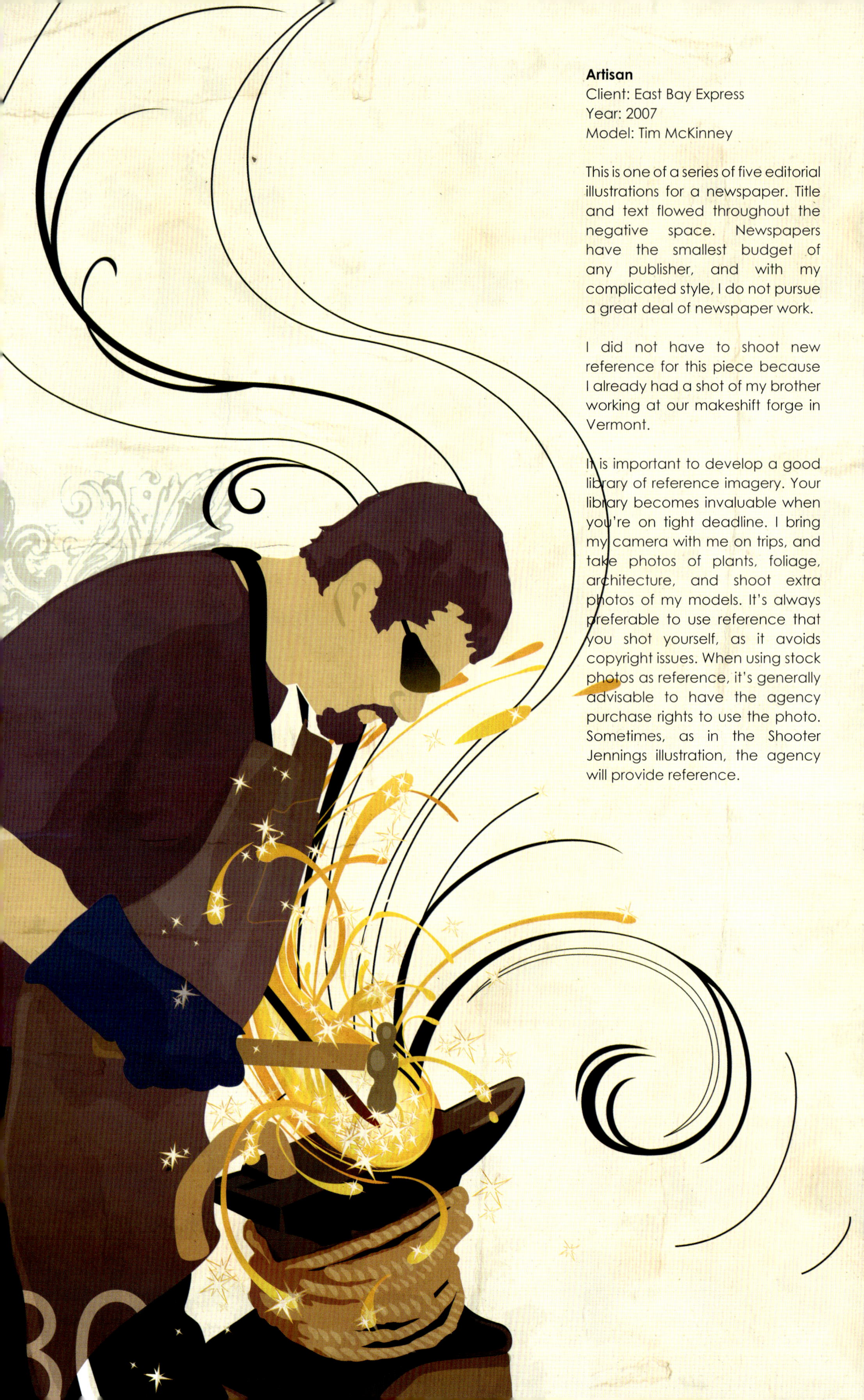

Artisan
Client: East Bay Express
Year: 2007
Model: Tim McKinney

This is one of a series of five editorial illustrations for a newspaper. Title and text flowed throughout the negative space. Newspapers have the smallest budget of any publisher, and with my complicated style, I do not pursue a great deal of newspaper work.

I did not have to shoot new reference for this piece because I already had a shot of my brother working at our makeshift forge in Vermont.

It is important to develop a good library of reference imagery. Your library becomes invaluable when you're on tight deadline. I bring my camera with me on trips, and take photos of plants, foliage, architecture, and shoot extra photos of my models. It's always preferable to use reference that you shot yourself, as it avoids copyright issues. When using stock photos as reference, it's generally advisable to have the agency purchase rights to use the photo. Sometimes, as in the Shooter Jennings illustration, the agency will provide reference.

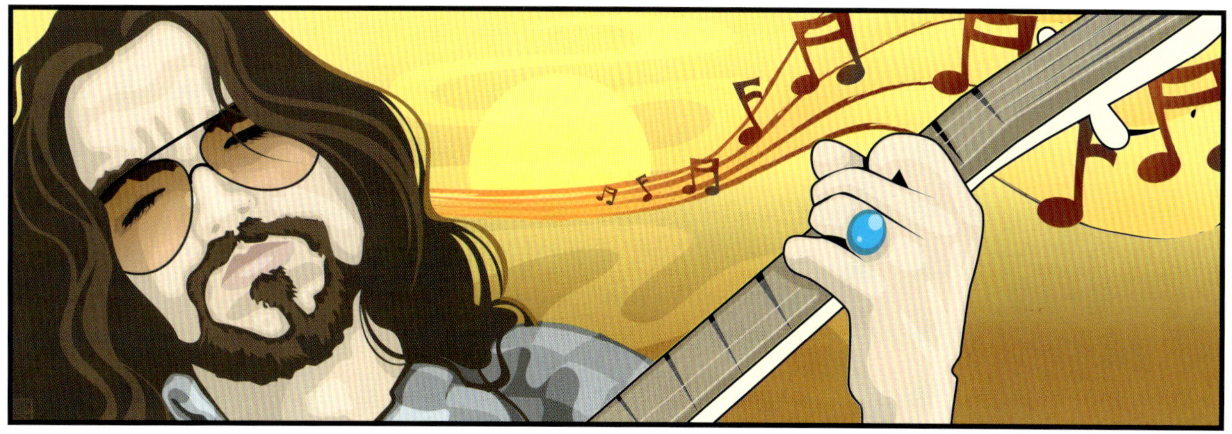

Shooter Jennings, IUD and Gay Porn
Client: Playgirl Magazine
Year: 2006

One of my crowning achievements in editorial advertising was getting my art director scolded for being too explicit for Playgirl Magazine. The art director thought that the series of illustrations I was doing for almost ten articles needed to be explicit to get the point across and gave me carte blanche to do what was necessary to communicate the articles' intent. Some were mundane articles, such as a feature on Shooter Jennings (Waylon Jennings' son). Some were truly editorial pieces, like the debate on whether IUDs are the right decision for the reader. Some were specifically titillating articles and stories, like the trend of women watching male gay pornography. They were fun pieces that I just could not bear to turn down.

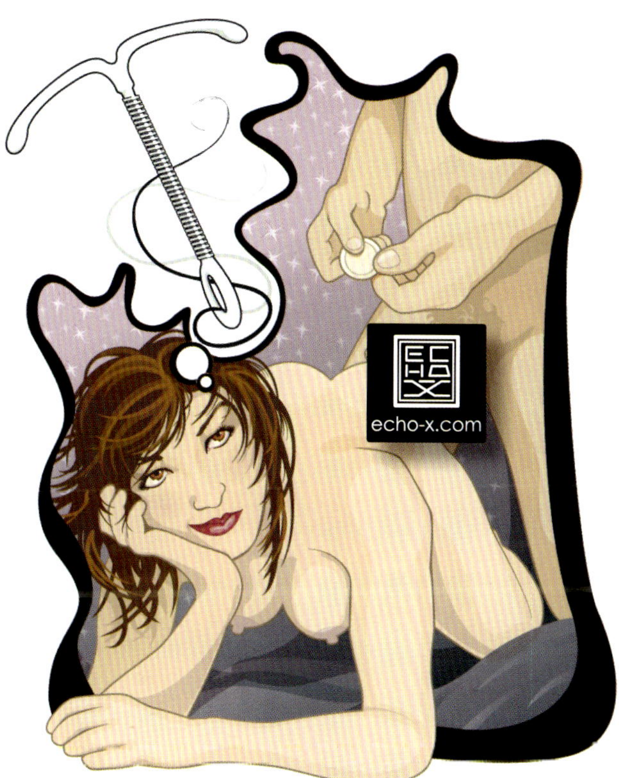

Hmmm....if I only had an IUD right now.

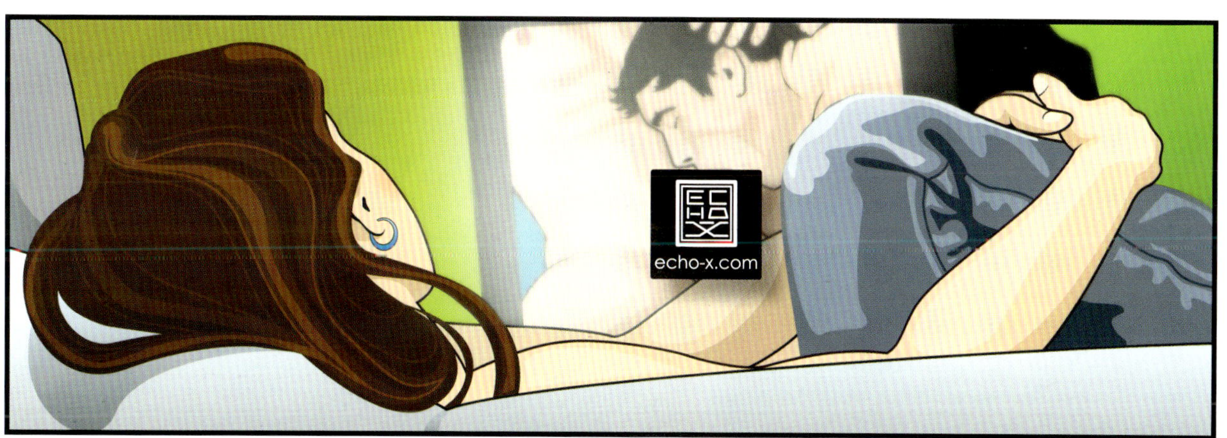

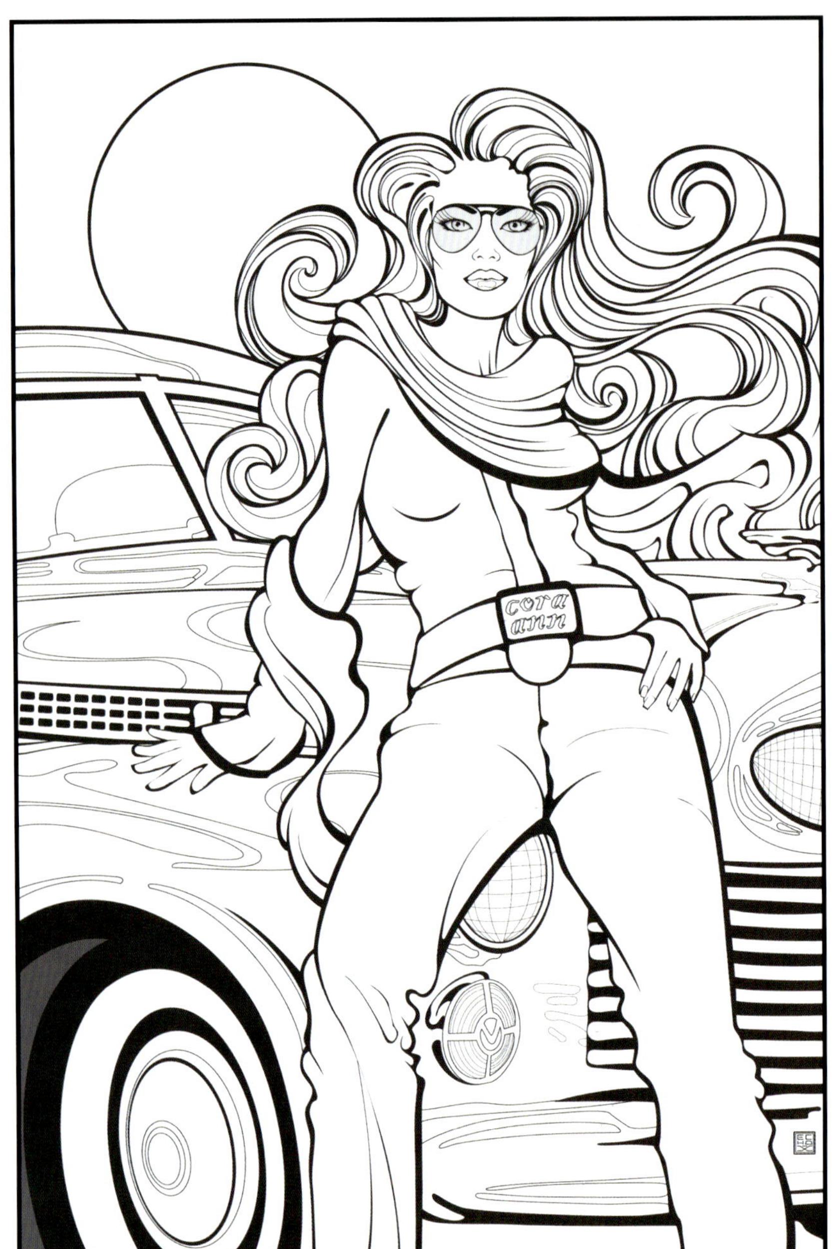

FACING PAGE
Burqa
Client: KONG
Year: 2010
Model: Meghan Perkins

LEFT
Mercury Girl
Client: Ravens
Year: 2009
Model: Echo Chernik

BOTTOM LEFT
Divorce
Client: Square Mile Magazine
Year: 2010

BOTTOM RIGHT
Banker
Client: Square Mile Magazine
Year: 2010

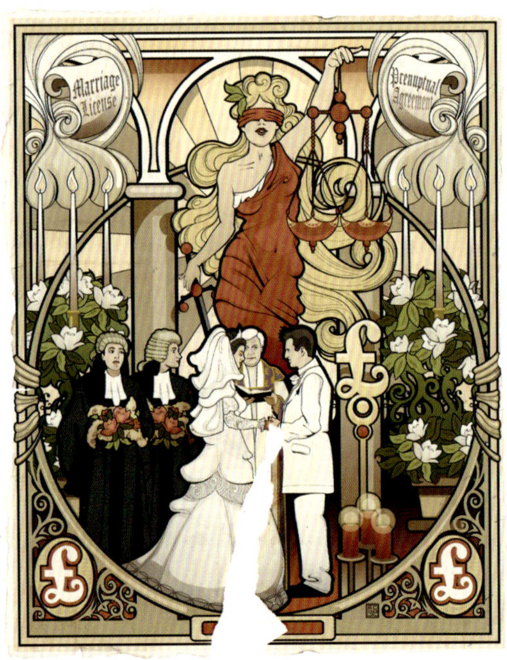

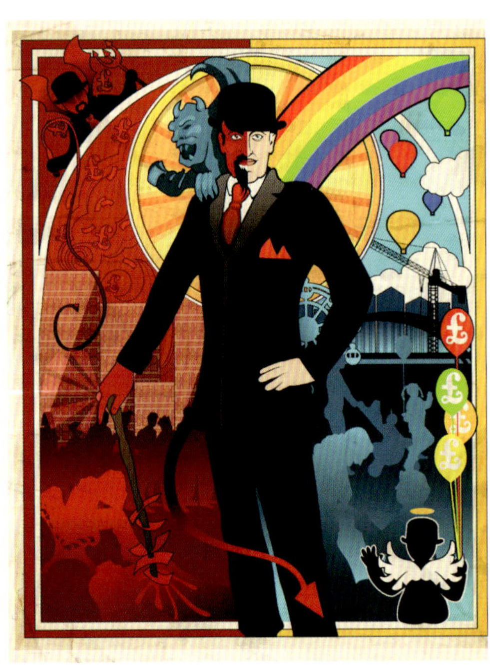

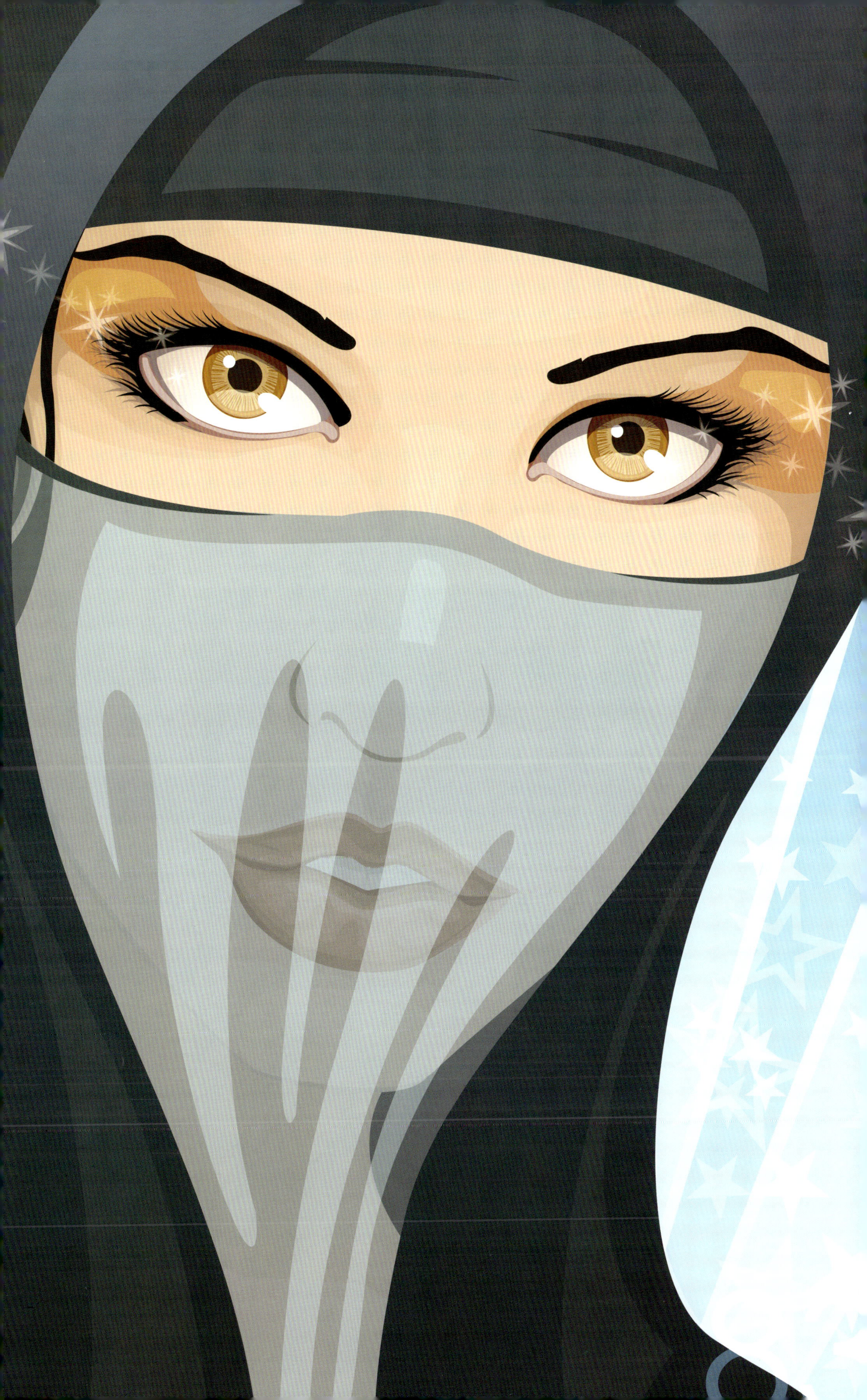

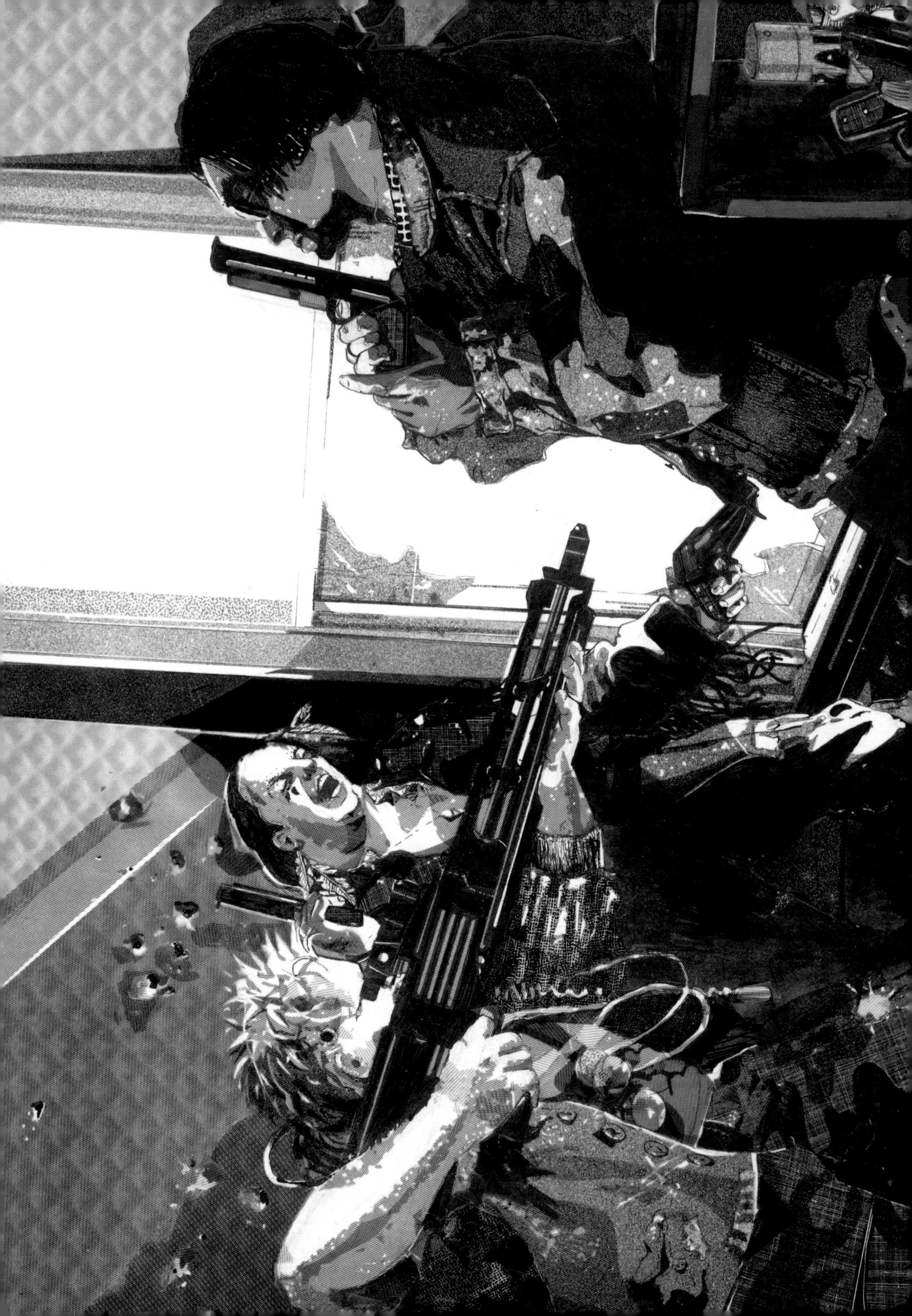

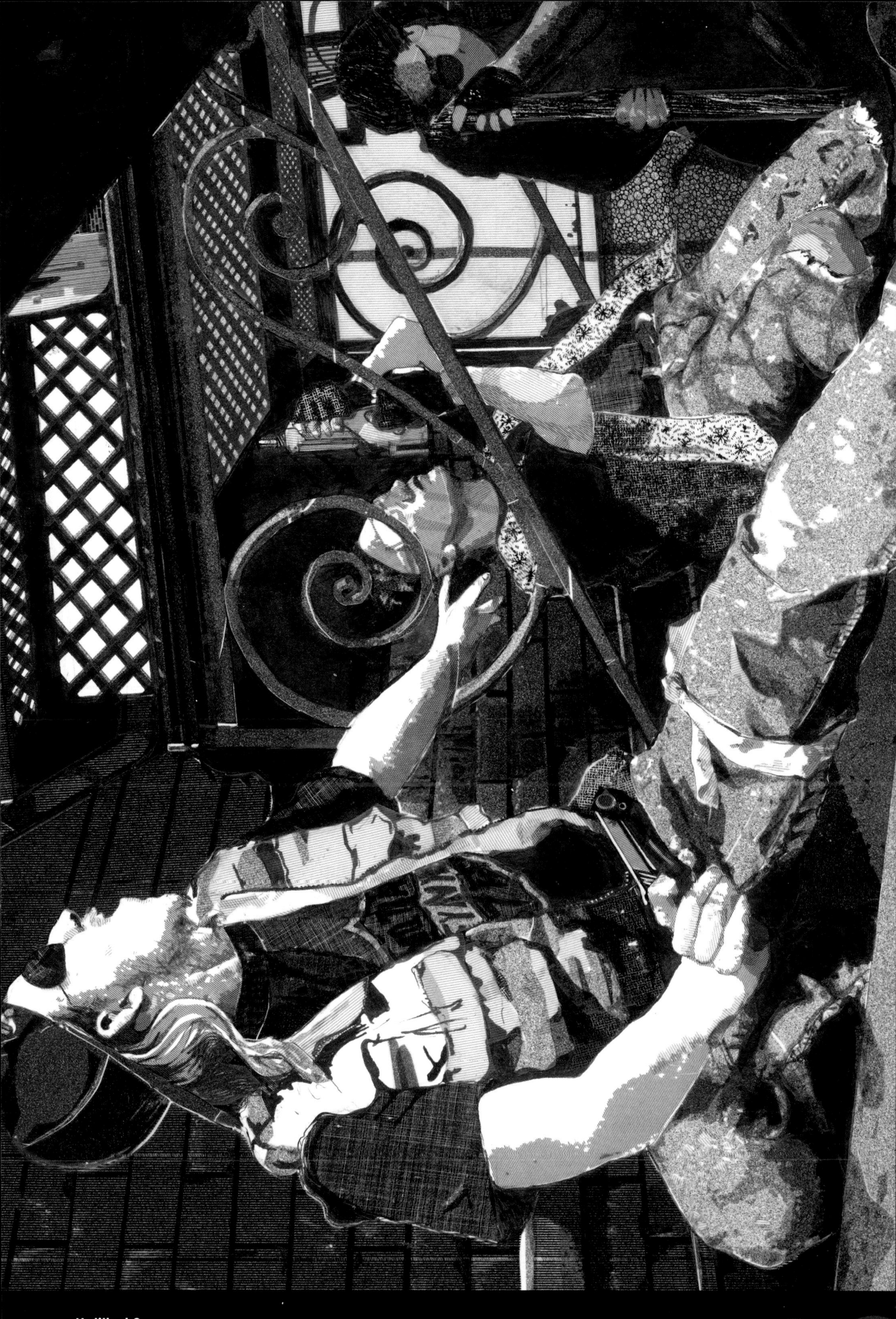

Untitled 2
Year: 1995
Models: Lazarus Chernik, Christian Fuller and others

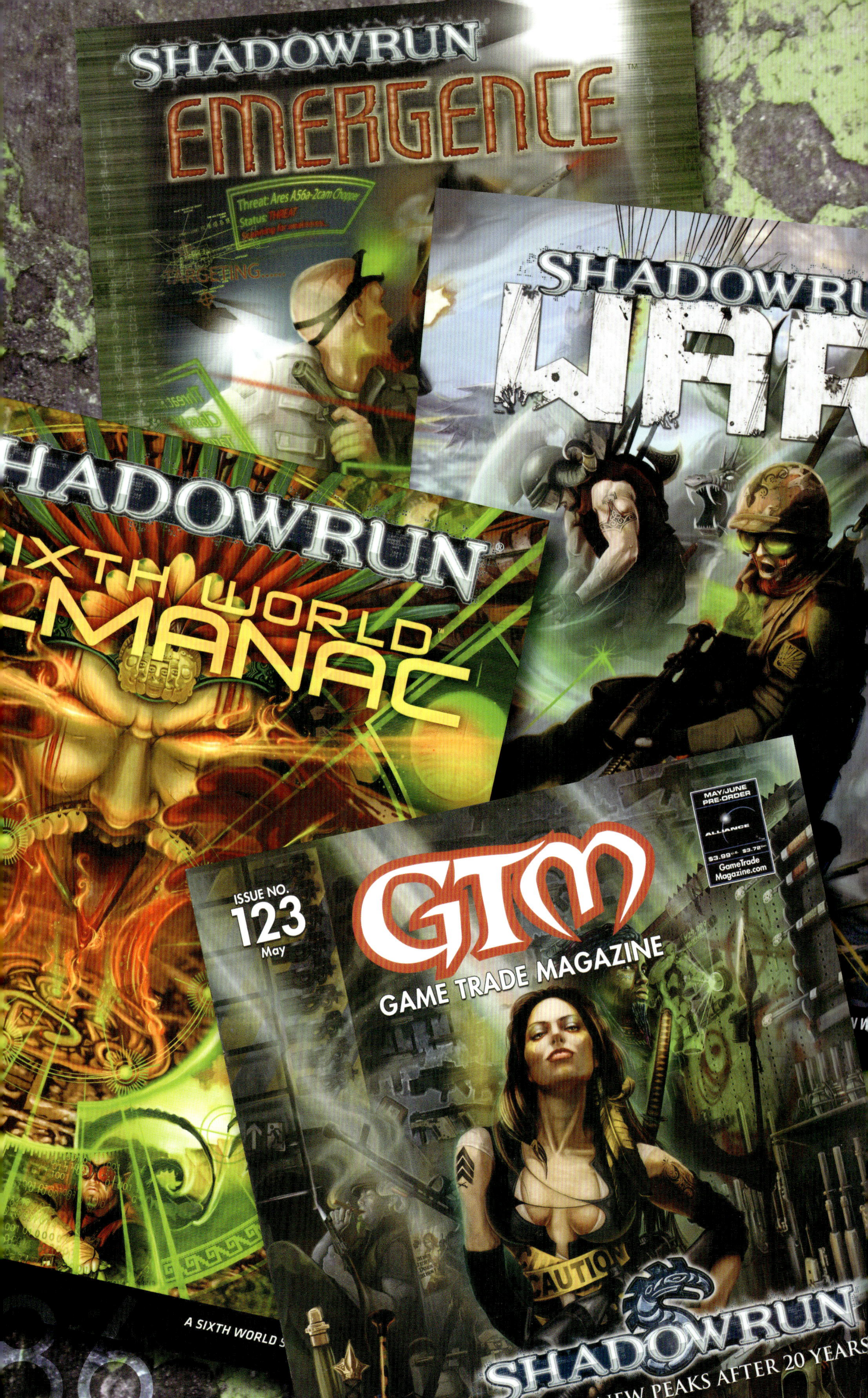
SHADOWRUN
EMERGENCE
Threat: Ares A56a-2cam Chopper
Status: THREAT
TARGETING......
WORLD
ISSUE NO.
123
May
GTM
GAME TRADE MAGAZINE
MAY/JUNE
PRE-ORDER
ALLIANCE
GameTrade
Magazine.com
CAUTION
SHADOWRUN
NEW PEAKS AFTER 20 YEARS

Origins

and GenCon and DragonCon and...

It is very difficult to land a big name gig out the door. You have to find someone to believe in you and start there. In my case, my launching pad was the role-playing game industry. We used to play the game Shadowrun™ two, three or sometimes four nights a week during my college years, so I was exposed to the frequent use of illustration in that industry. During my Junior year at Pratt, I needed to decide what I was going to do when I graduated. I knew that I wanted to illustrate right out of school and I needed published work right away, so I decided to start in the RPG industry.

You can have the most gorgeous personal pieces in the world, but to an art buyer a portfolio of unpublished work means "untried". Being published shows an art buyer that you are able to make deadlines and follow an art director's guidance. Being reliable is just as, or even more, important than being a talented artist in this industry. In advertising illustration, our deadlines are often days away, if that. Clients will spend months prepping and coordinating a project, and assign the illustrator a miniscule amount of time to make it work. Therefore, a good portfolio of published work shows the art buyer that you can deliver under pressure.

In order to woo an art buyer, you need a portfolio that shows the subject matter that they are interested in. I dedicated my senior year of college to studying all forms of black and white work. Woodblock, Pen & Ink, Wash, Screenprinting, and finally settling on the now archaic product: Zip-a-Tone (yes, you veterans just had a flashback). A dozen targeted pieces later and some footwork, I was granted eight pieces in White Wolf's *Wraith Players' Guide*. I was published before graduation.

The first five or six years (and hundreds of black and white illustrations) really taught me how to manage my business, keep deadlines, schedule my workload, experiment with my style and distinguish brands of ramen by sound alone. It was during these projects (specifically in *Mage: The Ascension*) that I started gravitating towards decorative art. Phil Brucato, the *Mage* line developer, was a big fan of my work and very encouraging towards an art nouveau direction. I did my first color art nouveau inspired pieces for his game *Deleria*, and from the publicity of those I was hired by Trek Bicycles for their "Le Tour de France" poster (see page 26).

If you're looking to break into illustration, you need a jumping point. In my case, I picked an industry where the pay is low, but creativity is high. The next few pages showcase a fraction of the hundreds of illustrations that I created for the industry before moving on to advertising work.

CLOCKWISE FROM TOP
Emergence, WAR!, Arsenal-Attitude, Almanac
Client: Catalyst Game Labs
Year: 2009-10 © InMediaRes Productions
Models: Meghan Perkins, Yaya Han, Tara Ryze, Alain Viesca, Sean Ambrioso, William "Just Some Guy" Zylstra, Ryan "The Machinist" Bobnik, Jesse "Bubbles" Cooper, Meghan Perkins, Lazarus Chernik, others and a dragon.

Shadowrun has been my personal hobby and passion since I met Lazarus. We play several times a week and it was Shadowrun that inspired me to do gaming art. When Catalyst finally asked me to do some covers (and others) for them, I aggressively put WAY more work into them than I could afford to. But some pieces are all about the blood and karma that you dump into them as an expression of the inner passion that drives you. They are not art nouveau, they're not advertising, they don't feed my body, but they nourish my soul.

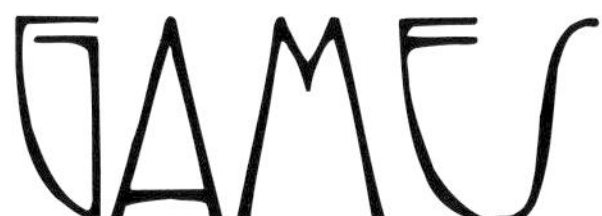

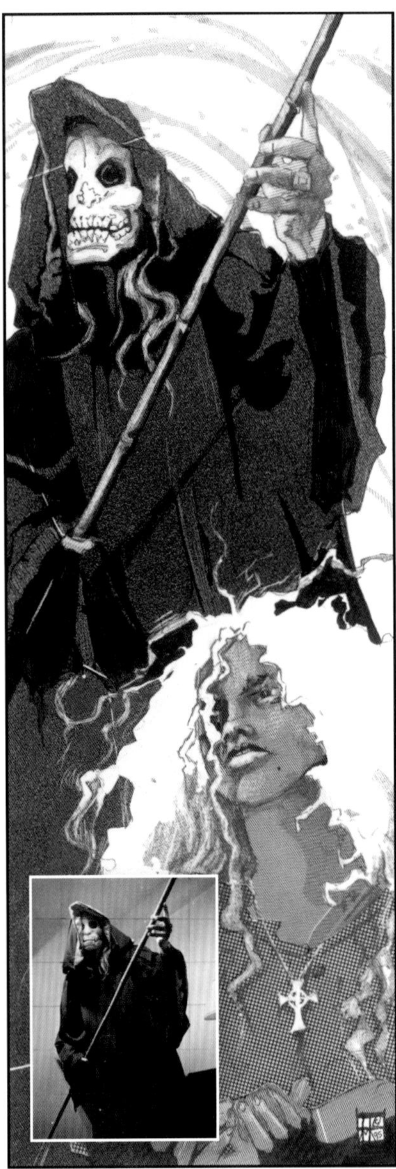
Laz is under the mask. I made the costume myself and we used it in live action role-playing for years.

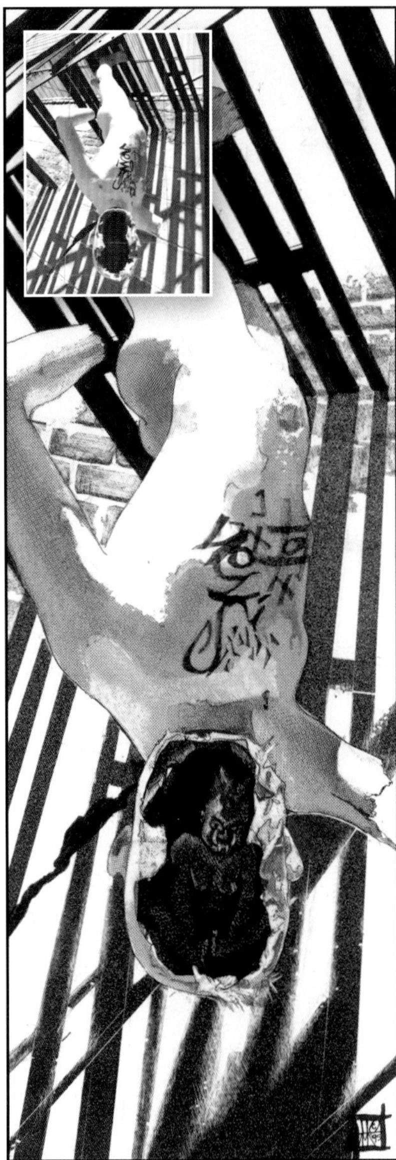
This was actually a mannequin my neighbors had hung under their stairs. I just added was the demon.

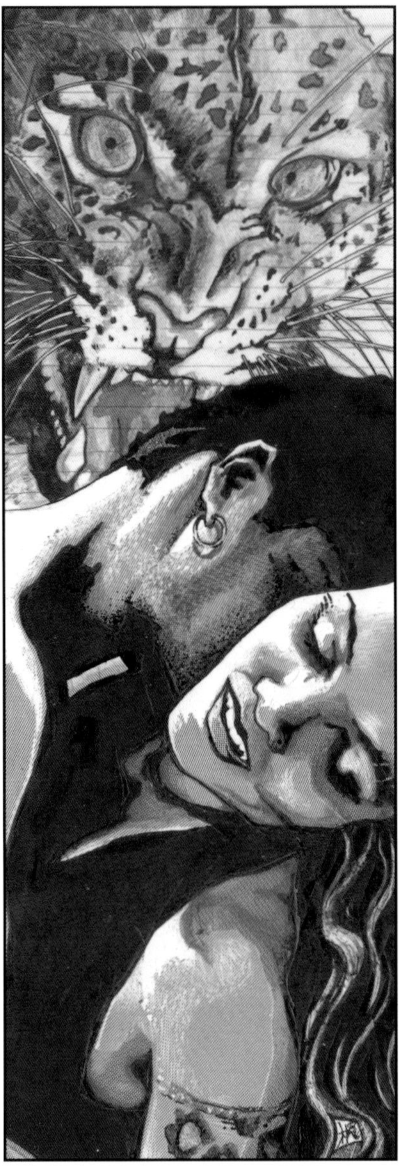
The textural quality of the medium is what kept me. It was like painting but with more control.

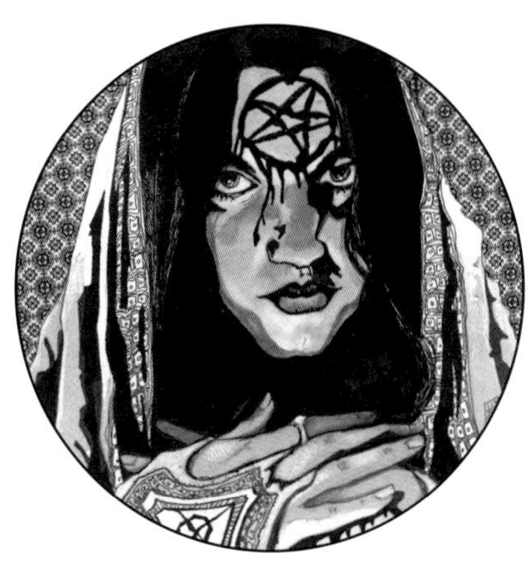

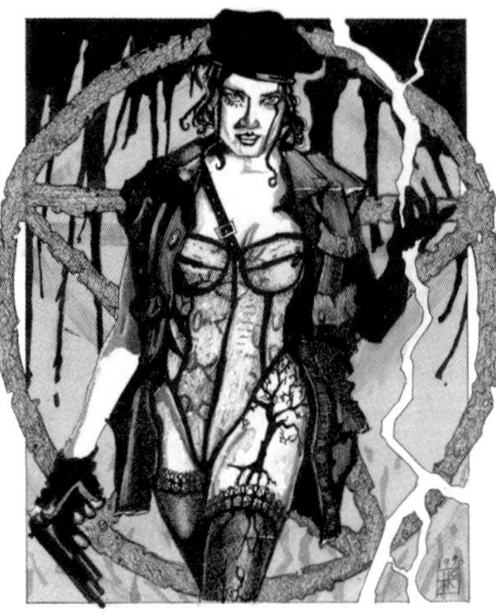

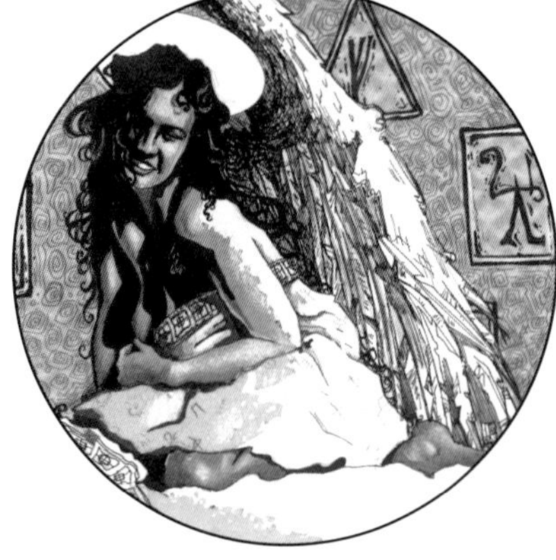

CLOCKWISE
Charon, Thing Under the Stairs, Jaguar Passion, Angel, Assassin, Pentacle
Client: White Wolf
Year: ©1995-1996 WWGS

My first assignments as a regularly working illustrator were for White Wolf's *Wraith: The Oblivion* - which was a new title at the time. Charon was my first piece ever. I was using a product called Zip-a-Tone (Letraset made a competing product called Letratone) which required me to cut-and-paste sheets of pre-printed adhesive acetate into every shape on the board, and manipulate it with an Exacto blade. I loved it. The budget was paltry, but I was working as an illustrator right out of college. No one else I knew could say that. This part of my life brings back fond memories, full of Ramen and Zip-a-Tone.

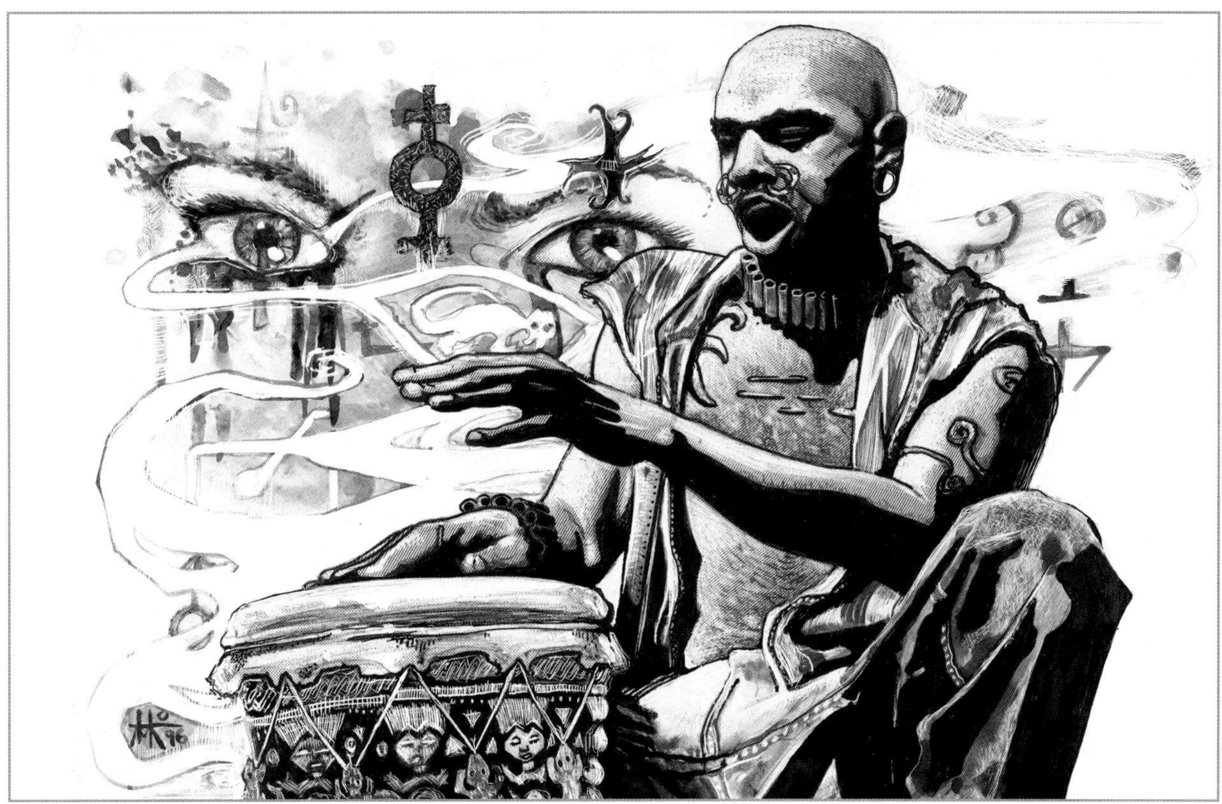

Drummer (TOP)
Aboriginal (BOTTOM)
Client: White Wolf
Projects: *Mage: The Ascension*
Year: ©1997 WWGS

When I mastered the medium, I blended it with others always pushing myself to the next level. Of course, I had an endless supply of models, because I actually played the games I was working on. My friends were always up for anything I could dream up. Sean played with us every week and I used his passionate personality to inspire me. Vicky was beautifully proud, and I made every effort to showcase her as best I could.

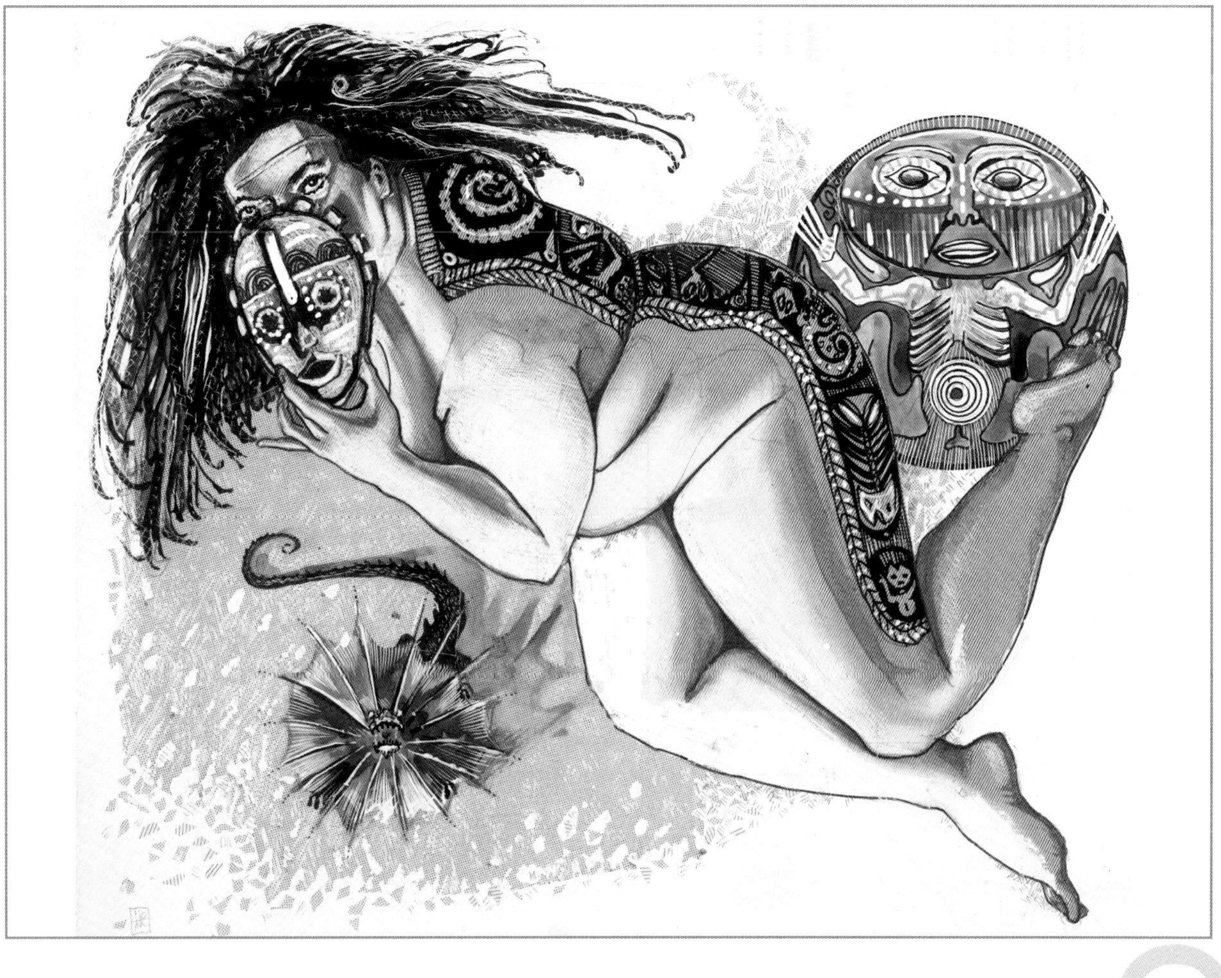

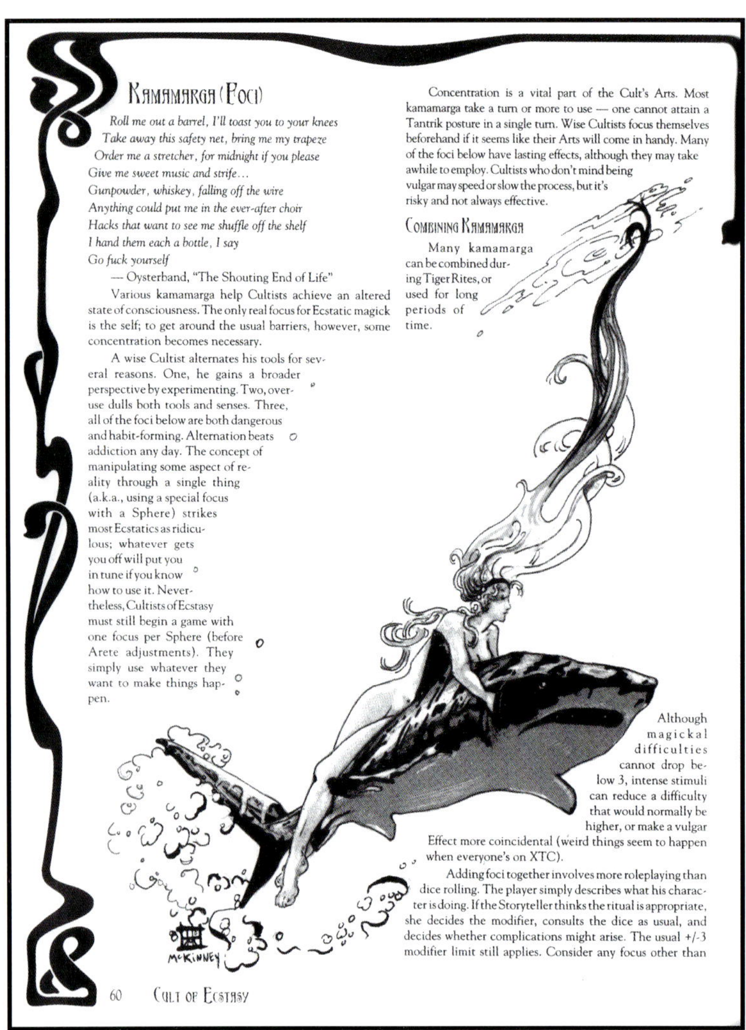

Kamamarga (Foci)

Roll me out a barrel, I'll toast you to your knees
Take away this safety net, bring me my trapeze
Order me a stretcher, for midnight if you please
Give me sweet music and strife…
Gunpowder, whiskey, falling off the wire
Anything could put me in the ever-after choir
Hacks that want to see me shuffle off the shelf
I hand them each a bottle, I say
Go fuck yourself

— Oysterband, "The Shouting End of Life"

Various kamamarga help Cultists achieve an altered state of consciousness. The only real focus for Ecstatic magick is the self; to get around the usual barriers, however, some concentration becomes necessary.

A wise Cultist alternates his tools for several reasons. One, he gains a broader perspective by experimenting. Two, overuse dulls both tools and senses. Three, all of the foci below are both dangerous and habit-forming. Alternation beats addiction any day. The concept of manipulating some aspect of reality through a single thing (a.k.a., using a special focus with a Sphere) strikes most Ecstatics as ridiculous; whatever gets you off will put you in tune if you know how to use it. Nevertheless, Cultists of Ecstasy must still begin a game with one focus per Sphere (before Arete adjustments). They simply use whatever they want to make things happen.

Concentration is a vital part of the Cult's Arts. Most kamamarga take a turn or more to use — one cannot attain a Tantrik posture in a single turn. Wise Cultists focus themselves beforehand if it seems like their Arts will come in handy. Many of the foci below have lasting effects, although they may take awhile to employ. Cultists who don't mind being vulgar may speed or slow the process, but it's risky and not always effective.

Combining Kamamarga

Many kamamarga can be combined during Tiger Rites, or used for long periods of time.

Although magickal difficulties cannot drop below 3, intense stimuli can reduce a difficulty that would normally be higher, or make a vulgar Effect more coincidental (weird things seem to happen when everyone's on XTC).

Adding foci together involves more roleplaying than dice rolling. The player simply describes what his character is doing. If the Storyteller thinks the ritual is appropriate, she decides the modifier, consults the dice as usual, and decides whether complications might arise. The usual +/-3 modifier limit still applies. Consider any focus other than

60 Cult of Ecstasy

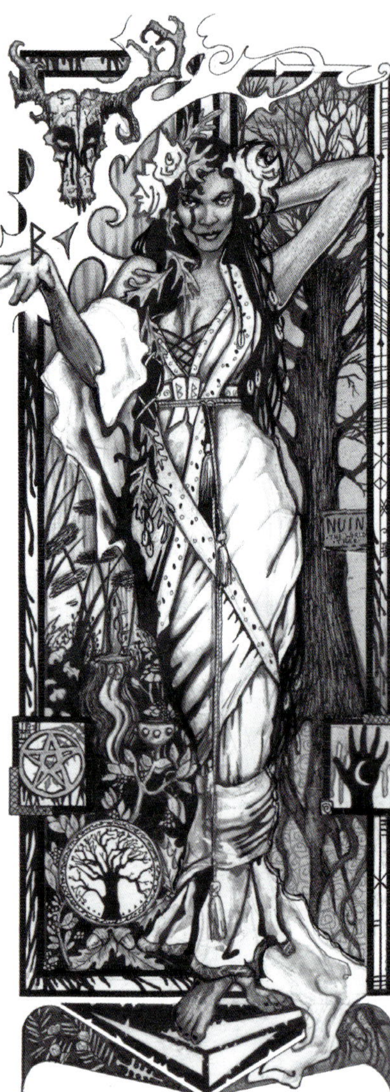

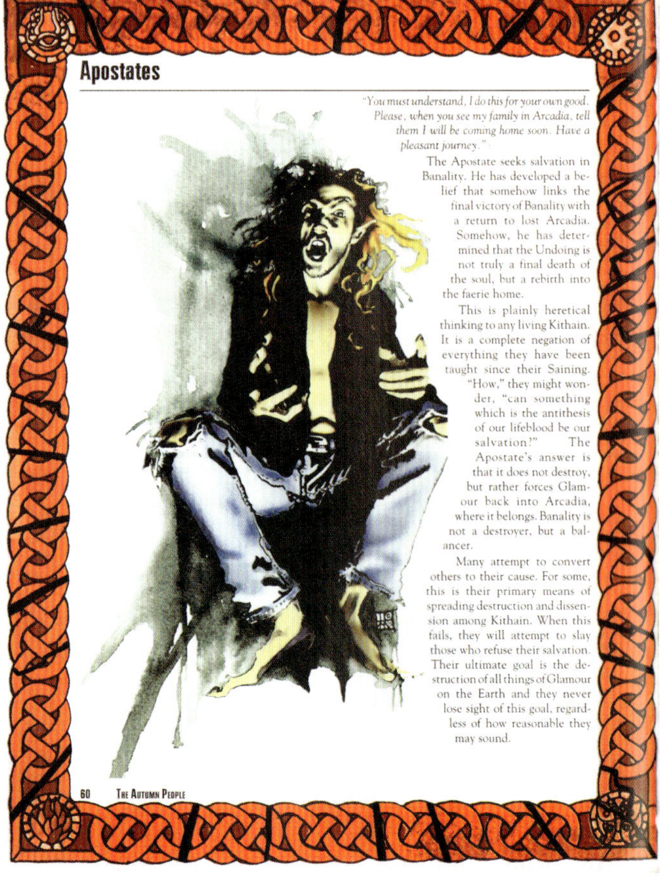

Apostates

"You must understand, I do this for your own good. Please, when you see my family in Arcadia, tell them I will be coming home soon. Have a pleasant journey."

The Apostate seeks salvation in Banality. He has developed a belief that somehow links the final victory of Banality with a return to lost Arcadia. Somehow, he has determined that the Undoing is not truly a final death of the soul, but a rebirth into the faerie home.

This is plainly heretical thinking to any living Kithain. It is a complete negation of everything they have been taught since their Saining. "How," they might wonder, "can something which is the antithesis of our lifeblood be our salvation?" The Apostate's answer is that it does not destroy, but rather forces Glamour back into Arcadia, where it belongs. Banality is not a destroyer, but a balancer.

Many attempt to convert others to their cause. For some, this is their primary means of spreading destruction and dissension among Kithain. When this fails, they will attempt to slay those who refuse their salvation. Their ultimate goal is the destruction of all things of Glamour on the Earth and they never lose sight of this goal, regardless of how reasonable they may sound.

60 The Autumn People

CLOCKWISE
Shark,
Verbena,
Apostate
Client: White Wolf
Models: Echo Chernik, Shanti Fader, Lazarus Chernik,
Year: ©1996-1997 WWGS

The dream project for many game artists in the 90's was White Wolf's *Vampire: The Masquerade*. While I never worked on that line, I quickly became a featured artist for *Mage: The Ascension* as it began its first edition (also White Wolf). In the process, I befriended the original line developer, Phil Brucato, and he would specifically request me for his projects. Phil is a fan of art and fell in love with all the personal touches I put into every work. He was the first client to compliment the symbolism I put into my pieces, and for "Mage", symbols were everything. Over time, I grew faster, and used that time to experiment with style. Phil helped me tremendously by being a fanatical supporter. There was no one else doing what I was at the time, and it was great. I also liked to push the nudity envelope, and was surprised at how few got cut.

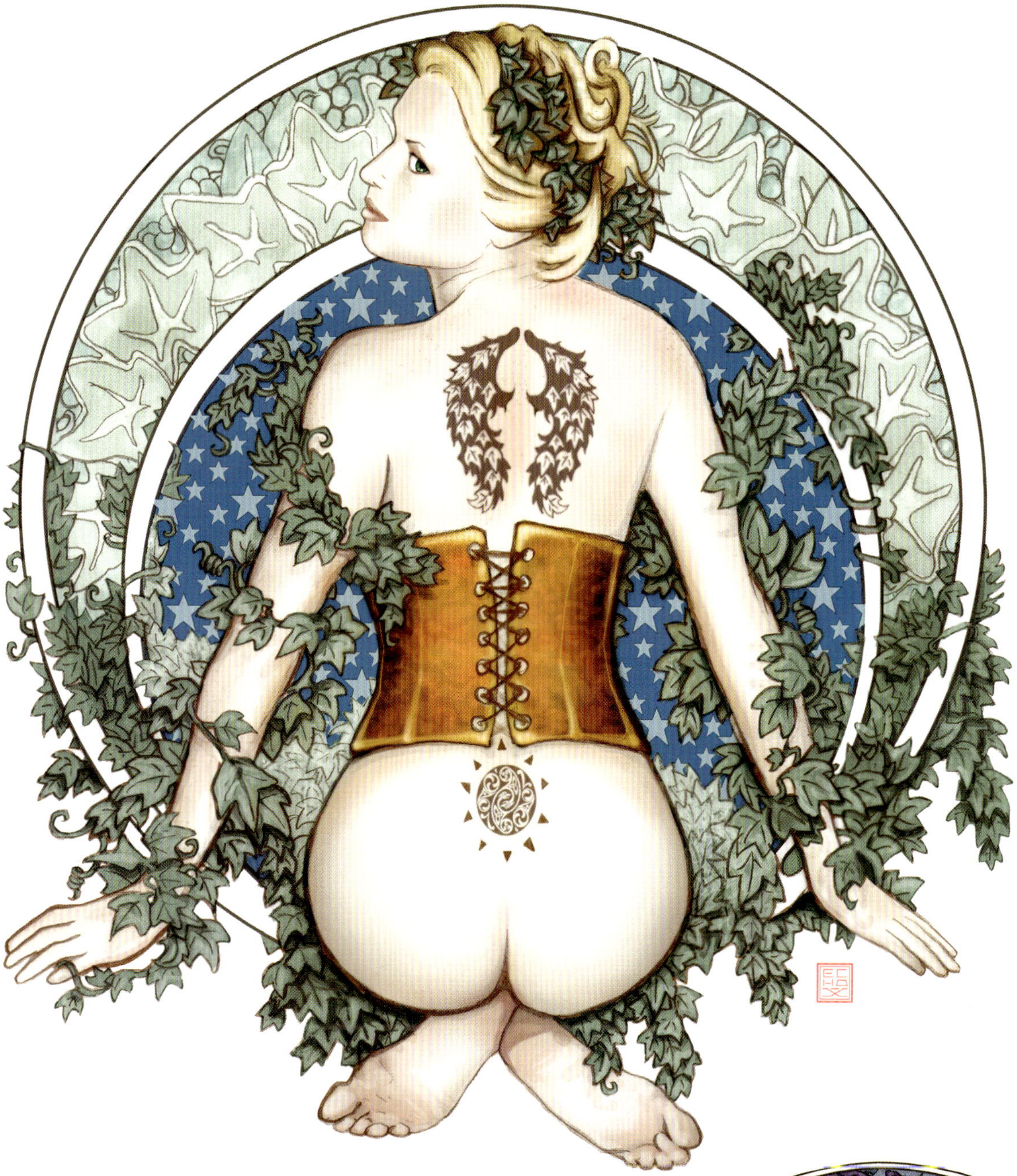

Ivy Florae (ABOVE)
Aelder Blood (RIGHT)
Client: Deleria
Year: 1999
Models: Darla Squeo

It took me years to earn the right to do great color work for a game company - and it was Phil Brucato again who believed in me. This time for his own game: *Deleria*. I had been given assignments by White Wolf for color, but for the price they paid, I could never spend enough time to get the feeling right. That, and being over-shadowed by great artists with quicker styles than mine, convinced me that a career in game art was the wrong path. Consequently, I turned to web design and teaching at the height of the Internet boom. It was a great time for me and I was able to think freely about what I wanted out of my illustration career. Then Phil called me and let me do anything I wanted. Having another job (two actually) allowed me to have fun and explore everything I enjoyed. From that, I finally integrated my vision for what would become MY interpretation of art nouveau. It seems like a lifetime ago now, looking back.

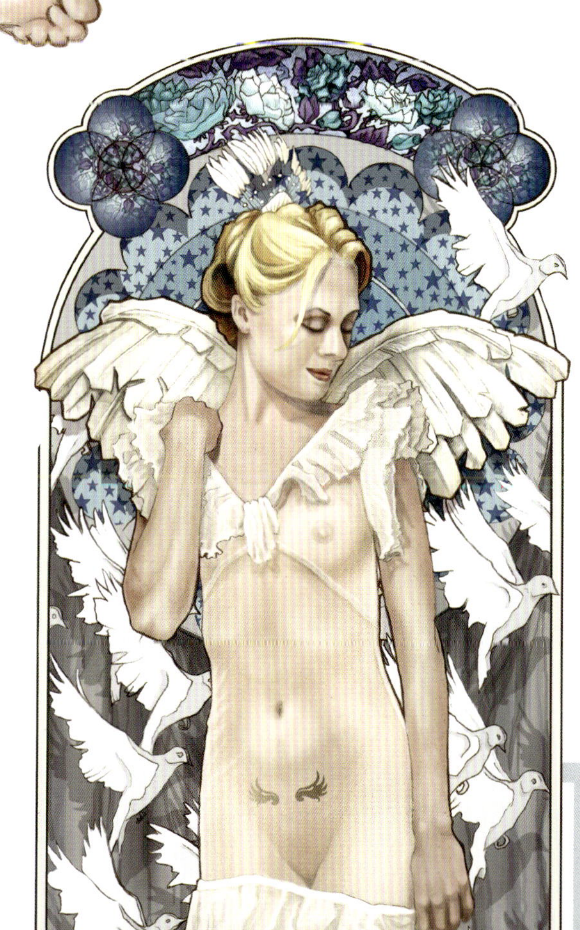

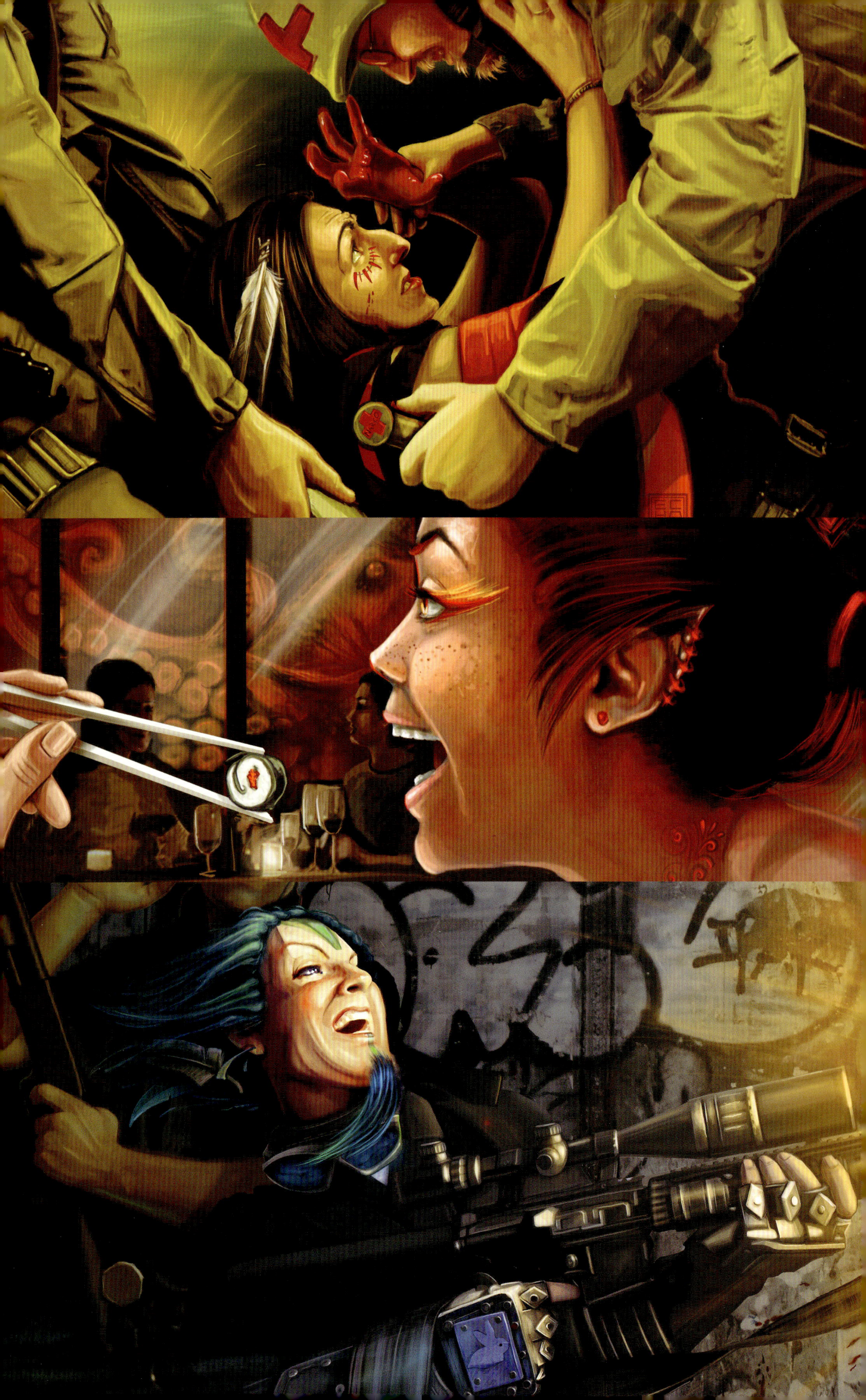

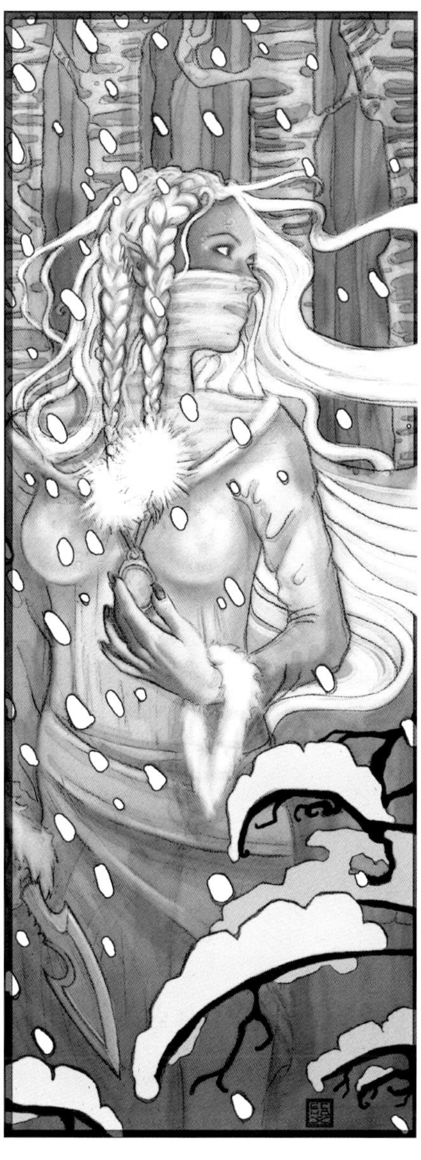

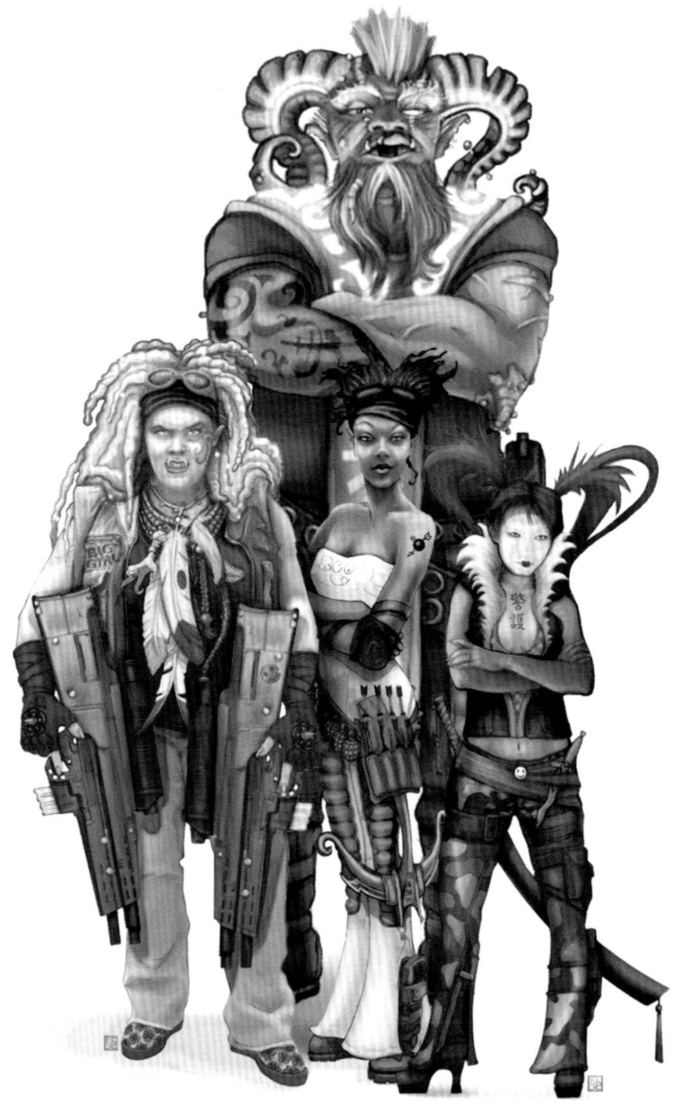

Snow and Wind
Client: ©2009 Fantasy Flight Games
Model: Darla Squeo

Four of the Five Major Shadowrun Races
Client: ©2009 Catalyst Game Labs (InMediaRes Productions)
Models: Denise Ritenour and others

Game art budgets are notoriously paltry, but it's fun. Ten years after Deleria, I sent a few feelers out for Shadowrun again. We never stopped playing the game, and after a decade of non-stop work I had a little breathing room to do something fun again. Surprisingly, the one game I had always played and had never contributed to suddenly became interested... and they needed covers. At first, I drew the spot illustrations to represent the main races in the game. No ornamentation - purely rendered. I successfully resisted the urge to draw characters we had played, but I did still use them for inspiration. For instance, the most tangible element of the game was established by Jeff Laubenstein, the games original art director and a fantastic illustrator in his own right. Because the future universe had so much potential for homogenization - the public became obsessed with affectations and personal adornments. After Jeff left the game, illustrators failed to realize this primary feature of the universe in their contributions. I made absolutely sure that every character I created looked and felt true to the game. Every freckle, tattoo, piercing, jewelry, clothing, weapon, armor and coif became a point of focus for my obsession with detail. Look for the smiley face, the cockatrice claw, the word "Boo" turned into a smiley, the scars, the Atari 2600 joystick, the bunny rabbit logo, the fiber optic hair, the octopus... it is all there for you. Besides, Just because I am well known for my art nouveau - that style alone is not what I'm all about as an illustrator. To me, it's all in the details. Shadowrun work for me, is a personal passion, and if you do not love what you do - why do it?

Docwagon (above-facing)
Gravity Bar (middle-facing)
Suppressive Fire (bottom-facing)
Client: ©2009 Catalyst Game Labs (InMediaRes Productions)
Models: Ryan Bobnik, Sean Ambrioso, William Zylstra, Sylena and others

Echo of the Future

What's next?

What about the next fifteen years? Am I going to give up commercial work to pursue my "own art"? At a certain point in their career, many of artists do and I get asked that question a lot. No. I intend to find a balance between my commercial work and my newly defined personal pieces.

The housing crash of 2008-10 was the first time in years that I was not up-to-my-eyeballs busy with commercial jobs. I still had more work than most illustrators, but chose to take that gap in my schedule to explore what could be done if I created pieces that were purely my own inspiration.

I have to admit, it is quite fun to create fine art works. They are fantastically received and will be featured in a book all their own, down the line. But I will not be weaning away from commercial work. I love advertising illustration. I am a commercial artist. I always have been, even before I studied Illustration at Pratt; however, I have begun being a little more choosy about the jobs that I accept, and leaving myself time to create new Echo pieces, as well as accepting the fun jobs. Unfortunately, I find most jobs fun, and difficult to turn away.

2011 is the beginning of the next decade of my commercial work. I am busy working on a series of thirteen culinary-inspired pieces for a huge gourmet market in Atlanta. This year has kept me busy with package design jobs, magazine covers and logos.

So, here is a peek at what you can expect to see in the next decade. I hope that my advice has been helpful and that you have enjoyed the art, Best of luck on whatever path you choose for yourself.

- echo
February, 2011

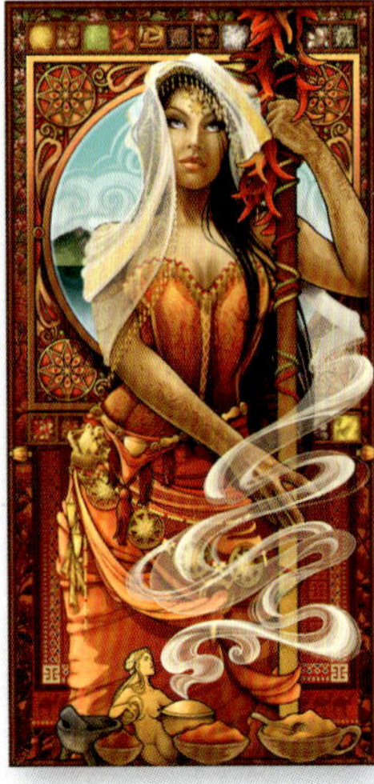

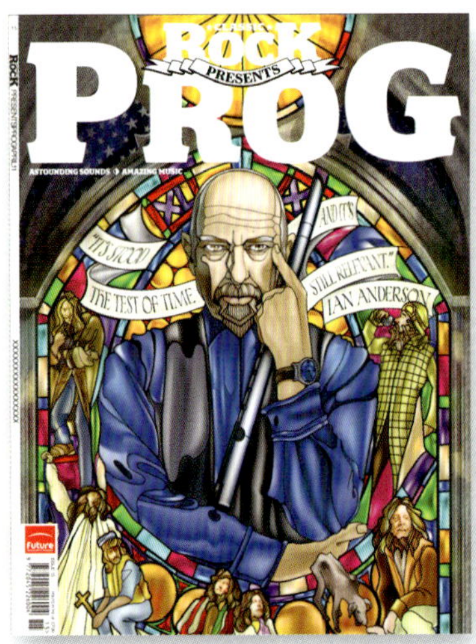

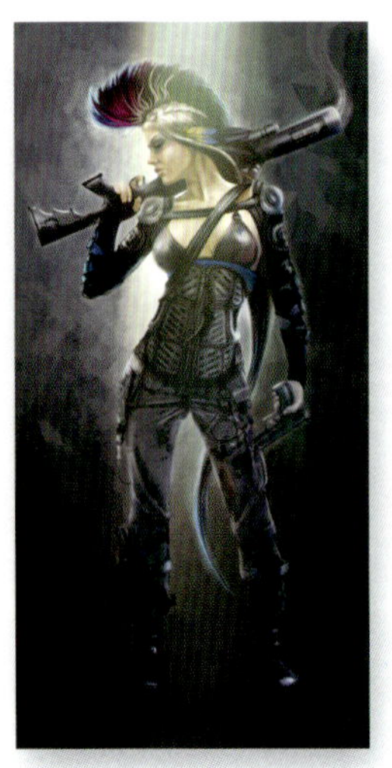

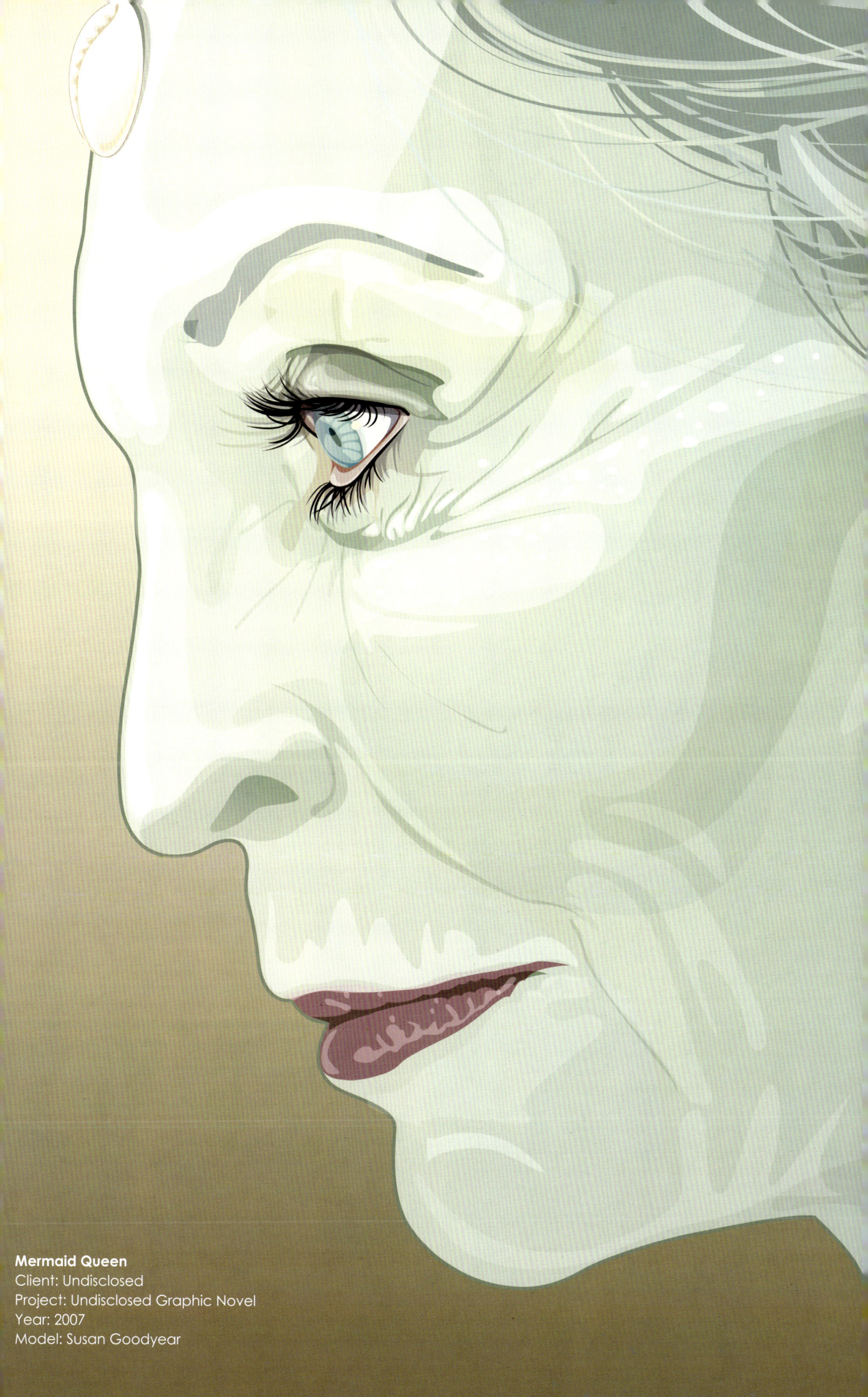

Mermaid Queen
Client: Undisclosed
Project: Undisclosed Graphic Novel
Year: 2007
Model: Susan Goodyear

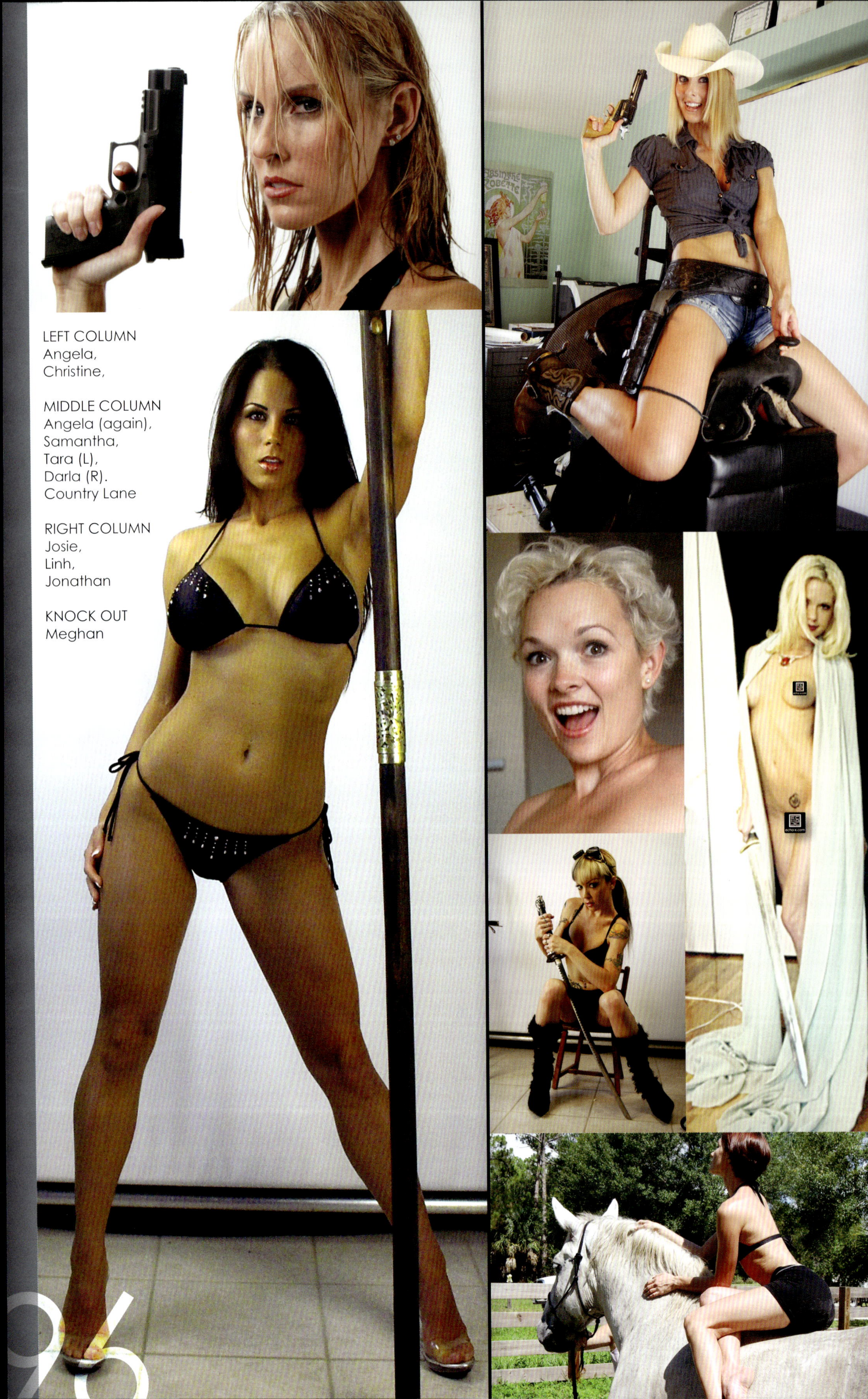

LEFT COLUMN
Angela,
Christine,

MIDDLE COLUMN
Angela (again),
Samantha,
Tara (L),
Darla (R).
Country Lane

RIGHT COLUMN
Josie,
Linh,
Jonathan

KNOCK OUT
Meghan

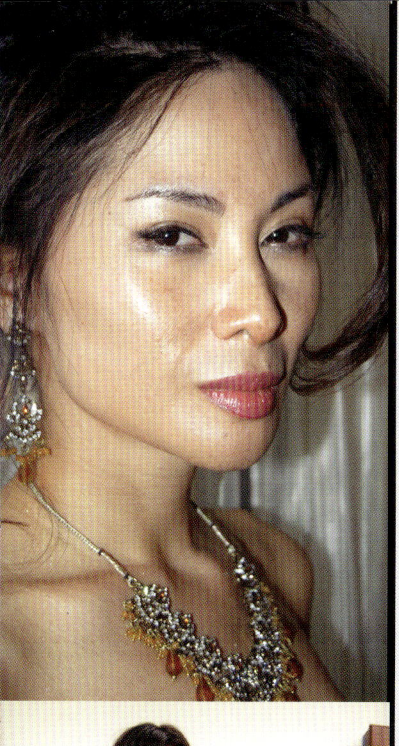

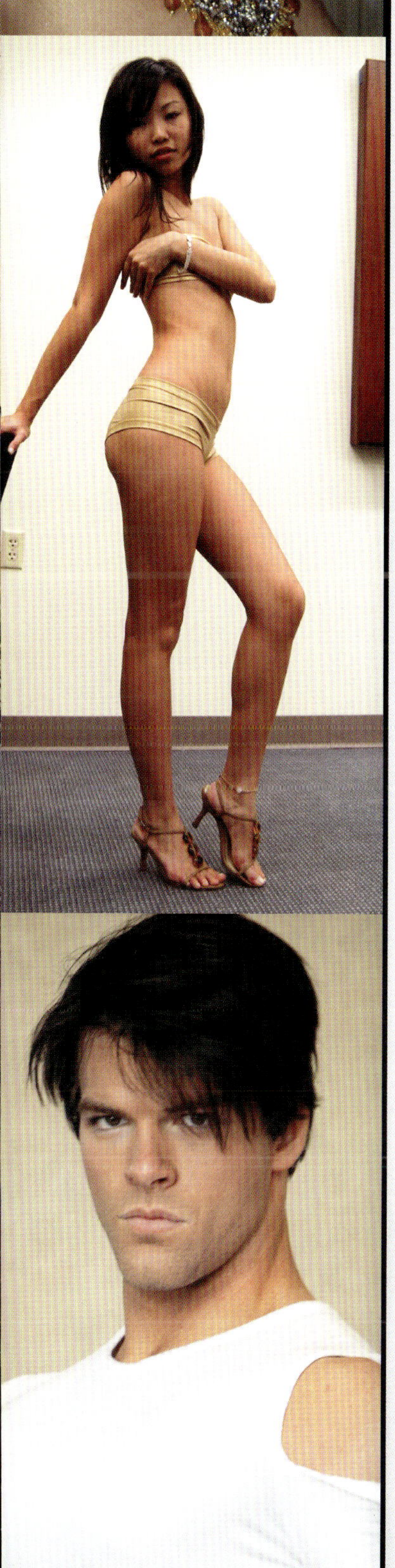

The Beautiful People

Do you work from models? Why yes, yes I do.

I generally shoot models in bikinis, with their hair pulled back. Costuming, hair and accessories are later supplied by my fertile imagination and from reference. Many artists rent props and costumes from specialty shops. I also befriend shop-keepers. Once I rented a horse. The model was patient and superb, even though it was the stinkiest horse I think I have ever smelled.

As an artist, I am drawn to features I know will illustrate well. Many attractive people do not draw well because they lack certain engaging attributes like strong cheek bones, riveting eyes or expressive lips. Professional models have hourly, half-day or day rates that are negotiated up-front - sometimes they split it with an Agent. I pay more when I have a particularly well paying job the shoot is for. Occasionally, my friends are the best fit for what I have in mind. Frequently, people will volunteer simply because they wish to be immortalized in my work. I've even approached people in public places and booked shoots on the spot.

When drawing from reference, I often use bits and pieces from several sources - and even several models. Eve, for instance, is a compilation of four different models.

I keep a large library of reference photos. After shooting what is needed for the current job first, I shoot for ideas that are in my head and generic shots to have on file. Sometimes it's years before I use that reference.

Visit http://www.echo-x.com/models

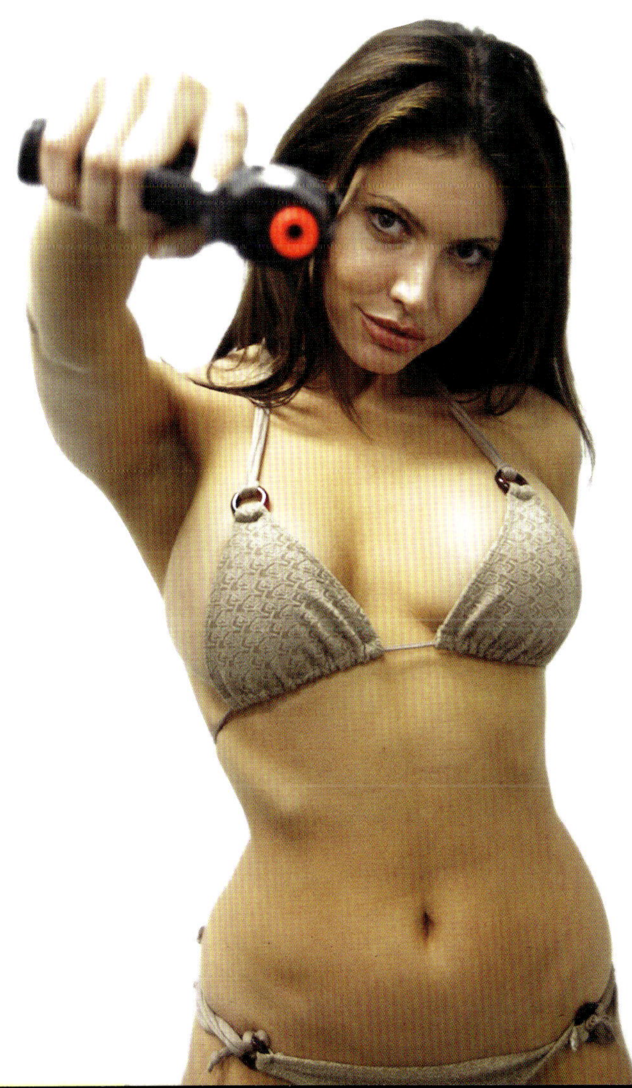

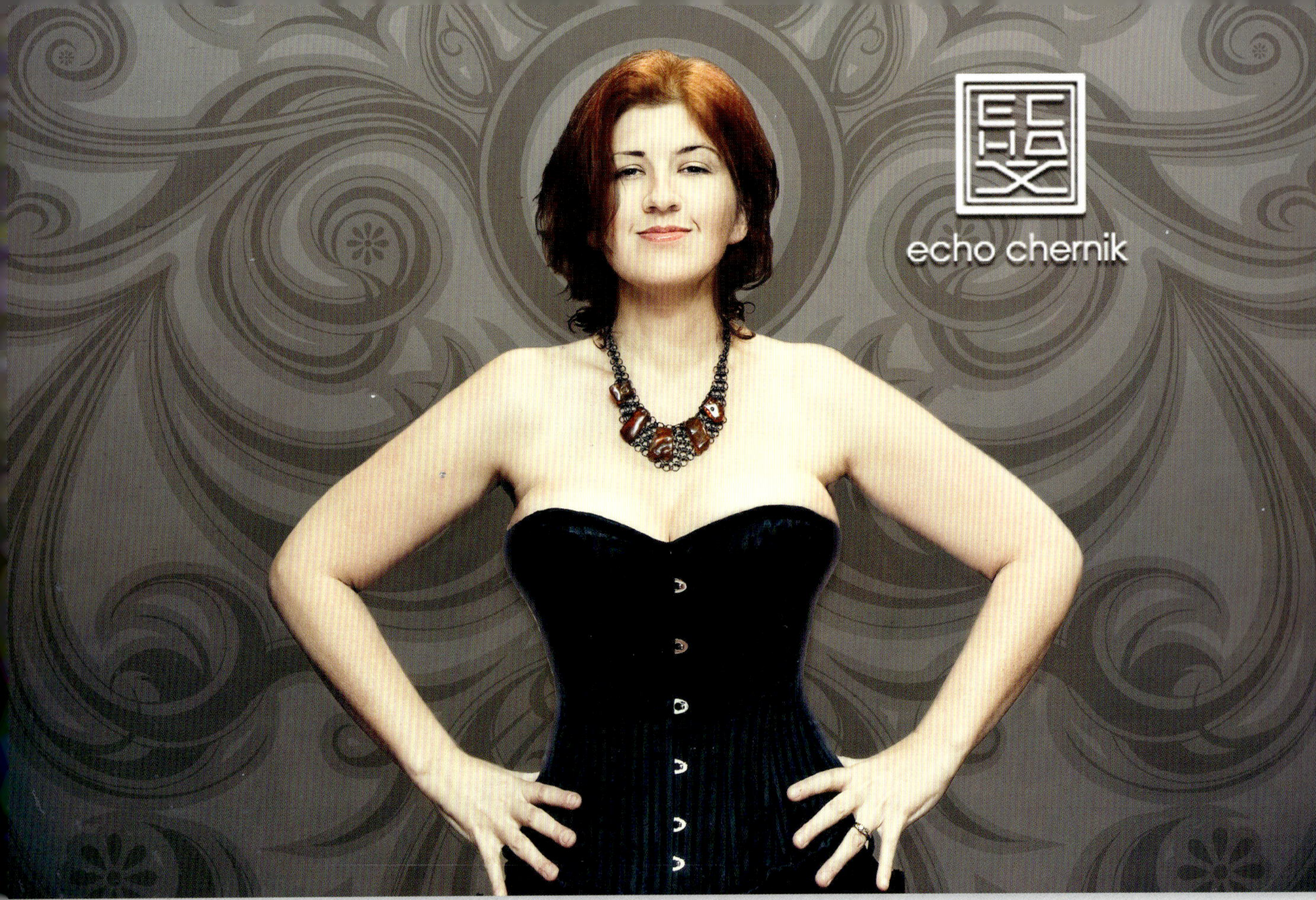

Biography

Echo Chernik grew up on a small farm in Connecticut. She loved to draw from a young age, and attended community college for Illustration while still in High School. In 1995, she graduated summa cum laude from Pratt Institute in New York City with a bachelors in Communication Design: Illustration. College sweethearts, she married Lazarus Chernik, creative director, in 1999. They work together fulltime as a creative team, and still roleplay Shadowrun every Friday night as they have for the sixteen years they've been together.

In 2009, Echo, Lazarus and their two creative daughters started the "summer tour" of comic book shows, as a family. You can learn more, and follow the exploits and adventures of the artist and her family on the tour blog at **http://www.echo-location.com**

What do you want to know?

What artists inspire you?
Besides the obvious, I am also a fan of Neoclassic art (David), Russian poster art, Japanese and primitive art. Two of my favorite works of all time is Hokusai's "Pearl Diver" and "Saturn Devouring His Son" by Goya. I'm also big into cyberpunk (William Gibson inspired) and other gritty futuristic genre art. I treasure the in-depth art history classes at Pratt, and the visits to the museums of New York City. There are some genres that I do not care for, but it's important to understand their evolution, and their roots.

Have you ever tried other media for your artwork?
I am a traditionally trained oil painter and have worked in most media including sculpture and print-making. I prefer digital painting because of the flexibility required for the commercial art field.

If you didn't become an illustrator, what else were you considering?
I was an E.M.T. in high school and seriously considered medicine, specifically brain surgery. I never wanted to do anything easy.

What do you think inspired you as a young child?
When I was young, my parents renovated a historic two family farmhouse. When naughty, I took my time-outs in a corner with a red and black painted door and gaudy peeling wallpaper. The wallpaper was a jaunty and monotone French toile straight from the 1960's and of a blatant erotic nature. Lovely men and ladies frolicked about in Victorian garb performing unspeakable acts to each other. I'm not sure my parents ever looked too closely at that wallpaper or at least thought it wouldn't affect me. I suspect that it may have influenced my artistic style ever so slightly.

Frequently Asked Questions

Forging out a career in illustration is like feeling around in the dark. The only way that you learn much of what I've learned is by experience, or having others share their experience with you. There is no rulebook. The instructor in me loves to share with others, so here is a selection of questions that I get asked often with the hopes that they will guide you.

When did you know that this was the career for you?
I have drawn avidly most of my life. In my Junior year of high school, my parents sent me to a summer arts program - and told me that if I still wanted to go into art when I came back they would build me a studio in the basement. The day after I returned my dad set up his old drafting table and the rest is history. Actually, I had to share the space with our gun range but I learned to draw around the shotgun reloaders.

Do you feel that working for a client limits your artistic scope or enhances it?
What others see as "limits and constraints", I see as a puzzle to solve. What is the best way to communicate the idea? What is the demographic? Where will this piece be featured? Do I need to create several versions? I thrive on solving visual puzzles and working with a team.

What did you learn in art school that prepared you for your career?
I know self-taught artists who are successful, and artists who went to school for art and are not. It is a matter of how much time and work you are willing to invest in yourself. I was fortunate to attend Pratt, a top-tier school. Pratt taught me to work in most media, and made me well rounded with art history and seasoned teachers. If you are fortunate enough to attend a good art school, focus on squeezing every bit of valuable knowledge that you can from the experience. If you are not, then you are responsible for developing your own learning base. Study art history, visit museums, learn techniques from other artists, and find open drawing sessions to attend and draw nude models. Drawing from life is invaluable. Once you can draw and paint in all media, you can develop your own path. Either road that you choose to go - you get out of it what you put into it. You do not make it in this field without dedication and the burning need to succeed. Pratt's motto is "Be true to your art and your art will be true to you." So study art history. Study your peers. Draw. Draw. Then draw some more. Learn to draw from life.

What did you not learn in art school that students should be prepared to learn elsewhere?
Business. I was fortunate that both my parents and brother were business majors, but there was a severe lack of training the freelance artist to excel at more than art. You must learn how to manage yourself and run a business including all of the paperwork, licenses, and bookkeeping that it entails. I am also lucky enough to have a Creative Director husband to bounce bids and proposals off of. He ran art departments for many years, and offers a great inside view to where a project is headed.

You talk about staying in the industry, what art related jobs did you do first, before succeeding?
Freshman summer of college I took on a fulltime unpaid internship at an ad agency. I also worked nights at Taco Bell to make up for the unpaid part. I learned a lot about how an advertising agency is run, including how to pull stats, and cut Rubylith. Junior and senior year, I worked at an art shipping warehouse on the west side of Manhattan. Marcel Duchamp's *Nude Descending a Staircase* passed through while I was there (we all went to peer at it in the crate), and I had lunch next to a huge statue of Lenin each day. Lazarus and I both freelanced in NYC through agencies for many years as production, web and graphic designers in conjunction to creating work for roleplaying games. I would supplement my advertising illustration with web design and logo creation, but eventually weeded out such jobs as I became more in demand. There was a market fluctuation after 9/11, and I compensated with teaching illustration at Pratt and Skidmore. A second such fluctuation happened in 2009-10 with the housing market, and initiated my movement into fine art, fantasy and comics shows. Versatility and the ability to adjust your business plan is what keeps you afloat.

Do you ever do work for free?
There is a preconceived notion among smaller clients that *"artists do what they love, so making art is reward enough"*. Let me reassure you that the requests for free work thin out as you become more established. Creation of work with the intent to get paid if the client likes it is called "spec work". Most of the time these jobs do not pay off. So, unless it is a project that you are collaborating on as a labor of love, then try to avoid spec work as tempting as it looks. You are a professional. You deserve to be compensated. On very rare occasions, I will create a style sample with the intent to win a client that I wish to work for. When we pitched Celestial Seasonings, I created a cloisonné-style sample as part of the proposal for presentation. Sketches and style-samples for client presentations are most often paid, with an additional amount to bring the art to finish, and an additional percentage on top of that if the art is used (this falls under licensing).

How do I turn my art into a business?
You are a business, and are going to need to learn about the paperwork involved with being a business. Most illustrators start out as a sole-proprietorship. You will need to create this sole-prop. by filling out forms with your local state to create a "doing-business-as" identity or "fictitious name" and set up a separate bank account. If you sell your art at art shows, you will need to register to collect and pay sales tax separately with every state you sell in. Tax law is a very complicated field so I did what any great businesswoman does - I hired professionals! There is nothing that says "audit me!" more than an income that fluctuates. I cannot stress this enough. You may also want to hire a book-keeper, but one thing that you do not want to skimp on is a good accountant and a good lawyer. Keep receipts for everything! You now live in the land of deductions. You can write off anything business related. This includes all of your art supplies, travel, your studio space and utilities - and even things that you do not expect, such as the open drawing class fee, magazines that you purchased for reference material, and art books. Your accountant may set you up with estimated quarterly taxes to pay. They may recommend that you incorporate. Save yourself a lot of trouble and hire professionals to help you set up your business structure! When in doubt, do an internet search on the subject and visit your state's department of revenue web site. Don't forget about health insurance. Call up a broker or call multiple companies yourself. They will seem very expensive but it is critical to never lapse in coverage. What most employees forget is that their employers pay for a large portion of their health insurance and so are protected from the full cost.

For the answers to more questions by echo, visit the book page at **http://www.echo-x.com/echonouveau**